Business Basics

BUSINESS BASICS

A Grounded Theory for Managing Ethical Behavior in Sales Organizations

BENNY BERGGREN NEWTON

Södertörns högskola

Subject: Business Studies
Research Area: Politics, Economy and the Organisation of Society
School of Social Sciences

Södertörns högskola
(Södertörn University)
Library
SE-141 89 Huddinge

www.sh.se/publications

Cover image: Benny Berggren Newton
Graphic form: Per Lindblom & Jonathan Robson

Stockholm 2021

Södertörn Doctoral Dissertations 187
ISSN 1652-7399

ISBN 978-91-89109-57-5 (print)
ISBN 978-91-89109-58-2 (digital)

Abstract

Background: Managing co-workers' ethical behavior in sales organizations is a complex social process. To start, sales organizations incorporate several actors to manage, often simultaneously, all with their own agendas. Ethics as a topic is convoluted because it encompasses context-based scenarios which may not have clear-cut right and wrong answers. The management process is an ongoing task managers deal with on daily basis, where mismanagement can lead to severe consequences.

The majority of existing research on this area tends to focus on single factors in the management process, not the whole process. While there are some research studies that presents models or integrated frameworks describing the management process, they are few in number.

Aim: The *aim* of this study is to derive empirical concepts and thereby try to develop a theory to facilitate an understanding of the process of managing co-workers' ethical behavior, where the purpose is to ultimately build an integrated framework. More specifically, this study aims to describe the involved actors' main concerns and the process by which these are continuously resolved.

Methodology: In order to achieve the aim, a method with an inductive approach was necessary. The orthodox *Grounded Theory* methodology was chosen as research approach since it can generate conceptualizations in an integrated framework which help explain the occurring social processes. Working from this approach means that the researcher develops a new theory that is grounded in empirical data, where the researcher inductively describes the social process.

The empirical data was mainly derived from interviews with actors within the field. The data was collected, coded and conceptualized in an overlapping procedure until an empirically derived theory emerged After the emergence of the theory, the empirical data was validated with existing academic literature.

Findings: The core category in this study is Business Basics and concerns the desire to continuously conduct business where the management of ethical behavior is a fundamental basis to achieve this. Five distinct categories, all related to the core category were revealed: Bureaucratization, Relationship Investing, Educationing, Monetary Managing and Intuiting. These categories are expressed in social and dynamic processes. They represent different activities, tools, influences and practices that managers can adopt in order to reach their main concern.

Contribution: As a contribution, this dissertation provides an integrated framework based on the actors own subjective experiences, describing the dynamic and social processes of managing co-workers ethical behavior in sales organizations.

Keywords: Management, Ethical Behavior, Business Basics, Sales Organizations, Grounded Theory.

Sammanfattning
(abstract in Swedish)

Bakgrund: Att hantera medarbetares etiska beteende i säljande organisationer är en komplex social process. Till att börja med inkluderar säljande organisationer flera aktörer som de kan komma bli tvungna att hantera samtidigt, där alla har sin egen agenda. Till detta inkluderar etik som ämne kontextbaserade scenarios där vad som anses rätt och fel inte alltid är tydligt. Dessutom är styrningen av sina anställda något chefer hanterar på daglig basis, där brister i ledarskapet kan leda till allvarliga konsekvenser för företaget.

Den mesta forskning som finns inom området tenderar att fokusera på enskilda faktorer i denna styrningsprocess, istället för på hela processen som sådan. Och det finns få studier som tar aktörernas subjektiva upplevelser av processen som utgångspunkt och som använder sig av integrerade modeller som beskriver hela processen.

Syfte: Syftet med denna avhandling är att härleda empiriska begrepp för att konceptualisera processen i hur chefer hanterar sina medarbetares etiska beteende i säljande organisationer. Ett delsyfte är därför att skapa en integrerad modell. Denna avhandling ämnar således studera aktörernas huvudangelägenhet och den process med vilken denna angelägenhet löses.

Metod: För att nå syftet behövdes en metod med induktiv ansats. Ortodox grundad teori valdes som metod då den har förmåga att kunna generera konceptualiseringar till en integrerad modell som förklarar de pågående sociala processerna. Att arbeta från denna ansats betyder att forskaren utvecklar en ny teori, där forskaren induktivt beskriver de pågående sociala processerna.

Det empiriska datamaterialet samlades i huvudsak in via intervjuer med aktörer inom fältet. Detta kodades och konceptualiserades i en överlappande process tills en empiriskt härledd teori skapats. Därefter validerades teorin med befintlig forskning.

Resultat: Kärnkategorin i denna avhandling heter Business Basics. Den handlar om en önskan hos chefer att kunna fortsätta göra affärer där hanteringen av deras medarbetares etiska beteende är en grund för att kunna uppnå detta. Fem olika kategorier, alla relaterade till kärnkategorin, har framträtt: byråkratisering, relationsinvestering, utbildning, monetärhantering och intuition. Dessa kategorier uttrycks i en social och dynamisk process och representerar olika aktiviteter, verktyg, influenser och metoder.

Bidrag: Denna avhandlings bidrag är en integrerad modell, baserad på aktörernas subjektiva erfarenheter, där den dynamiska och sociala processen beskrivs för hantering av medarbetares etiska beteende i säljande organisationer.

Keywords: Management, Etiskt beteende, Business Basics, Säljande organisationer, Grundad Teori.

Acknowledgements

For Adam!

It has been a long journey writing this dissertation and I dedicate it to you. You are what truly brings joy, happiness and meaning into my life, I love you so much.

I would also like to thank the important people in my life who all were somehow part of my writing journey. On a personal level, I would like to first and foremost thank my wife Natanya for all the love and support you have given me. Thank you for putting up with me during this crazy ride, for being there for me all those endless nights and weekends I was away writing.

To my parents – Gun and Svante. Thank you for your love and support, I would not be here if it were not for you, your encouragements and the way you raised me. To my brothers and sister and their families, thank you for helping me out with all those little things to make life easier during this research process.

On a professional level, I would first like to thank my main supervisor. Thank you Professor Lars-Johan Åge, without your guidance, wisdom and (great) patience, this dissertation would never have happened. Your mentoring, clear directions and encouragements provided me with not only the necessary guidance an aspiring researcher need, but it also facilitated me to discover my research voice and grow as an individual.

Thank you Professor Aihie Osarenkhoe for your wisdom, contributions and genuine concern during my ups and downs. Your input into this dissertation along with our general discussions during work at both the University of Gävle and at the Makerere University have helped me greatly with my understanding of research conduct and practices. Thank you Professor Erik Borg for your knowledge and contributions to this project from its proposal to its completion. I am indebted to you all for your unique and respective important roles you have had during my doctoral studies.

Additionally, I would also like to thank my colleagues (to which many I call friends) around the world whom all somehow also contributed to my writing process. This includes Dr. Michelle Rydback (My sister in crime), Mr. Mats Lövgren, Dr. Tommy Gerdemark. Dr. Jonas Kågström (My friend in need), Dr. Maria Fregidou-Malama, Dr. Agneta Sundström, Professor Tomas Brytting, Dr. Paulina Rytkönen, Dr. Hanna Grylin, Dr. Jaana Kurvinen, Dr E., Dr. W., Mr. Martin Ahlenius, Dr. Olivia Kang, Dr. Signe Jernberg, Miss Annika Lake, Mr. Peter Lindberg, Dr. Zahra Ahmadi, Mrs. Elena Ahmadi, Mr. Jonathan Robson, Miss Lina Lorentz, Mrs. Kristina Mickelsson, Dr. Ehsanul Chowdhury, Mr. Jonas Molin, Miss Nina Daskalova, Professor Rodrigo Lozano, Professor Akmal Hyder, Dr. Mats Landström, Dr. Pär Vilhelmson, Professor L-T Eriksson. Mr. Tomas Källquist, Dr. Apostolos Bantekas, Miss Maria Kulander, Mr. Anders Hedman, Miss Amelina Söderberg, Miss Anna Engvers, Miss Eva Persson, Mrs. Ng De Gracia, Dr. Andy Lowe, Dr. Romeo V. Turcan, Herr Jakobsson, Dr. Mabel Komuda, Professor Jotham Byarugada, all my respondents participating in this dissertation, other colleagues at the faculty of business and economics at the university of Gävle and Södertörn University, and last but certainly not least Mr. Gerard Betros at the USQ in Australia.

Benny Berggren Newton – Gävle, January 13th, 2021

Table of Contents

Figures and tables

Figures

Tables

Words and Concepts

Basic Social Process: A Basic Social Process are basic and pervasive in social life and can be found regardless of structural social units and variation of time. I.e., it transcends the boundaries of time, individuals or place (Christiansen, 2006).

Cover Price: Is when a broker uses incorrect pricing to increase the interest in a home. The broker deliberately sets a price that is lower than the value of the home or the price that the seller is willing to sell for.

Dynamic Process: The interaction between two or more seemingly opposite tendencies.

Franchising: Franchising is a form of co-operation between two owner-independent parties (Franchise Arkitekt, 2011) where one has the right to sell a company's products (or services) in a particular area using the company name (Cambridge, 2008a, p.567) In brief, franchising means that someone who has a successful business concept offers others to apply this for their own business activities (Axberg 1993).

Franchisee: The franchisee is the party that runs its own company and hires a well-proven and profitable business concept (Fernlund & Ideström, 2009).

Franchisor: The franchisor is the party that owns a well-proven and profitable business concept which it then leases.

Organizational Culture: An organizations culture for this dissertation refers to underlying values, beliefs and different ways of interaction at the workplace that to different degree contribute to that organizational settings social environment.

Staged Bidding Process: When someone places a bid and only has the intention to increase the bidding and not to actually win the bidding process in order for the seller to get much money as possible for their home.

Stakeholder: Those individuals or groups who are affected by and have an interest in the actions of the enterprise (Hitt, Black, Porter, 2005)

Social Process: A social process is the social interaction between individuals and groups, where this interaction can occur again and again.

Abbreviations

AMT	Administrative Management Theory
ARN	Allmänna Reklamationsnämnden
BSP	Basic Social Process
CEO	Chief Executive Officer
FMI	Fastighetsmäklarinspektionen (Real-Estate Brokers Inspection Authority)
GT	Grounded Theory
HR	Human Resources
HRM	Human Resource Management
Ph.D.	Doctor of Philosophy
SLT	Social Learning Theory

Main Terminology

English	*Swedish*
Adaptation Process	Anpassningsprocess
Board of General Complaints	Allmänna-Reklamationsnämnden
Bureaucratization	Byråkratisering
Business Perpetuating	Affärsfortlevning
Clarity	Tydlighet
Compassing	Kompassering
Competitions Authority	Konkurrensverket
County Administrative Board	Länsstyrelsen
Cover Price	Lockpris
Educationing	Utbildande
Ethical Regulations Authority	Etikregelverket
Fellowship Building	Kamratskapsbyggande
Finance Supervisory Authority	Finansinspektionen
Fingertip Feeling	Fingertoppskänsla
Franchisee	Franchisetagare
Franchisor	Franchisegivare
Gut-feeling	Magkänsla
Implementation Process	Implementerings-process
Maintenance Process	Underhållsprocess
Monetary Managing	Monetärhantering
Occupational Health	Företagshälsan
Paragon of Virtue	Förebild
Real Estate Brokers Law	Fastighetsmäklarlagen
Real Estate Brokers Inspection Authority	Fastighetsmäklar-inspektionen
Relationship Investing	Relationsinvestering
Sense of Justice	Rättspatos
Staged Bidding Process	Falsk budgivning
Staff Welfare	Personalvård
Termination	Uppsägning
Well-read	Påläst

Foreword

In the spring of 2014, I attended a one-day seminar for real estate students initiated by the very top management from one of Sweden's biggest real estate agencies. The focus for the day concerned ethics, ethical behavior and how to act in accordance with it.

After attending the full day seminar, observing different activities and discussions, several thoughts triggered my curiosity. The more I thought about the seminar, the more I came to realize two things. One, the co-workers' ethical behavior seems to be of importance for managers in sales organizations. Two, the actual management process of it seemed convoluted and hard to comprehend, it is simply not a straight forward process.

As my curiosity grew, I wanted to understand what managers actually do to manage ethical behavior. I wanted to understand what underlying processes it encompasses. Finally, I also wanted to understand why the management of ethical behavior is important to the manager? This became the focal starting point for this dissertation.

1. Introduction

Managing a co-workers' ethical behavior is a complex social process where the reasons for this argument include that:

- Ethics is convoluted because it encompasses context-based scenarios that may involve no clear-cut right and wrong answers.
- Ethics is of importance for the sales organizations, where mismanagement can lead to severe consequences.
- Sales organizations incorporate several actors that managers have to manage.

Before establishing this more prominently, I feel the need to provide a short introductory narrative to illustrate the challenges managers in sales organizations may encounter:

> As a franchisee for a real estate company with over 15 co-workers you have just hired a new broker. You know that this employee is relatively new in the business and creating a customer network might be difficult in the beginning. You get a feeling that there might be a risk that this person will experience your company's commission-based salary system as stressful before getting acclimatized. Based on earlier experiences, you know that this type of stress has caused past sales people, while not breaking the law, some sales people have started to take short cuts to the extent that their behavior were not aligned with your business philosophy. As a consequence, you strongly consider offering the new employee a guaranteed income for the first months until he has established his own customer network.
>
> That same day, you get informed by the franchisor that they are going to implement new rules for the brokers regarding conduct and practices during client meetings. These rules apply to the whole franchise and as a result, you put this at the top of the agenda for the next upcoming department meeting. However, you also realize that some of the rules can be perceived as confusing, and misunderstandings might therefore occur. In order to communicate these rules as effective as possible, you realize that one meeting is not enough. You also feel the need to arrange a half-day workshop with special focus on these rules. You reason that this is a great opportunity to further inform, clarify and discuss with the employees for how they are expected to behave.

> During all this, you have also noticed that two employees seem unhappy and act in an inappropriate behavior at work. After one-on-one conversations with both, you find out that the two are at odds with each other. One feels that the other has deliberately stolen customers from her. While neither have acted completely wrong in this matter, you can see why both feel the other is to blame. Since there is no definitive right or wrong in this issue, you decide to play it by ear for how to best maneuver this situation towards a solution.
>
> You also fear that this conflict might negatively affect the other co-workers and the overall mood at the office as well, which in turn might also affect customers. Based from earlier experience, you know that a negative atmosphere might result in co-workers becoming careless due to a negative attitude. To avoid this from happening, you decide to invite your colleagues to your home a Thursday evening to play poker in an effort to get to know each other better.
>
> About ten minutes before the poker evening starts, you get two messages. One from the newly staffed broker and one from one of the individuals who was in the conflict. Both wrote that unforeseen things had come up, and could therefore not participate. Your hopes for reconciliation in the evening between the two just went out the window. Later in the evening, you overheard a noteworthy remark about the newly staffed broker. The person said that he could not understand as to why I would hire such a "dodgy individual". He continued with saying that he knew that the newly staffed broker had systematically acted extremely questionable at two previous workplaces, and that is why he stopped working there.

As can be seen in the example, there are many ethical considerations a manager must consider. Ethics as a topic is no doubt complex where it was noticed that in common usage, individuals often use the terms "ethics" and "morals" interchangeably and can therefore be confusing. Crane and Matten (2010, p. 8) explained that "Morality is concerned with the norms, values and beliefs embedded in social processes which define right and wrong for an individual or a community." Ethics on the other hand is suggested to "concern the study of morality and the application of reason to elucidate specific rules and principles that determine right and wrong for a given situation. These rules and principles are called ethical theories" (Crane & Matten, 2010, p. 8).

The discourse of these theories can roughly be divided into consequentialist theories (teleology), non-consequentialist theories (deontology) and virtue ethics. Ferrell, Fraedrich and Ferrell (2015) explain teleology as a look at the consequence of one's action in regards to right or wrong from a philosophical standpoint. Unlike teleology, which focuses on the consequences, deontology focuses on "the rights of individuals and the intentions associated with a particular behavior" (Ferrell et al., 2015, p. 161). Virtue ethics is explained as correct actions that are those undertaken by actors with virtuous characteristics.

These ethical theories have a long-standing history which can be traced all the way back to the ancient Greeks where the most prominent figures in Greek philosophy are Socrates (ca 469–399 BC), Plato (428–354 B.C.) and Aristotle (384–322 B.C.). Since then, several more prominent philosophers in ethical literature have emerged, philosophers like Niccolò Machiavelli (1469–1527) and his book *The Prince* along with Immanuel Kant (1724–1802) and his categorical imperative, British economist John Stuart Mill (1806–1873) and his ideas regarding utilitarianism. Evidently, ethics is not a new concept, instead it has been discussed and developed for thousands of years. As a result, ethics as a topic for study has also branched out into several different parts of our society where business is one.

1.1 Ethics in Business vs. Business Ethics

According to De George (2005), while ethics in business and business ethics are separate areas, they are related to each other. Ethics in business concerns the application of ethical norms into business-related contexts, while business ethics concerns the development of the academic field of ethics in business.

Business ethics can be roughly divided into three branches. The first branch (1) of business ethics concerns a normative approach. It examine questions of how we should and are expected to act at work (from a moral standpoint). The second branch (2) of business ethics concerns an empirical and descriptive approach (Applied ethics). It examine questions of why ethical and unethical decisions occur at work. The third branch (3) concerns the adoption of ethics in businesses. It concern the integration of ethics into business and related practices (De George, 2005).

These three branches form business ethics as a topic for which there are several academic definitions. While Lewis (1985) suggest that no universally accepted definition exists, Shaw and Barry (2001, p. 4) define business ethics as "the study of what constitutes right and wrong, or good and bad, human conduct in a business context". De George (1987, p. 203) explains that business ethics "deals with a set of interrelated questions that are untangled and addressed within an overarching framework" while the term ethics in business is a more general term often used in public discourse and media in the context of business scandals.

Despite the numerous definitions, business ethics is a contemporary phenomenon where some scholars claim it lacks history while others disagree (De George, 1987). Its academic history can be traced back to the 1960s, originating in North America where both De George (1987) and later Ferrell et al. (2015, pp. 9–13) summarized the development of business ethics into a timeline:

- 1960s – The rise of business-related social issues, where focus for research tended to be aimed on civil rights issues, increased employee-employer tension.
- 1970s – The emergence of business ethics as a field, where focus for research tended to be on employee militancy, human rights issues, disadvantaged customers.
- 1980s – Business ethics was acknowledged as a field of study, where the focal point for research tended to aim at bribes and illegal contradicting practices, influence peddling, deceptive marketing.
- 1990s – Business ethics was institutionalized where focus for research tended to aim towards organizational ethical misconduct, financial mismanagement.
- 2000s – Increased focus on business ethics where focus for research tended to be aimed at sustainability, global issues, cybercrime, etc.

In recent years, business ethics has grown more important for organizations due to the impact business have on society today and the globalization (Kotler, 2011). Ferrell et al. (2015) provides more arguments of its importance since business ethics contributes to employee commitment, investor loyalty and higher customer satisfaction. Business ethics helps us to understand malpractice, its causes and how to improve human conditions at work. Crane and Matten (2010) stress that business ethics can provide us with the ability to assess the benefits and problems associated with different ways of managing ethics in organizations. Additionally, while research topics within the field of business ethics seem to go in trends, there are a number of recurring topics being researched. Three prominent topics within business ethics that attract research interest on a recurring basis are:

- Organizational unethical behavior
- The ethical decision-making process
- Ethical leadership

Organizational unethical behavior is explained by Andreoli and Lefkowitz (2009, p. 310) as "employees breaking organizational and societal norms motivated by greed, and/or egoistic self-aggrandizement or as a retaliation for perceived inequities." Existing studies not only encompass business in general, but also encompass studies with specific focus on sales organizations.

Examples of prominent studied topics are lying (Grover, 1993), bribery (Steidmeier, 1999), fraud (Micewski & Troy, 2007), discrimination (Brief et al., 2000), sexual harassment (Asgary & Mitschow, 2002) and abusive behavior (e.g. Decoster, 2013) to name a few. Another example is rewarding and disciplining co-workers. For over 30 years several studies have appeared how not only managers in general, but also managers in sales organizations both reward and discipline unethical co-workers (Bellizzi & Hasty, 2003; Bellizzi & Hite, 1989; Strout, 2002). The overall conclusion in these studies is that managers often do not match the level of discipline with the objective seriousness of the unethical behavior (Bellizzi & Bristol, 2005).

Studies as early as 1978 revealed that rewarding individuals conducting business, despite unethical practices, increased the probability of them engaging in such practices in the future (Hegarty & Sims, 1978). It is later claimed by Treviño and Brown (2004, p. 72) that unethical practices are not necessarily performed by individuals who have low moral values. Instead they suggest that "most people, including adults are followers when it comes to ethics," i.e., the researchers suggest that individuals are influenced by the practices of others.

From what I understand after reading studies and literature about organizational unethical behavior is that the topic is closely related to studies concerning the ethical decision-making process. Studies which relate to this topic can be traced back to the late 1950s. For example, in 1959 Simon presented an article about theories in decision-making in which he discussed "how much psychology economics needs, the goal of the enterprise and decision premises," Simon (1959) came to the conclusion that since the business environment's complexity increases, more information is needed regarding the different processes and mechanisms that an individual can use to reach his or her goals. Ever since, several researchers have developed different models and conceptual frameworks, explaining the inherent processes of when and how individuals make ethical decisions in organizations.

Three of the most prominent models covering ethical decision-making in organizations are Treviño (1986), Wotruba (1990) and Jones (1991). Treviño (1986) notes that while situational and individual factors affect the outcome of an individual's ethical decision, it is the person's cognitive moral development which is the most fundamental element in the actual ethical decision-making process. Wotruba (1990) on the other hand focuses on a broader picture than just the ethical decision-making process. Focus is more on presenting how sales managers can analyze how sales people arrive at certain ethical decisions, and from there manage their behavior. Jones (1991) also developed a model where he added external factors (there described as the "environment") affecting the ethical decision-making process.

Since then, studies with a focus on the ethical decision-making process have expanded, focusing on either single factors or on a more holistic and comprehensive view. As late as 2007, both Ingram, LaForge and Schwepker (2007) and Ferrell, Johnston and Ferrell (2007) made further developments on the frameworks of Treviño (1986) and Jones (1991). Ingram et al.'s (2007) objective was to enhance an individual's ethical judgment where focus was on how sales leadership and sales management control strategy indirectly affect co-workers' ethical decision-making process. In more recent research, Heyler, Armenakis, Walker and Collier (2016) attempt to unveil the complex nature of the intervening steps between a person's moral awareness and the unethical/ethical outcome in his or her decision.

The third prominent topic within research of business ethics is *Ethical leadership*. Ethical leadership is an area directly related to business ethics and organizations since managers often are said to set the ethical tone for the organization. For example, many of the existing studies like Ferrell, Weaver, Taylor and Jones (1978) have come to the conclusion that the top managers' ethical behavior has an influence on their co-workers' ethical behavior. Ever since, researchers within the field like Brown (2007) have studied both positive and negative leadership in order to better understand its impact at the workplace. In more recent research, Belak and Milfelner (2011) and Shin et al. (2015) have, like Ferrell et al. (1978), linked managers to playing a key role in organizations for influencing the co-workers' ethical behavior, further solidifying its importance when managing their employees.

In current literature, many researchers make distinctions between being a "leader" and being a "manager" (e.g. Pielstick, 2000). Being a manager does not automatically make that person a leader. A person can be appointed to a leading position as a manager, making him or her to be a formal leader (Pielstick, 2000). However, there can also be informal leaders in an organization that co-workers prefer to listen to (Pielstick, 2000). Treviño, Hartman and Brown (2000) divided the concept of ethical leadership into two sub-concepts, (1) a moral person (ethical individual) and (2) a moral manager (ethical leader). Heres and Lasthuizen (2012) further expand on Treviño et al. (2000) discussing "moral manager" in terms of being a role model.

Specific studies on role models are not a new topic of research. For example, Bowlby (1969; in Neubert, 2009) discussed its impact as early as the late 1960s. The concept of a role model can deal with how managers (as role models) can manage co-workers' ethical behavior. Researchers like Belak and Milfelner (2011) and Neubert et al., (2009) both stress that being a role model is in fact the most important factor for influencing co-workers' ethical behavior when practicing ethical leadership, suggesting that it is sometimes not enough to be a manager. The manager needs to act virtuously. This claim gets support from Mayer et al. (2009), who also found a positive relationship between being a role model and co-workers' ethical behavior.

One of the first studies on the effects of role models related to sales management was conducted by Rich (1997). The researcher found positive relationships in their hypotheses that sales managers who acts as a role model increase the level of overall performance by the salesperson. Rich (1997) also found that acting as a role model also has a positive effect on employee trust towards the manager.

In conclusion, clearly there is a lot of research within business ethics relating to not only organizations but also sales organizations per se. In turn, this suggests that ethics is important to sales organizations and therefore needs to be addressed.

1.2 The Importance of Ethics in Sales Organizations

Research suggests that salespeople in sales organizations have more day-to-day close interactions with customers than in other organizations (Weeks & Nantel, 1992). These salespeople often operate unsupervised and therefore their activities can more easily go unnoticed by management. In turn, this can create incentives to act unethically if given the opportunity. In fact, several researchers agree that salespeople in sales organizations are usually more exposed to unethical behavior than in other businesses (e.g. Román & Munuera, 2005). One recent example is that the real estate business seems to have been exposed to an increase in unethical behavior lately (Oneberg, 2019). If a co-worker should decide to engage in unethical practices, research shows that customers exposed to unethical behavior are more likely to seek other alternatives (e.g. Rich, 1988), where up to 47% of the consumers would not buy from an organization they believe is not "good" (Joyner & Payne, 2002). I thereby argue that acting ethically is of importance for sales organizations.

As a consequence for addressing the importance of ethics in sales organizations, I have come to realize three things. For this dissertation, I also need to address (1) what a sales organization is; (2) what an "ethical salesperson" is; and finally, based on these definitions along with the discussions above, (3) provide my own definition of ethics.

1.2.1 Defining a Sales Organization, an Ethical Sales Person & Ethics

I found that defining a sales organizations was more difficult than initially thought since current research seems to include many organizations when discussing sales organizations. Singh (2013) describes it as an organizational unit that distributes and sells products and services to consumers. It consists of individuals working alone or in a group where their main objective is to sell products and services to increase sales and thus expand the share of the market (Singh, 2013). Kurbel (2013) defines a sales organization as "a legal entity that is responsible for selling goods and is liable for the sales (product liability, compensation claims)."

This suggests that the concept of a sales organizations is broad. It can be a supermarket selling fruits and milk or an organization selling DVD movies. Focus for this dissertation is on sales organizations who sell more complex products and services where the salespeople working there are more involved in the sales process. The salesperson plays a pivotal role in the consumers' purchasing decision since these products require high product involvement by the customers.

Trust in the salesperson is necessary since the business transaction includes large sums of money. Buying a bad movie-DVD or spoiled fruit has far less impact on the consumers' economy while buying a defective house can have severe and long-life economic consequences for the buyer. A more appropriate definition of a sales organization for this dissertation is:

> A sales organization is an organization where the salesperson conducts larger sales transactions and has a great influence on the consumers' business decisions. (Author, 2019)

The suggested definition allows me to narrow down on the spectrum of what sales organizations are for this dissertation. In turn, this enables me to be more selective when approaching sales organizations for the data collection.

As for defining an ethical salesperson, I argue that a salesperson working for a sales organization is evaluated by others in how they act, not only at work but also in private life. If the salesperson should decide to keep important information away from another person or diminish an issue that is normally considered important, it is most likely that (s)he will be judged by that other individual as being a person of low moral character and of a deceptive nature, i.e., acting unethically.

This can signal to both current and potential customers that the salesperson is not trustworthy who thereby loses legitimacy. A salesperson therefore is responsible and needs to protect their own character in order to be perceived as having high moral standards by others at all times, not just during working hours, for these customers to be willing to conduct business.

To exemplify, a car salesperson can diminish or withhold information that can be of importance to a potential customer. For example, a family with young children is in the dealership where they show great interest in purchasing a particular car. What the salesperson knows is that this car has scored specifically low ratings for protecting children in numerous crash tests. Yet by selling this car, the salesperson receives a higher commission than selling other cars due to the higher price of this car. The salesperson might have no legal obligation to tell the family about these low safety scores for protecting children. Also, if this information gets to the family by someone other than the salesperson, (s)he can always protect him/herself by claiming these tests are easily found online where it is the responsibility of the buyer to look this up. Yet, the salesperson is expected to be honest and knowledgeable, thereby also expected to provide important information to the customer.

Consequently, it is a complicated situation for the manager to manage since (s)he cannot control what is being said or not between a salesperson and another individual. The manager's organization might not only end up losing money due to dishonest salespeople, but their whole company might be branded by such negative attributes.

Based on the example above, it is evident that I believe that the approach of a salesperson should be based on character and integrity due to its strong resonance in business contexts since customers and other stakeholders often need to rely on the salesperson's ethical behavior to maintain legitimacy among customers. Consequently, the ethical salesperson's actions should be manifested in a set of virtues like honesty, wisdom, loyalty, patience, friendship, and modesty — both at work and in private life.

In other words, the way I perceive it, an ethical salesperson working for a sales organization needs to act virtuously. Their behavior is closely related to the previously mentioned "virtue ethics" due to the traits that are necessary for the salesperson, whose behavior is inductively evaluated upon by others. Virtue ethics for this dissertation was earlier explained as the "correct actions that are those undertaken by actors with virtuous characters."

That is, a salesperson acts, then their action is determined by others, like their manager, whether or not the action is deemed ethical. In deontological and teleological ethics, an action is made after ethical consideration has been applied. Therefore, I assert that:

> An ethical salesperson is determined by the expectations from the managers, the society and the law in a particular context. (Author, 2019)

As a result of the given discussions above (chapters 1.1–1.2.1), I find the current definitions of business ethics to be too delimiting to appropriately fit sales organizations as defined for this dissertation. The reason is that the definitions of business ethics tend to focus solely on purely business-related situations and activities. Ethics on the other hand is an umbrella concept in which business ethics is included along with many other concepts.

In sales organizations (as defined for this dissertation), ethics transcends the boundaries of work, the manager can at times need to take into consideration situations outside work as well. Consequently, a broader definition is needed in order to grasp every aspect of the management process. I define ethics in sales organizations as:

> The study of morals practiced by a group or an individual concerning issues of right and wrong for a given situation, including how their ethical behaviors are perceived outside the actual business context (Author, 2020).

Thus, managing ethical behavior in sales organizations for this dissertation are those work-related attempts to formally and/or informally manage ethical issues through practices, policies and programs.

1.3 Approaching the Gap

Despite the salesperson's responsibility to act virtuously, I contend that it is ultimately the manager of the sales organization who is responsible for ensuring that the ethical behavior of the co-workers lives up to the expectations of the customers, the sales organization and society. Research shows that neglectful leadership can be a potential source for unethical behavior in co-workers (Treviño & Brown, 2004) and that the manager plays a key role to influence co-workers' ethical behavior (Huberts, Kaptein & Lasthuizen, 2007).

It is therefore important for managers to understand how to manage co-workers' ethical behavior in accordance with current expectations in society. However, after writing about ethics, sales organizations, salespeople, and the management process, it is clear that this can be a complicated process for the manager to manage and even grasp.

After reviewing existing literature on the process for how managers manage their co-workers' ethical behavior in sales organizations, my general impression is that most of it tends to focus on single influencing factors like trust, ethical leadership and economic conditions. There are seemingly few studies which attempt to explain the whole, or at least larger parts of, this process. In total, 22 articles and related literature were found that to different degrees explain this process in comprehensive way (See Table 1.1).

Moreover, not all studies have specific focus on sales organizations but rather on businesses in general. Also, much of the existing research is based on quantitative data. This leaves out the voices of the respondents. As a result, I miss studies encompassing the following three dimensions:

- Research which presents an integrated framework that explains the process of managing co-workers' ethical behavior
- Research with specific focus on sales organizations
- Research that is based on the actors' (managers) own subjective experience

Existing literature may capture one or at best two of these three dimensions. The most prominent attempt was made by Stead, Worrell and Stead (1990) who presents an integrated framework which describe how different processes relates to each other when managing ethical behavior.

However, their focus is on business organizations in general and not sales organizations per se. Two other notable articles with specific focus on sales organizations are Román and Munuera (2005) and Schwepker and Good (2007). However, neither of these presents an integrated framework for managing ethical behavior that describes the different social processes occurring.

An overview of the current field is provided in Table 1.1 below revealing which dimensions each literature encompass.

Table 1.1: Missing Dimensions in Literature

Authors	Dimensions		
	Dimension 1 Integrated frameworks	**Dimension 2** Specific focus on sales organizations	**Dimension 3** Based on managers' own subjective experience
Bellizzi & Bristol (2005)	No	Yes	No
Bolander et al. (2017)	Yes	Yes	No
DeConinck (1992)	No	Yes	No
Gellerman (1989)	No	Yes	No
Hawes & Rich (1998)	No	Yes	No
José & Thibodeaux (1997)	No	No	No
Lee & Cheng (2012)	No	No	No
Madhani (2015)	Yes	Yes	No
McDonald & Nijhof (1999)	Yes	No	No
Murphy (1988)	Yes	No	No
Robertson et al. (2003)	No	No	No
Román (2011)	Yes	Yes	No
Román & Munuera (2005)	Yes	Yes	No
Schnebel & Bienert (2004)	No	No	No
Schwepker & Good (2007)	Yes	Yes	No
Stead et al. (1990)	Yes	No	No
Treviño & Brown (2004)	No	No	No
Treviño & Nelson (2016)	Yes	Yes	No
Treviño et al. (1999)	No	No	No
Treviño et al. (2006)	Yes	No	No
Vardi & Wiener (1996)	Yes	No	No
Wotruba (1990)	Yes	Yes	No

This table suggests that no previous research has attempted to articulate and present (1) an integrated framework for managing co-workers' ethical behavior that at the same time specifically focuses on (2) sales organizations that are (3) based on the managers' subjective experience.

Consequently, a gap in current literature has thus been revealed as illustrated below (see Fig 1.1).

Figure 1.1: The Gap

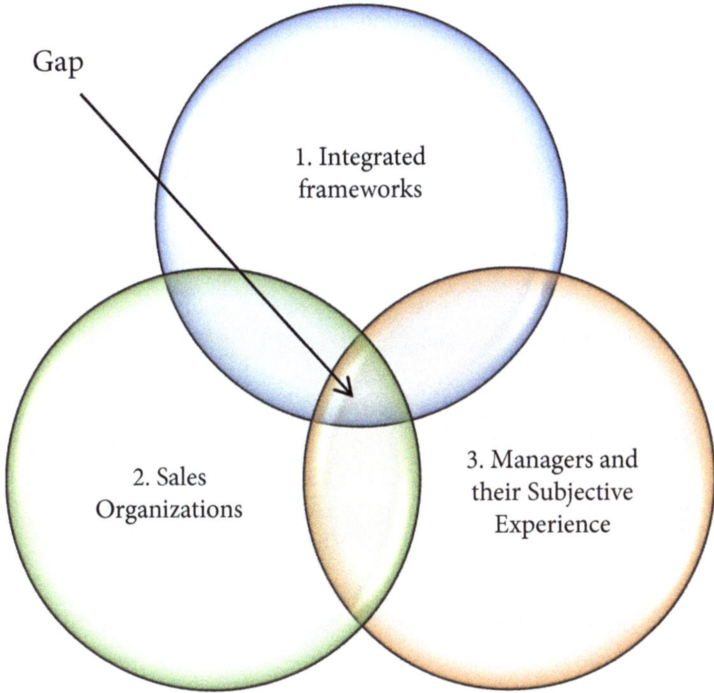

1.3.1 Research Question, Objective and Aim

In summarizing arguments, I have argued that:

- Ethics as a topic includes *social interactions.*
- Management of ethical behavior is a complex social process
- There is a gap in existing literature regarding integrated frameworks that focus on sales organizations that are based on the managers' subjective experiences.

Consequently, the following two research questions have been made:

1. What are the managers' main concerns with respect to managing co-workers' ethical behavior in sales organizations?
2. How do the managers resolve their main concerns?

Since I have not encountered any studies based on the actors' own experience within the field, a decision was made that there is a need for an inductive research approach. This will facilitate me as a researcher to deliver a more comprehensive framework. As a consequence, the following three objectives emerge:

1. To identify the main concerns of managers in sales organizations with respect to managing co-workers' ethical behavior.
2. To discover and identify the issues these managers find most challenging and important.
3. To gain an understanding for how managers' main concerns are not only resolved but also processed.

In short, the *aim* of this study is twofold:

> (1) Derive empirical concepts in order to conceptualize the social process of managing co-workers' ethical behavior in sales organizations and (2) present the findings in an integrated framework.

In order to discover the *main concerns* of the actors, Gasson (1998) stresses that it is required to conduct a deep investigation of the "real life" situations of the particular problem. Therefore, choosing an appropriate methodology needs to be made on the basis of what allows me as a researcher to investigate these "real life" situations that are relevant to these managers' main concerns.

1.4 The Need for an Explorative Study

To start, despite existing literature often mentions the word 'social process', it is difficult to find a clear definition of the concept. However, there are academic voices like Parry (1998) who suggest that management can be perceived as a social influence process. Others like Macuh (2005) describe a social process as "the interaction between an individual and the environment". A social process for this dissertation is best explained as the social interaction between individuals and groups, where this interaction can occur again and again.

An inductive explorative approach can contribute to gaining new insights in such process since such approach can help recognize the actions and the experiences of the studied actors in a way that is not directed by previous research. Exploratory research can be explained as an approach to investigate an underdeveloped idea of an undefined problem or phenomenon. For an exploratory research approach, the starting point for the researcher is with a general idea that will be further developed to discover issues and develop new concepts. The notion of having a general idea as a starting point can also be applied for this study. It was clearly noted in sections 1.1–1.3 that the general idea is that ethical behavior of co-workers seems to be of importance for managers in sales organizations. Stebbins (2001) wrote a book about the exploratory research approach and defines it as:

> Social science exploration is a broad-ranging, purposive, systematic, prearranged undertaking designed to maximize the discovery of generalizations leading to description and understanding of an area of social or psychological life. Such exploration is, depending on the standpoint taken, a distinctive way of conducting science – a scientific process – a special methodological approach (as contrasted with confirmation), and a pervasive personal orientation of the explorer. The emergent generalizations are many and varied; they include the descriptive facts, folk concepts, cultural artifacts, structural arrangements, social processes, and beliefs and belief systems normally found there. (Stebbins, 2001, p. 3)

By this definition, it is clear that the inductive exploratory research can help me gain a deeper understanding of the management process since its driving force is to discover. By "discover" I mean that the studied actors of the field seemingly know their story, but they may not grasp or articulate the whole process. Therefore, there is an indication that there are aspects of their knowledge that are up for discovery.

Since this study is inductive and exploratory, the reader will find that it differs from other more traditional deductive studies. To start, focus of the research can change throughout the course of the study depending on what is revealed in the empirical data. Moreover, the researcher does not attempt to logically apply their own preconceived ideas and hypotheses to existing theories. Instead, the purpose for a researcher using this approach is to interpret what is found in the empirical data.

Therefore, due to the nature of an exploratory approach, it is necessary to find the underlying issues and problems with the help from actors in the field. In order to better explain these processes, there is a need for "real life examples" of what the studied actors actually do to manage their co-workers' ethical behavior enabling me to create a theory that is grounded in those experiences.

As a consequence of trying to understand those real-life examples, there is a need for new terminology and new concepts. New terminology and concepts that are close to the studied subjects' everyday language gives me and the readers a better understanding of the studied actors' own description of the empirical field (Brytting, 1991). Consequently, there is a need for research with a generative capacity, where generative capacity refers to one's ability to create something new in a certain context (Avital & Te'Eni, 2009).

As a result, in more traditional research the literature review comes before the empirical findings. In this study, the empirical findings will come before the literature review, where the empirical findings are validated (grounded) through the existing literature. Moreover, the reader can also not expect this dissertation to test hypotheses since I aim to understand and explain a social process. In that sense, an exploratory approach is more hypothetically generative, even if that is not an explicit aim of the study. Consequently, while testing pre-existing hypotheses is not the focal point for this study, that does not exclude that hypotheses may emerge from the empirical data that later can become suggestions for future research.

In inductive research there are several approaches, where the orthodox Grounded Theory (GT) methodology was chosen as the most suitable approach for this dissertation. Orthodox GT as a research approach was introduced by Dr. Barney Glaser and Anselm Strauss (1967). While visiting hospitals they encountered problematic issues in regards to the process of dying among patients and their interactions with their relatives. At an early stage, they suspected that to understand the interactions, both saw the patients and their relatives as a key to their understanding.

In order to gain a better understanding of these complex interactions, Glaser and Strauss (1967) conducted systematic interviews with both patients and their relatives. Their research approach in their study, *The Awareness of Dying* (Glaser & Strauss, 1965), later paved way for the orthodox GT approach (Glaser & Strauss, 1967) which is still used today throughout different research disciplines.

However, as I understand, GT as a methodology is not commonly used within social sciences. Still, the methodology contributes to social sciences with helping to expand the research front forward. GT has a reflexive starting point and is a useful methodology since it has a generative capacity that enables me to reflect on and analyze data to both discover social interactions and generate new theories (Parry, 1998). Using GT can help me as a researcher to:

- Fulfill the purpose of this study since it has the capability to conceptualize complex social processes.
- To fill the gap in existing literature by delivering an integrated framework that is based on the actor's subjective experiences in a particular field.

In conclusion, by conceptualizing concepts (called categories in this dissertation) that are empirically derived, increased understanding of the process of managing co-workers' ethical behavior in sales organizations is achieved. While there are many different versions of GT to use for researchers, a more in-depth discussion concerning what version of GT should be used is provided in the methodological chapter (see chapter 2).

1.5 Limitations to Consider Before Reading Subsequent Chapters:

For this dissertation, before reading any further, there are limitations that need to be addressed.

- Focus on this dissertation is the management process of ethical behavior in sales organizations from a managerial perspective. Consequently, this dissertation will not include any philosophical discussions of ethics, business ethics and different perspectives.
- There are academic voices like Carroll (1991) arguing that there is a distinction between the law and ethics. Others like Crane and Matten (2010) argue that the law needs to be perceived as the minimum acceptable standards of ethical behavior, where the law is a codification of ethics into specific rules. I share Crane and Matten's perception on the law, that it should be perceived as a codification of ethics into specific rules and perceived as the minimum acceptable standard of ethical behavior. Several other academic voices also discuss the relationship between ethics and the law (e.g. Shum & Yam, 2011; Ferrell et al. 2015). However, focus for this dissertation is on the management process of

ethical behavior in sales organizations. Consequently, no philosophical discussion will be made concerning ethics and its relationship to the law.

- Due to the similarity in linguistic roots, the terms "moral" and "ethical" are perceived as synonymous and are therefore used interchangeably in this dissertation.
- Other interchangeable words used throughout this dissertation are:
    - Co-worker, employee, salesperson, broker and real estate agent
    - Ethics and business ethics

1.6 Overview of the Dissertation

Below is an overview of the dissertation.

1. Introduction

In the first chapter a discussion of ethics and business ethics as topics and the importance of ethics in sales organizations. Definitions of a sales organization, an ethical salesperson and ethics are then provided. This chapter concludes with a presentation of a gap in current literature, along with an objective, the aim and limitations, and concluded with the suggested research approach.

2. Methodology

The second chapter presents the chosen methodology for this dissertation. Discussions regarding methodological considerations are provided along with a rationale for choosing the particular methodology. Moreover, the procedures of this study, important terminology and epistemological considerations are also presented.

3. How the Substantive Theory Emerged

The third chapter provides a description and illustrations of the research process, how the core category along with its categories and sub-categories emerged. In short, this chapter presents the developmental stages of the emerged theory.

4. Theory

In the fourth chapter, the empirical findings reveal the emerged theory. First, a presentation of the core category is provided. This is followed with a presentation of each of its related categories and sub-categories to which several empirical examples are provided.

5. Validating the Theory

The fifth chapter is the validation chapter. A limited number of existing research studies from the literature are synthesized with the empirical findings in the developed theory. This chapter constitutes new information that clarifies and provides more angles and strengthens the theory. Additional interesting discoveries and thoughts relating to the emerged theory are also highlighted.

6. Conclusions

In the final chapter, a summary of the developed theory is presented as well as personal reflections regarding the empirical findings and the research process. Both theoretical and managerial contributions are then provided, which in turn is followed by a presentation of the limitations and suggestions for future studies. This dissertation is concluded with final words from the author.

References

In this section, the reader find all the references used in this dissertation.

Appendices

The appendices provide the reader with additional and supplementary readings related to this dissertation.

2. Methodology
The Orthodox Grounded Theory

One of the characteristics of the orthodox grounded theory methodology is that the steps during the study are conducted simultaneously at various times. Consequently, Glaser (1978) claims that orthodox GT, as will be seen in this chapter, is not an approach which tells you exactly what to do step-by-step. Instead, as soon as the study starts, the research process is often conducted in a non-linear fashion, where data collecting, writing memos, analyzing, coding, etc. overlap.

From Glaser (1978), the process of orthodox grounded theory (GT) research can be broadly summarized in the following different steps and procedures:

- **Data Collection:** Choosing data collection should be based on a general problem founded in a sociological view, rather from a conceptual framework since these frameworks can be preconceived. By having this attitude, Glaser (1978) suggests that the researcher is "open" and thus the categories will emerge through conceptualization. Collecting data progresses until saturation is reached.
- **The Substantive Open Coding Process.** This step consists of looking at the data and continuously comparing it in order to conceptualize categories.
- **The Emergence of the Core Category:** In the third step, the emergence of the core category occurs (which includes categories, sub-categories and data incidences).
- **The Substantive Selective Coding Process:** When the core category has emerged, the process of substantive selective coding begins for the researcher, meaning all new data is compared with the core category.
- **The Theoretical Open Coding Process:** Here the researcher writes theoretical memos which elaborate on theoretical categories. A theoretical outline is then conducted by sorting those memos. Memos allowed me to write creative theoretical forays with help from the categories and the data.
- **The Grounding of the Emerged Theory:** The final step is to integrate the empirical categories with existing literature in a validation process.

The methodology chapter is divided into nine main sections. The first section is the short introduction to this chapter. The second section provides a rationale for choosing orthodox GT as method, why the word orthodox is used, a brief discussion of ontological and epistemological aspects underpinning the emerged theory and finally a brief discussion of Tabula Rasa. The third section consists of discussing the data collection process and the importance of conceptualizing data. The fourth section outlines the substantive open coding process when conducting research from an orthodox GT methodology. The fifth section provides a discussion of the emerged core category in regards to orthodox GT along with related categories and subcategories. The sixth section outlines the substantive selective coding process when conducting research. The seventh section presents the theoretical coding process along with the memo writing and theoretical sorting procedures. The eighth section discusses the validation process of orthodox GT studies. The ninth section presents the evaluation criteria for orthodox GT-studies. Lastly, a brief summary and conclusion are provided.

2.1. Rationalizing for Orthodox GT Studies

To choose the appropriate method in research can be a difficult task for a researcher (or in this case, for a Ph.D. candidate). One can ask when orthodox GT is suitable as a research method. To start, this methodology was created by Glaser and Strauss in the 1960's since they thought there were too few theories from real data that was collected in a systematical way. Smith, Flowers and Larking (2009) describe GT as:

> Grounded theory was originally developed in order to offer researchers a clear, systematic and sequential guide to qualitative fieldwork and analysis. This was operationalized via a rather technical sounding vocabulary (e.g. 'co-axial coding') and a highly structured procedure for the development of theory. Taken together, these features probably account for its great success in making a space for qualitative research in social scientific disciplines which were largely dominated by positivism (p.201).

From what I have encountered throughout my PhD. studies, I understand that researchers often tend to want to put orthodox GT into the qualitative data analysis family of research. This method does not belong in this family since, while it is inductive and general, the researcher can still use both qualitative and quantitative data. Instead, the orthodox GT methodology should be placed on a branch by its own (Glaser, 1998, p.30).

The main objective for researchers using orthodox GT as a methodology "is to generate a theory that accounts for a pattern of behavior which is relevant and problematic" for the involved actors (Glaser, 1978, p. 93). Gustavsson (1998, pp. 37–39) lists a number of instances when orthodox GT is an appropriate method to use. Orthodox GT is good for researchers to use for those who aims to study and interpret:

- **Social interactions** – Since this dissertation aims to study the management process of co-workers' ethical behavior in sales organizations, social interactions were studied.
- **Phenomena which lack theory** – Understanding new structures, behavioral patterns or other activities which are created by humans. As seen in chapter 1, managing co-workers' ethical behavior in sales organizations seemingly lacks an integrated framework explaining the social activities taking place.
- **Experiments which aim to explain and understand a basic social process (BSP)** – I wanted to understand and explain the management process of ethical behavior in sales organizations, i.e., I wanted to explain and understand a BSP.
- **Useful to give an in-depth look at areas which are relatively unknown to the researcher** – Since the management process of co-workers" ethical behavior in sales organizations was an unknown area before undertaking this study, this was another strong argument to choose orthodox GT as research approach.

Moreover, orthodox GT is exploratory, giving it a reflexive starting point and has a generative capacity (Parry, 1998). This enabled me to reflect on and analyze the empirical data in order to both discover social interactions and generate new theories. The researcher is also supposed to generalize and find regularities in large populations with these theories. In order to generalize data, you as a researcher need to understand what is "going on," thus an exploratory approach is needed, something an orthodox GT approach can help with (Blatter & Haverland, 2012).

Since I thereby wanted to understand what was "going on", it was therefore a need for an exploratory methodology. Orthodox GT helps with this since it is exploratory and aims to find meaning in and investigate social phenomena, without having created hypotheses or expectations beforehand (Åge, 2009). Additionally, the selection of orthodox GT as methodology to use when conducting research should be based on clear conventions, with no room of discussing how various alternatives in methodology fulfill the objectives differently (Åge, 2009). Due to the described gap in chapter 1, there was a need for an inductive approach where orthodox GT has inductive elements and therefore could help me to fill this gap.

Orthodox GT is also detailed and systematic, something which allows researchers to be not only flexible, but also provides them with creative freedom during the research process. Clearly, orthodox GT was deemed as a suitable approach to use since I wanted to look at complex social process which lacked a conceptual theory and to which I had very little knowledge about.

In concluding this section there is also need to explain the aforementioned basic social process and its features since it is an important and recurring theme. Glaser's (1978) explanation of a BSP can be summarized in the following two bullet points:

- Core features for BSP's are that they are basic and pervasive in social life.
- A BSP can be found regardless of structural social units and variation of time. It means that the basic process of for example "honeymooning" can be found both in 17th-century India as well as today in Sweden, i.e., a BSP is stable and durable over time. At the same time, a BSP can "account for change over time with considerable ease of meaning, fit and workability" (Christiansen, 2006, p. 43).

Thus a BSP transcends the boundaries of time, individuals or a place (Christiansen, 2006). There are many examples of BSPs where one earlier given example was "honeymooning" which describes the BSP of getting familiar with a new partner or a new job, etc. Another example is "business maneuvering" which describes the BSP of complex sales. Moreover, as readers will experience when reading this study, when a BSP is being conceptualized, it can be denoted as a gerund in orthodox GT – a word that is a verb but that functions as a noun, where an "-ing form" is applied to the category, most usually to the core category (Glaser, 1978). Denoting a gerund for the core category in this dissertation – Business Basics – was not made since it was deemed more appropriate without. However, four of the core category's five related categories was denoted with a gerund since it describes an ongoing process. For example, the BSP of educating individuals became Educationing.

2.1.1 Explaining the Word "Orthodox"

There are several different methodologies in research that are labelled as a "Grounded Theory" approach, each with different sets of procedures (e.g. Strauss & Corbin, 1990a; Charmaz, 2006). Due to that fact, it is ill-fated since it is either unsuitable or incorrect labelling, or sometimes both, which makes these "GT" studies misleading.

The first version of Grounded Theory was introduced by Dr. Barney Glaser and Dr. Anselm Strauss in 1967 and is often referred to as *orthodox* GT. Glaser (1998) and Gustavsson (1998) both discuss the tools that uphold the actual rationale for conducting an orthodox GT-study and its prescribed procedures. This was later further elaborated upon by Christiansen (2008):

1. An analyst using the orthodox GT methodology does not know beforehand what they are looking for. As a result the main issue is to "let the patterns emerge by staying open" instead of forcing, preconceiving, logically deducing the derived data, then testing it, and ultimately trying to verify any hypotheses. Instead, the core category needs to be discovered (emerge) via patterns in the derived data. The researcher should therefore by default focus on what really goes on, and by doing this, the researchers' interest in the field of research is maintained. Furthermore, orthodox GT is modifiable since more categories can be discovered with new data – there are no final or ultimate solutions so to say.
2. Additionally, the core category's' significance is of great importance since focus of the research is about the interest of the participants. Any interests that are pre-framed (preconceived) needs to be avoided. Focus should not be on people or units, but rather on behavior.

According to Glaser (1978), other methodologies may claim to be a "Grounded Theory," but in reality they have moved away from using the aforementioned two points. Consequently, many researchers are seemingly making up their rationale in order to be able to apply the GT approach. Therefore, those researchers are using different types of procedures in their respective "GT" studies. Subsequently, these procedures are modified and/or are an adapted version of the procedures of orthodox GT.

There can be many reasons as to why a researcher labels his or her research as "GT" but are using different procedures. For example, Christiansen (2006) suggests that it may concern the researchers' inability to work in accordance with the prescribed procedures of the orthodox GT methodology and instead makes certain adaptations along the way when conducting research. It can also be that the researcher makes a deliberate choice to use other procedures, replacing the procedures in orthodox GT.

Glaser and Strauss eventually went separate ways in the academic field due to differences in perception of Grounded Theory. One key difference is that Strauss (and Corbin, 1990b) recommends the usage of specified theoretical frameworks (Christiansen, 2006). The original intention behind orthodox GT is that the emergence of a theory should not be generated through a researcher's preconceptions and assumptions, but instead be generated through the studied actor's subjective experiences. This is something Strauss and Corbin's version is not always likely to reach (Harttman, 2001) which in turn suggests that the rationale of their version of GT differs from Glaser's rationale of what a GT study is supposed to be. Harttman (2001) notes that:

- Strauss and Corbin (1990b) do not strive to seek for the core category in the first stages of the research. This suggests that an emphasis is put on how the core category delimits the study.
- Unlike Strauss and Corbin (1990b), Orthodox GT do not have any procedures that are strict in terms of being able to avoid pre-framing and not stay open in order for the data to emerge. Instead, they rather suggest forcing the data through some previously selected theoretical perspectives like symbolic interactionism.

Also, the procedures of Strauss and Corbin's (1990b) GT-version differs from the original rationale. Strauss and Corbin's version provides a more pre-framed and detailed guiding when it comes to the different stages in the research process. As a consequence, researchers who are in the process of deciding which of the GT versions suit them best need to take certain factors into consideration:

1. GT's original rationale for using it – the emergence of the theory (without pre-framing it).
2. If the researcher believes in and/or prefers the *emergence* of data or the *sorting* (forcing) of data.

Based on the two previous points it is apparent in this dissertation that I, believe in emergence and consequently prefer orthodox GT. I do not believe in forcing data since it is then no longer a procedure of the actors' telling their story. By forcing data, I feel that the study instead becomes the researcher's preconceived story. I have an interest in the actors' main concern and their resolving of it – not my resolving of a pre-conceived problem.

Still, it is worth stressing that there is nothing wrong with the other approaches, they are simply not genuinely true as an orthodox Grounded Theory, they are just different, not superior or inferior. Arguments between methods can go on forever in a rhetoric wrestling match, where Glaser (1978, p. 19) states that "A researcher just chooses and uses the method he chooses. He likes one method over the other for essentially personal abilities, skills and reasons". I chose orthodox due to a personal preference for emergence and the methodology's ability to help me understand and explain a, for me unknown area of research.

2.1.2 Philosophical Considerations

As for ontological and epistemological considerations in orthodox GT, Barney Glaser (2004), later cited by Christiansen (2006) wrote:

> Man is a meaning-making creature. Consequently, social life is patterned and empirically integrated. It is only a question of applying a systematic and rigorous method for discovering and explaining these patterns. Thus, just do it. (p. 61)

This statement can be interpreted as that there is no need for discussions of ontology or epistemology since the researcher is limited to being a meaning-making creature. In supporting arguments both Glaser (1978) and Lowe (personal communication, May 11, 2016) explain that the orthodox GT methodology is based on a latent structure analysis. It is therefore suggested that such studies does not need to have an epistemological justification. Researchers like Glaser (1978) and Lowe (personal communication, May 11, 2016) both suggest that individuals using orthodox GT as a research approach should avoid empty epistemological rhetoric.

Though, by reading literature related to GT (e.g. Glaser, 1978, 1998; Brytting, 1991; Christiansen, 2006; Gustavsson, 1998; Åge, 2011), it was realized it is not as simple as initially thought to dismiss the ontological and epistemological aspects. To start, by reading GT-related literature, it is clear that it exist different positioning perceptions relating to GT. For example, while Charmaz (2006) is positioned in the interpretivist paradigm, Strauss and Corbin (1990a) are positioned in the constructionist paradigm (Levers, 2013). The latter paradigm suggests reality is interpreted and constructed by each individual, where reality only exists within our mind.

However, in 1967 when Glaser and Strauss laid the foundation for orthodox GT with their book, its very title – *The Discovery of Grounded Theory* – suggests that there is a theory out there, awaiting discovery. Consequently, this implicitly suggests that there is a reality above and beyond human influence, independent from the human mind, i.e., reality is both unitary and knowable, waiting to be discovered. While I agree with this perception of reality, it is only agreed to a certain extent.

While reality is observable and conceptualizable, I also favor the idea that reality cannot be observable in its entirety but rather in partial fragments and glimpses, where nothing is absolute. One can argue that it is only possible to see the end result of an action or a structure, while actions and structures behind the end result are unobservable. This notion makes me critical towards the idea of arriving at the truth through mere observation. Instead, the key to arriving at the truth goes through reasoning where parallels of this perception can be drawn to the research of this dissertation.

For example, during an interview with a respondent, the importance of salaries for how to manage co-workers' ethical behavior was brought up for discussion. During another interview with a different respondent, the importance of reward systems was discussed in the same context regarding the management of ethical behavior. The conceptualization process facilitated me with a realization that both respondents discuss monetary-related aspects for how to manage their respective co-workers' ethical behavior, where the category represents a concept of the reality. Thus, this example may reflect a glimpse or fragment of the reality for how managers manage their co-workers' ethical behavior.

With this mindset for how reality works, additional reflections were made. These reflections concern an evaluation criteria for orthodox GT-studies – the characteristic of being modifiable (Glaser, 1978). By perceiving the reality as observable in only fragments and glimpses, this implicitly suggests that reality is modifiable, i.e., there is no definite theory "out there" presenting a definite truth. By being modifiable, if new data emerge, this allows the substantive theory to come closer to "the truth" for how managers manage their co-workers' ethical behavior in sales organizations – but never to arrive at the one final truth for how their reality works.

After coming to an understanding of how orthodox GT relates to reality, other problematic aspects emerged. By using an orthodox GT approach, the majority of data were collected through interviews. The actors' reality is constituted through both dialogical and intersubjective processes (Åge, 2011). Therefore, hermeneutical elements were by default present.

Since the knowledge from these interviews was constituted through observable contextual experiences and perceptions, it should be noted that it is a possibility that some of this knowledge may be fallible — possible misunderstandings could have occurred. In an attempt to solve this, if I encountered unclear issues in the derived data, I would contact that specific respondent for further clarification.

However, there are several prominent features in the orthodox GT methodology which also relates to positivism and are thereby in line with the word "discovery." These features relate to the evaluation criteria of the methodology — fit, work and usability (see section 2.8.3 for the evaluation criteria).

As originally intended by Glaser and Strauss (1967), orthodox GT methodology research occurs in the "real world." Therefore, an emerged theory needs to both "fit" and "work" in the substantive area of research, otherwise the generated theory is not relevant (Åge, 2011, Levers, 2013). This contends with my generated theory for how to manage co-workers' ethical behavior in sales organizations. For example, the positivistic elements correspond with "fit," but fit as in usage and action, not as fit by testing the theory. The positivistic elements also correspond with "work," as the emerged theory's ability to predict and explain the social process, in this case managing co-workers' ethical behavior in sales organizations.

Additionally, positivists like Karl Popper (1972) stress that true knowledge should be free from the researcher's own biases. In a similar vein, Levers (2013, p. 3) contends that "the removal of human bias leads to the discovery of knowledge." In contrast to these academic voices, I oppose the existence of the unbiased researcher, where this consequently becomes a discussion about tabula rasa. Therefore, since one can ask if it is possible to construct a theory (meant to explain a social process) free from biases like pre-understanding and preconceiving this becomes a discussion about Tabula Rasa.

2.1.3 Tabula Rasa

Tabula Rasa is an important measure that benefits the researcher conducting an orthodox GT study. It refers to having no, or at least as little pre-knowledge and pre-understanding of the field of study as possible (Glaser, 1978; Christiansen, 2006). I.e. the researcher needs to have a so-called beginner's mind - to become tabula rasa (Glaser, 1978; MacInnis, 2011). Having a beginner's mind help limits preconceiving and biases, thus helping the researcher to not lose contact with the empirical domain.

As an aspiring GT researcher, I was therefore expected to undertake the study with an empty head, not having the mindset of how things should be, i.e., avoid preconceiving the emerged data. But working as a PhD candidate at a university suggests that this person is specialized and trained in related fields. Some scholars may therefore strongly suggest that I do not have a blank or even a beginner's mind, and rightfully so, to a certain degree.

While many of these researchers, usually not familiar with working from an orthodox GT approach, dispute the possibility of having a blank mindset. Researchers like Gustavsson and Åge (2014) suggest this critique is a mere excuse of neglecting the engagement and discovery aspects of the research process. Instead, they stress that this argument fully preserves the existing theoretical perspectives and suspending pre-knowledge (temporarily) can be reached through training. An experienced supervisor or coach who has used the orthodox GT approach themselves can have tacit knowledge about this and can thus be helpful for the novice researcher.

As stated earlier, I firmly believe that no person can become tabula rasa, a belief also shared by Glaser (1978). It was therefore realized that overcoming potential biases was necessary where several measures were undertaken.

- First, one measure to avoid being influenced is to conduct the literature study after deriving the data (Glaser, 1978). Consequently, no in-depth literature study were conducted before I started to collect data. The literature study for this dissertation occurred after the emergence and saturation of the core category (see chapter 5). This hopefully helped ensuring that the emerged theory was derived from the data and not me.
- Second, there is a need to be not only aware of but also acknowledge potential biases (Glaser, 1978). The pre-conceived notions about sales organizations are mainly based on conversations with friends and reading about scandals in the media, i.e., second-hand information. It has made me feel that sales organizations may suffer from a stigma of being branded with having unethical practices when conducting business. If this is the actual case, I have no idea. However, whether or not it is true is beyond the point for this study, the interest for this study is solely on the management process.

- Third, going into the field of research there is a need to suspend the mind from the potential biases, or as Glaser (1978) suggests, being close to the mind of a humble and innocent child helps the researcher suspend these biases. While being familiar with ethical concepts and important ethical theories, the author was not familiar with the actual management process of ethical behavior. The knowledge and experience within the field was very limited, both on an academic level and on a personal level. This hopefully facilitated me to be more open for new information, making it easier to discover hidden categories and not trying to force the derived data into categories.
- Fourth, by being close to the data at all times throughout the research process helped as an aspiring researchers to not lose track of the field.
- Fifth, literature warns against logical elaborations suggesting that the researcher needs to be aware of the possibility of unintentionally activating it to the research (Glaser, 1978). When relying on logical elaborations, the procedures of orthodox GT are abandoned. Therefore, throughout the whole research process an active attempt was made to be aware of not activating logic. As a result, the key is to not only be aware of and acknowledge what is "known," but also be open to the possibility of discovering a new category. I realize that this is a thin line to walk on for the researcher. Within the orthodox GT literature, this is known as "theoretical sensitivity" (Glaser, 1978). It means that I need an understanding which facilitate my ability to conceptualize but at the same time without it being overshadowed by the aspect of discovery of the actual research endeavor (Gustavsson & Åge, 2014). This is something I gained help with from both supplementary literature like Glaser (1978) and from my supervisor.

The above presented measures helps a researcher to temporarily suspend logical deductions and biases, which in turn helps preventing from interfering with the derived data. It was essential that any ungrounded assumptions, elaborations, logical deductions and preconceptions were minimized in order to tell the story of the actors of the studied area. If this was not achieved, it is possible that my pre-understanding and preconception could have subconsciously affected me throughout the research process. Hopefully, I achieved to temporarily suspend potential biases and preconceived notions to a satisfactory level.

2.1.4 Concluding rationale for Orthodox GT studies

In conclusion, in orthodox GT studies the objective is to discover an emerging theory, where the discovery of the absolute truth is close to impossible. Instead, I recognize that discoveries are perceived as partial segment approximations of reality, constituted through observable experiences and perceptions. By temporarily suspending my logical deductions and biases, hopefully this helped me come closer to the so-called truth – without actually ever reaching it.

As a result, there is no claim that the substantive theory for this dissertation presents the one final truth for how managers manage their co-workers' ethical behavior in sales organizations. Instead, it is my own understanding (as unbiased as possible) for the observable experiences and perceptions of the respondents that is reflected in this study. To better illustrate this perception, generating a theory can be compared with two artists painting a picture of the same object. Although there will probably be similarities between the two paintings, they will never look exactly alike. This also applies when generating a theory. The theory one researcher generates will not look exactly the same as if another researcher within the same substantive field would have generated it.

Thus, the word "discovery" in Glaser and Strauss's (1967) title is accurate in suggesting that there are indeed theories out there awaiting to be discovered. It may just not look exactly the same depending on who discovers it.

2.2. Data Collection

The focal starting point for any orthodox GT is that everything can be data and thus be included in the substantive theory (Glaser & Strauss, 1967; Gustavsson, 1998). This includes not only primary- and secondary data, but also both qualitative- and quantitative data as well. In orthodox GT, collecting primary and secondary data are gathered and obtained via theoretical sampling. As for primary data, the theoretical sampling process can include several types of data. Below, the primary data marked in bold are the type of data included for this dissertation:

- **Interviews**
- **Observations**
- Surveys
- Case Studies
- Focus groups
- Content analysis of documents
- **Seminars**
- **Notes from observations**
- **Transcripts from interviews**
- **Notes from interviews**
- **Subjective impressions which were not clearly stated by the observed**
- **Written Memos**
- Own experiences
- Library studies
- Summaries from scientific conferences
- Other unrelated literature with distant tie to theoretical cross connections
- Serendipity – An unexpected and unintentional discovery when you are searching for something else.

As I wanted to gain a deeper understanding by analyzing the process of how managers manage their co-workers ethical behavior in sales organizations; the main source for empirical data was to conduct open interviews, which is also in accordance with what Glaser (1978) suggests for the orthodox GT approach.

To achieve this, individuals in leading positions were approached. This did not just include the very top management like the CEO, it also included individuals who works in other managerial positions like middle managers and HR managers as well.

To find suitable respondents, managers for different sales organizations were initially contacted by phone where I presented myself and the study. However, some of these were reluctant to participate in an interview and declined. This turned out to be problematic, so to access more respondents there was a need for a different strategy. Therefore, I used my own connections, approaching a colleague who had operated as a franchisee within the real estate industry and an old classmate who is an active franchisee within the real estate industry. It turned out that both had connections to several managers in sales organizations, not just within the real estate industry but also in other relevant industries as well. This resulted in five more potential respondents.

Another strategy was to ask a respondent who had just been interviewed if (s)he could recommend anyone else to approach. This snowball sampling strategy also proved to be fruitful and provided me with several more respondents. There were also times when randomly looking up phone numbers on the organization's homepage for contact details. Most contacts with the respondents started with a phone call where I introduced myself and who had recommended them. Very seldom did my first contact occur in any other fashion (e.g. via email).

In total, 38 individuals were approached and was turned down by 13 of these for various reasons. In total, 25 interviews were conducted, where eleven respondents were identified by the author himself while the remaining fourteen interviews were identified through snowball sampling.

These 25 interviews were conducted across four industries – Real Estate, Car Sales, Pension Insurance Advisors and Private Investing. The locations for these sales organizations were spread across six different Swedish cities. The interviews took between 23 to 85 minutes to conduct with an average of 49 minutes. In total over 1233 minutes were recorded and transcribed. Of these 25 interviews, five respondents were women while the remaining interviews were with men (see Appendix 2 for a summary of the respondents). The average years of experience within their respective industries for the respondents was 19 years. The respondent with most years of experience had 42 years of experience while the respondent with fewest years of experience had three years of experience. Conducting open-ended questions allowed me flexibility to ask follow-up questions. Asking open-ended questions ensures emergence of categories (Glaser, 1978, p. 44).

It should be noted that in the early stages of the study, the questions were asked more broadly since I did not want to add any of my own preconceptions and pre-knowledge. Below, three examples of questions are provided for what could be asked during the interviews.

- "Can you tell me about what a typical day at work consists of?"
- "How do you manage your co-workers' ethical behavior?"
- "Can you tell me about instances when a co-worker had acted wrong and how you solved that instance?"

However, as the research process progressed, categories and ideas emerged. This eventually allowed questions to become more specific. Examples of questions asked throughout the conducted interviews and how they evolved to become more specific are found in Appendix 3.

Since some approached respondents were reluctant to agree to participate in an interview, presumably since it involved discussing ethics, I needed to make them feel comfortable and able to trust me. I attempted to solve this by not only ensuring them full confidentiality (as I did for all respondents), I also emailed these individuals a general description of myself, my role, and if they were still unsure, I sent them examples of questions that I could potentially ask during the interview. See Appendix 4 for how an email could look that was sent to the respondents.

Collecting data progressed until saturation is reached. Reaching saturation in the derived data means that no new categories or sub-categories are found when collecting data and comparing the incidents with each other. After having conducted 20 interviews, I felt saturation had possibly been reached. However, new incidences were encountered which were not exactly the same while their basic underlying meaning remained the same. To ensure saturation, four more interviews was held and then one final (no. 25) interview was conducted. Still, no new underlying basic meanings, no new categories or sub-categories were discovered. As a consequence, saturation of my empirical data was confirmed and the collecting of empirical data was stopped.

Regarding the interviews, in orthodox GT literature some scholars suggest that recording interviews can interfere with the respondent's willingness to be honest, and therefore advise against it (e.g. Glaser, 2016; Lowe, personal communication, May 12, 2016). Åge (personal communication, January 13, 2015) however, made an important note that taping can be necessary for novice researchers within the orthodox GT field due to his or her unfamiliarity with the methodology itself. Moreover, an individual who is aspiring to become a Ph.D. is expected to present a substantial amount of material of his or her data collection that are analyzed. If not, he or she might not be taken seriously and thus fail to attain his or her research to be recognized by scholars. Therefore, it was decided, with the blessings of the respondents, to record all interviews which were later transcribed, after which memos was written, coded and conceptualized.

However, as suggested in the text above, the interviews were not the only source of empirical data used for this dissertation. For example, throughout this research process, memos were written (see section 2.6.1) and two seminars for real estate students named *Ethics in practice* were attended. As can be read in the foreword, it was during the first seminar where the interest for the studied area started was ignited. Ideas of the topic for this dissertation emerged. Later on, during the research process, another opportunity presented itself to attend the same seminar, held for a new class of real estate students. I could then attend with more focus than earlier, where the aim was to observe, ask questions to the individuals holding the seminar, take notes and write memos of how management wants real estate students to act ethically.

I was also inspired, albeit little, by secondary data in the form of articles in newspapers about scandals occurring in sales organizations. For example, one scandal was unveiled in 2006 by Swedish newspaper Expressen where brokers used unethical tactics like staged bidding processes and cover prices (see the Words and Concepts section) just to attempt increase the bidding (Sundsten, 2006). This inspiration led to asking questions related to the different scandals, where the respondents were asked how he or she would have solved the situation if they were placed in such a social context. See section 2.8.4 and Appendix 3 for examples regarding these questions. Needless to say, all collected data provided me with a broader understanding of the field of study.

2.2.1 Conceptualizing and its Importance in Orthodox GT

A conceptualized category can say a lot about an entire social process in a simple and comprehensive way. Therefore, the conceptualization process is the most important process in orthodox GT since that is where the categories emerge. To think in categories is to understand a problem or a situation which is abstractly experienced via connections or patterns (MacInnis, 2011). This is central to us as humans when attempting to understand our world and how it works. In accordance with this description, the featured categories can be representations of ideas that can be anything from pictures to verbal, mathematical or metaphorical abstract patterns since humans continuously construct symbolic universes via objectifications with categories (Gustavsson et al., 2014).

Jarowski (2011) stresses that managers can via categories and their interrelationships obtain influential knowledge. This knowledge can provide an umbrella perspective or a broad orientation of a complex social process that may help practitioners and researchers alike to think in broader contexts about the topic. Relevant conceptualizations for any orthodox GT should be able to (1) discover latent data (Glaser & Strauss, 1967); (2) Simplify the complexity of the studied area via the categories in order to make the complexity somewhat feasible (Glaser, 1998); and (3) "grab." By grab I mean that the category should not be limited to a specific substantive area; the conceptualized category needs to have a more general application (Glaser, 2001). It is also important that the conceptual categories both "work" and "fit" for the particular social setting. Therefore, these two aspects of the conceptualization process are not only important but they are also part of the evaluation criteria for any orthodox GT studies (see section 2.8.5). By working and fitting for a particular social setting, conceptual categories reach a higher level of generalization.

The basis for conceptualization in this dissertation was inspired by Gustavsson et al. (2014). In order to ensure the emergence of categories, it is important to not only have a beginner's mind, but also to find the core category since it explains most of the process and provides an umbrella perspective that depicts the main concern of the stakeholders. Therefore, orthodox GT is a research approach which aims to explain and conceptualize the main concern of the involved actors and its recurrent resolving within the specific area of concern.

In other words, the author's agenda of research is to conceptualize the managers' main concern in sales organizations and to conceptualize the recurrent solving of their main concern. As will be seen in coming sections, the importance and the need for conceptualizing categories into an emergent substantive theory is the whole point of orthodox GT.

2.3. The Substantive Open Coding Process

The coding procedure for any orthodox GT study is done on two levels: (1) *substantive* coding (which includes both *open* and *selective* coding procedures) and (2) *theoretical* coding (Gustavsson, 1998). In this and the following sections, these analytical processes are explained based upon how I as a Ph.D. candidate coded my data.

The logic behind both the substantive coding procedures is for researchers to generate categories via stable, but latent patterns in the derived data. After discovering these patterns, I proceeded to label them in accordance with each underlying meaning and/or how they were signified by their respective characteristics. For example, I labelled one category 'Monetary Managing' for how to manage co-workers' ethical behavior since it consisted of several stable patterns. Examples of related stable patterns (later called sub-categories) were salary systems and rewards. For further reading about the remaining categories for this dissertation and their related patterns, please see appendices 5a–e.

In the process of substantive open coding, everything and anything can be coded if it is deemed necessary where the sole purpose is to discover the core category. My focus for substantive open coding was to fracture data and thus discover categories and their respective sub-categories through coding or conceptualizing processes. Eventually, I ended up with a core category, five categories and several sub-categories, each relating to one of the five categories. The sub-categories and their respective categories gave me an indication of how the derived data fit together in various stable patterns. Not only did I gain a familiarity with the categories in this procedure, but the categories also became grounded in the data.

Furthermore, while other procedures associated with coding are described later in this chapter, it is important to stress that a researcher can go back to this coding procedure despite finding the core category (Gustavsson, 1998). I did this on several occasions during my research with the result that new categories emerged and some categories were abandoned. For example, a category labeled Ethical calibration was completely removed since not many respondents discussed it. This also happened with the initially proposed category named Brand protection. In the early interviews, one respondent discussed the importance of protecting their brand, but was not discussed again and the potential category was therefore eventually eliminated.

As for the core category, a researcher can come to have doubts after he or she has encountered it about whether or not this core category is truly emergent. I initially thought that I had found a core category and called it "Business Flourishing." However, doubts arose as I felt it did not truly represent what a core category was supposed to be (see section 2.4 for a more detailed discussion of what a core category should represent). Consequently, when going back the substantive open coding process, more data was collected and conceptualized. Eventually, a new core category emerged and was ultimately called "Business Basics."

Additionally, a researcher can also encounter other doubts like when to stop the substantive open coding process and when to start with the substantive selective coding process instead. Glaser provides much insight on how to manage these problems in several of his books (e.g. Glaser 1978; 1998; 2001), much of which was taken to heart during this research process.

In Figure (2.2), inspired by Gustavsson (1998), the direction of my analytical process is explained. The arrows in the figure displays the substantive open coding's focus – Where the focus directs from the derived data into categories and their respective sub-categories, and ultimately the categories are directed toward the core category. The data incidences (referred to by Gustavsson (1998) as indicators) along with the sub-categories and the categories are integrated with the core category. These accounts for how the main concerns of what is observed are continuously resolved.

Figure 2.1: The Relationships between Open Coding, Categories, Memos and the Core Category (inspired by Gustavsson, 1998, p. 63)

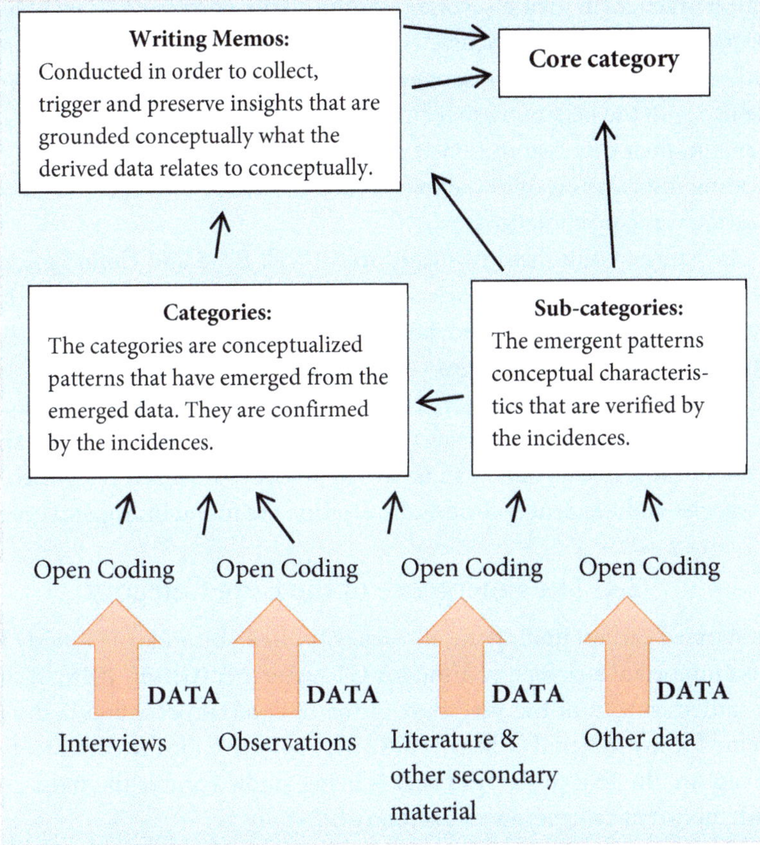

As for the substantive open coding process, two examples from the substantive theory is provided for how one of the categories emerged, how it was conceptualized and how it was linked to the core category. To start, when conducting interviews, some respondents discussed that before instructing their co-workers about a desired ethical practice, some stressed the necessity to be well-prepared (an incidence). In a similar vein, others discussed the importance to read up on the topic before instructing (another incidence). Memos were written with the help of these incidences in the data. In turn, it provided me with an indication that it was important for the managers to be well-read about the topic before instructing others. Thus, the category of *Well-Read* was conceptualized.

As a second example of conceptualizing a potential category, during some interviews, some respondents discussed how they communicated desired ethical practices to their co-workers. Some discussed in the context of having formal meetings, others discussed in the context of having informal meetings, while other respondents discussed sending emails, etc. Again, by writing memos with the help of these incidences, it became apparent that the central theme in their discussions (albeit expressed differently) concerned communicating information onto their co-workers. Thus, the category of *Communication* was conceptualized.

As it turned out, these two categories (Well-Read and Communication) were demoted to sub-categories during a sorting procedure since it was realized that both concerned how to educate co-workers in how to act ethically. From this, the category of Educating was conceptualized.

Then, when the core category emerged, it became apparent that Educating is a focal part in how managers in sales organizations manage their co-workers' ethical behavior. A summary of all conceptualized categories, sub-categories and incidences for this dissertation are found in Appendices 5a–e.

2.4. The Emergence of the Core Category

As stressed earlier, finding the core category in an orthodox GT study is the most important task for any orthodox GT researcher (Glaser, 1978). It should be undertaken from the very start of the research process and is the main theme for my material (Glaser, 1978). The objective for the core category is to capture the BSP in the field that is being studied and is the most central and important category in an orthodox GT study.

There are several reasons as to why it is the most important category. For example, one essential characteristic is that the core category is at the very top of the conceptual levels where it explains most of the variation of a BSP. It should also conceptualize the main concern of the involved actors and their recurrent resolving (Glaser, 1978). Another important characteristic is that the core category is the category which links the substantive theory together through all other categories (Glaser, 1978). It is therefore related to all other categories of lesser levels and their respective sub-categories.

It is evident in the empirical findings (see chapter 3) that the core category for this dissertation (Business Basics) manages to capture these characteristics. Not only is Business Basics on the highest conceptual level in the substantive theory describing a social process, it also links all other categories together explaining the main concern of the actors and their recurrent solving of it (see chapter 4).

It is imperative that the core category has the ability to explain the main concern of the involved actors. Therefore, as an inspiration, I used the following criteria that both Glaser (1978, pp. 93–96) and later Gustavsson (1998, p. 80) listed to determine the core category for this dissertation:

1. The core category has to be a central category related to as many other categories as possible. It is also more related to the categories than any other categories are. This centrality is a condition that is a necessary criterion in order to make the core since it indicates that a large part of the variation accounts in explaining the behavior or phenomena.
2. The core category occurs frequently in the derived data and is perceived as a stable pattern due to it recurring frequently.
3. Relates not only easily with other lesser level categories but is also meaningful to these categories.
4. Even though it accounts for most of the variation in a certain behavior, the core category can be perceived as a dimension of behavior. The involved actor's main concern and the recurrent solution to their problem can eventually come to represent not only a problematic issue but also two (or more) related facets. For example, if a particular core category is discovered in the substantive area of sales and managing business ethics in sales organizations, it can explain a problem or a social process in the sales organizations. At the same time, it could also possibly explain how and why the organization can/should continue to pursue a certain behavior or course of action when they meet customers, managers, co-workers and other involved actors. In fact, due to the aim of this study, there is a chance that advantages with this may be found in the data, where managers and co-workers alike use it to their own advantage.
5. It provides clear implications for a general theory.
6. It allows by its characteristics as much variation in the analysis as possible.
7. The core category's relation to the other lesser-level categories makes the core category very variable. The conditions can easily vary, and the core category is modifiable via these dependent variations.

While an exact number of criteria for deciding a core category in orthodox GT cannot be decided, according to Glaser (2001), the quality of the core category should also be based on the researcher's trust in and reliance on his or her own judgment. The judgment can be gained not only through the researcher's own insight, but also through his or her familiarity with the conceptualization of the derived data during the "open coding process." In order to better rely on my own judgment and insight when determining the core category in accordance with the above given criteria, I re-read the empirical data several times and compared it with the criteria. This provided me with a confidence that it was indeed a core category that had emerged.

This enabled me both to take in critical considerations as well as know how to think regarding my own judgment which ultimately made me confident in the core category. Additionally, Glaser (1978) also stresses that it is important for a core category to have the characteristic of grabbing implycations formal theories have despite being substantive theory. As Glaser (1978, pp. 95–96) explains, "the analyst can talk of hospital shifts and immediately realize the implication of shifts as a basic social condition in any work operation and start to conceive of generating a formal theory of work shifts."

It is not only crucial that the core category explains most of the variation, it also becomes very problematic for the researcher as well. The core category is what directs and drives the involved actor's behavior. This means that in orthodox GT studies, the agenda of the involved actors are deliberately being watched by the researcher where any preconceived professional notions that the researcher may have should be avoided. This may not be easy for inexperienced researchers using this methodology.

2.4.1 Substantive Categories and Sub-Categories

As mentioned, the core category connects all other categories. According to Glaser (1998), a "substantive category" can be explained as those categories of the substantive theory which reflect the studied area of research. As I did in my substantive theory (Business Basics), substantive categories (e.g. Educating) are used to construct the substantive theory based on their relationship.

Christiansen (2008) goes further and explains the substantive categories as a stable pattern consisting of a set of descriptive incidents (keywords in the data). This stable pattern not only describes the area of research, but may also summarize the derived data's empirical substance. At the same time, theoretical categories (or sub-categories) characterize potential relationships between the substantive categories.

There are several levels in the conceptual hierarchy between the substantive categories. Below the core category are the closely related categories. In the lower level of conceptualizations, there are the sub-categories, each closely related to a category. A sub-category has the category's conceptual characteristics where Glaser (1992, p. 38) describes them as a category of a category. This means that it is on a lesser conceptual level than a category or a core category and can define and explain what the category stands for. To exemplify, for this dissertation each of the five emerged categories consists of several sub-categories. For instance, the category of Monetary **M**anaging consists of three sub-categories (Salary Systems, Rewards and Goals) with all sub-categories having a lesser level of conceptualization compared to the category.

As experienced during this research process, a sub-category can initially have been thought of as a higher-level category, but during the research process can be demoted. For example, a category named "External Ethical Controlling" was initially conceptualized. It was later demoted due to being at a lower conceptual level and placed in the Bureaucratization category.

At the bottom of the conceptual levels are the descriptive incidences of the emerged data along with possible keywords. These data can be extracts from interviews which give incidences about the sub-categories. Examples of these for my substantive theory are found in the appendices (5a–e). Below is a summary of the categorical hierarchy:

The Categorical Hierarchy

- Core category
- Categories
- Sub-categories
- Data & Descriptive incidences (e.g. keywords)

The time after the researcher has "discovered" the core category, not only does he or she still continue to write memos, but the researcher also starts a methodological procedure of *selective coding* when analyzing the derived data.

2.5 The Substantive Selective Coding Process

After discovering the core category, the researcher starts the methodical procedure of *substantive selective coding* when analyzing the derived data. This meant that during this stage of the study that the objective, in accordance with Glaser (1978), was to compare all new data only with the core category and potential relationships therein.

Consequently, this coding procedure allowed me to delimit the process to the indices, sub-categories and categories that were related to the emerged core category. The purpose for conducting this type of analytical process was not only for the core category to be saturated, but also to find and saturate the lesser levels of any substantive categories that somehow related to the core category.

This allowed me to be more specific when asking respondents questions. For example, as noted earlier, at an early stage in the research process, the questions were asked in a broad and general way. During the substantive selective coding process, more specific questions were asked like "Can you tell me how salaries affect your co-workers' ethical behavior".

Additionally, when a researcher is conducting this analytical process, (s)he can find it helpful to start organizing the memos (s)he has written. The reason for this is to discover theoretical codes and then go back to the selective coding yet again. As can be seen in chapter 3, I present several drafts of the substantive theory before reaching saturation. It was between these drafts I sat down with my written memos, trying to organize them into groups based on relationships and from there create potential categories.

In Figure 2.3, also inspired by Gustavsson (1998), illustrates for how the substantive selective coding process proceeded in this dissertation. For example, the arrows show the substantive selective coding's direction of focus. As can be seen, the primary focus is directed (mainly) from the core category to the incidences of data, opposite direction compared to conducting substantive open coding (see Figure 2.2).

This procedure further established the relationships between the core category and its related categories. Eventually no more new data was found, which signaled that saturation in the empirical data had been reached.

Figure 2.3: The Process of Selective Coding (inspired by Gustavsson, 1998, p. 83)

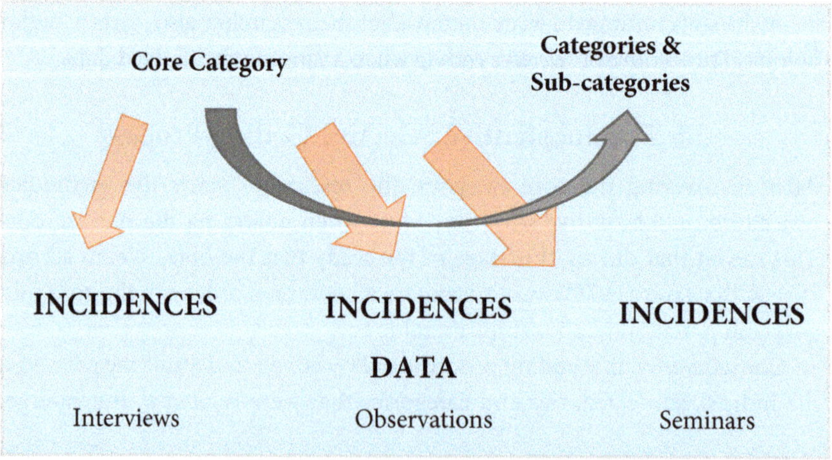

2.6 The Theoretical Coding Process

While the substantive coding process provided categories and sub-categories, etc., I It was also necessary to look into how these related to each other. Looking for the relationships between the categories is therefore called the theoretical coding process (Gustavsson, 1998). Other researchers like Christiansen (2006) refer to the theoretical coding process as the coding of the coding. The theoretical codes are what integrate substantive theory as they explain all the relationships between not only the core category and other categories, but also categories with sub-categories.

This process consists of writing memos (section 2.6.1) and the sorting of these (section 2.6.2) in order to find any possible relationships between the codes. The theoretical coding process was therefore undertaken during this study to identify any theoretical codes in the data that had emerged and their potential relationships. Throughout the years, researchers like Glaser (e.g. 1978; 1998) have identified several theoretical codes and coding families. If the reader wish to become more familiar with these, please read Appendix 6 for recommended readings.

As with any process in orthodox GT, I noticed that theoretical coding can occur throughout the whole process of research, overlapping with other processes. For example, I could be theoretically coding, but still write new memos about new potential categories. The reason for this is simple; this coding process aims to link categories together via relationships and several codes can be discovered throughout the whole research process.

2.6.1 Writing Memos

The bedrock of generating a substantive theory is writing memos (along with the coding and constant comparing). Writing memos can be conducted from day one when using an orthodox GT approach (Glaser, 1978). Therefore, it is extra important during the process of coding that the researcher should have a pen and paper nearby since (s)he may get sudden insights, hunches and ideas which may emerge. If an immediate note is not made about the idea or hunch, they are likely soon to be forgotten.

With this in the back of my mind, if I had no pen and paper available, I used a recorder on my cellphone to construct ideas relating to the memos. For example, there were times when I had to take a quick pause at the gym in order to record a notion I had instead of risk losing my train of thought.

Moreover, researchers get conceptual familiarity with the data by constantly comparing it. Having read much literature about orthodox GT, it became evident that constantly comparing the data is an essential process. It helped me to see patterns, relationships and conceptualize when writing memos. Writing memos frequently throughout the research process led me to the following benefits:

- The emergence of various new ideas and insights regarding categories were triggered by the writing of memos.
- Gaining new ideas and insights regarding the categories' grounding via saturation based on the interchangeable indices.
- Triggering new ideas and insights about theoretical codes – like relationships between different categories.

For example, one written memo was named "Clarity." It concerned how managers need to display clarity towards their co-workers of what is expected in how to ethically behave. To exemplify, if managers do not display clarity in regards to how they expect their co-workers to act in certain procedures, not only can it lead to unintentional unethical behavior, but also lead to frustration for the involved actors. In turn this frustration can lead to both intentional and unintentional unethical behavior. It is therefore important to educate co-workers by being clear about what is wanted and expected. This memo became a category and was later demoted to become a sub-category, placed under the conceptualized Educating category due to their close relationship.

Still, *writing memos* can be perceived as category-describing and thus a transitional step to the conceptual explanations. However, many of the memos were in actuality not only emerging categories and memos of categories, they could also be incidences in data that linked the categories. Subcategories and categories tend to pattern out when the data incidences convert to becoming interchangeable. Consequently, all data needs to be recorded throughout the whole process of research, therefore memo writing turns into an "ever-going" work for the researcher. While some memos eventually became categories or sub-categories, other memos were either disposed or merged with other memos.

One example of a disposed memos is the elimination of the "three processes." During the process of research I initially thought I saw a relationship between the existing categories and three distinct processes (see section 3.4.1). However, after a discussion with T. Brytting (personal communication, November 20, 2019), a well-versed scholar in orthodox GT, this led me to further the theoretical coding of these processes. I realized that the processes had very little relationship to the categories (see section 3.6) and were therefore eliminated altogether from the substantive theory.

2.6.2 Theoretical Sorting

The theoretical sorting process can not only be conducted at any time during the process of research, but it can also, if required, be conducted several times. At times, the theoretical sorting led to more writing of memos and more collecting of data (interviews) since it was just another form of me constantly comparing. As can be read in chapter 3, I conducted six major sorting procedures (there described as drafts). However, it also happened that I could do a minor sorting in order to detect or dismiss a specific relationship between categories. One instance concerns the Compassing category since I felt this category was difficult to grasp. After further conceptualizations, it was re-named (back) to "Intuiting" because it more appropriately connects to the sub-categories and describes the process.

When sorting, using the software of a computer is not to be recommended, instead theoretical sorting needs to be manually conducted through a pair of scissors (Glaser, 2003). The sorting process in this study was conducted by the conceptual levels and by categories, where the analyzed data and the memos were included in the process. Since sorting was conducted via the conceptual levels and via categories, every memo of every category was cut out, along with every index of coded data. I then proceeded to sort all the pieces into a sufficient number of boxes, where every box can represent a certain substantive category or sub-category.

Even though theoretical sorting is a process that requires constant comparison, I found it was still different compared to constantly comparing during the substantive coding process. Here, every substantive category was connected through the theoretical codes to other substantive codes found in the data. The emergence of the theoretical codes was enabled by the sorting process, where the theoretical codes' data incidences can in the sorting process emerge in the data (Glaser, 1998). Normally, during the process or sorting, this is where most of the theoretical coding occurs.

Being heavily influenced by Glaser (2003) when theoretically sorting for this study, I had my memos cut out on paper and placed them on the floor in my office. I sat down and started to sort them into different piles (boxes) of where I deemed them to fit best (into potential categories) in the categorical hierarchy. The reason for this was to distinguish categories from sub-categories and incidences as well as if some categories needed to be re-named. Additionally, the possibility of having to derive more data or re-code the derived data can be revealed in the theoretical sorting process – as happened in the Compassing category which was re-coded to Intuiting.

2.7. The Grounding of the Emerged Theory

When the researcher is confident enough about the theory (s)he has discovered, the researcher then proceeds to look for relevant existing theories which (s)he can analyze and ultimately integrate and synthesize to the theory. This procedure is called the validation of the empirical data in existing literature and can be read in chapter 5.

The reviewing of existing literature is not determined contextually, but rather determined conceptually as part of the delimiting process (for this dissertation, category by category and sub-category by sub-category). The categories rather than contexts are examined when conducting a literature review with orthodox GT, since it is from the categories the data has emerged. The literature read by the researcher is perceived as new data and needs to be related to the categories and its sub-categories. The literature also needs to be constantly compared (Glaser, 1998) and by constantly comparing existing literature during the grounding (Validation) process, it may lead to the emergence of new sub-categories in the theory.

Therefore, the integrated literature in the data can potentially lead the researcher to further modifications. For this dissertation, no new categories (or sub-categories) emerged during the validation process. Moreover, corrections of existing literature may also occur. Theories emerged via the orthodox GT methodology are always modifiable since they describe a social process of what is going on where new relevant categories can emerge. If a researcher should miss something in the conceptualization process or in the literature review, the modifiability of orthodox GT is still not undermined. Consequently, as stressed in section 2.1.1, there is no ultimate theory in orthodox GT to discover that is seen as final.

It should also be noted that the literature review of an orthodox GT-study is not only all funneled down to the significance of the core category and the categories, but also funneled down to the significance of the theoretical codes and other related lesser-level categories. When there is no relatedness of importance to the core category in the context of the read literature, that literature will simply be excluded from the synthesizing process. As can be read in the validation chapter (chapter 5), researchers can include literature from another disciplines or contexts to the theory (Glaser, 1998; Christiansen, 2006). The key here is the conceptual relatedness to the theory, not what discipline it belongs to. As the reader will experience with this dissertation, including literature from other disciplines were made. Moreover, due to the frequent abundance of existing literature, the validation chapter in orthodox GT studies tends to be kept short compared to literature reviews in studies using other methodologies.

Also, in orthodox GT studies, the researcher has the option to write a stand-alone chapter solely focusing on the validation of the empirical data where its structure can be based on the outline of the final sorting (Glaser, 1998). Early on during the research process the approach of including a stand-alone chapter was chosen. However, after the final sorting it was decided that the structure of this chapter (chapter 5) needed to be based on the final sorting in order to make it more comprehensible for the reader.

2.8. Important Aspects in Orthodox GT studies

As the reader of this chapter by now probably have come to realize, the orthodox GT methodology differs greatly from other common methodologies in social sciences. Since the methodological paradigm is different for researchers using orthodox GT, this chapter will not only focus on explaining the methodology's procedures but it will also present the evaluation criteria for orthodox GT studies and measures undertaken to ascertain the honesty of the respondents.

2.8.1 Evaluation Criteria for Orthodox GT

As any conducted research, orthodox GT studies also need to be evaluated. When using an orthodox GT research approach, the research should be evaluated upon the principles on which it is based. This means that those more traditional criteria that are used in positivistic research (e.g. the validity and reliability criteria) are not applicable to Orthodox GT (Gustavsson, 1998). Validity measures something that is predetermined, in orthodox GT nothing is predetermined. Regarding reliability, if it should be included as an evaluation criterion, the researcher should test the theory in a customary way. But when generating a substantive theory, it needs to be measured in other ways (Christiansen, 2006).

In orthodox GT research, it is the final product that should be assessed as quality criteria In short, Gustavsson (1998) address four main criteria for how an orthodox GT study should be assessed: if the theory is (1) *grounded*, its (2) *theoretical* aspects, its (3) *processual* aspects and (4) *personal* considerations:

1. There are three prominent (1) grounded criteria (Fit, Work and Usefulness). They concern how close the substantive theory is to the data: (a) How adequately does a category mirrors (Fit) the derived data and what it is supposed to express. Here, the validity criteria corresponds with fit, but fit as in the ability to be authentic, not as fit by testing. (b) Does the theory's ability to explain and predict a BSP and/or a complex phenomenon. For example, the theory for this dissertation explains the management process of managing ethical behavior in sales organizations. (c) If the theory both fits and works, it is relevant (Useful). If the theory is relevant, it provides the studied actors with not only an enhanced understanding for the field but also with tools to solve their recurrent main concern.
2. There are three theoretical quality criteria to consider. To start, as earlier noted no emerged orthodox GT theory is ultimate or final, nothing is set in stone. As a result, the substantive theory's ability to be (a) modifiable is important to consider when evaluating. As new data emerges, the theory is modified – without the previous theory ceasing to be valid. The study's ability to (b) discover new relationships and insights should also be evaluated and is closely tied to the researcher's ability to conceptualize. The final (c) important theoretical quality criteria are the theory's ability to *generalize* a process through the categories. The researcher must be able to have high abstraction levels in their categories. It is a balance for the researcher to be sufficiently abstract in the emerged theory (and categories) without losing the responsiveness of the specific area.
3. The research process of the study also needs to evaluate the skills of the researcher. This includes the actual process and how the study came about, if the researcher discovered a BSP and managed to link relationships. For example, problems I encountered during my research concern the sheer volume of the data and the complex interplay between categories. To solve this, I continuously compared the data and frequently to conceptualized and re-conceptualized to ensure this.
4. The *personal quality criteria* refers to the researcher's personal traits like engagement and managing understanding. Managing understanding refers to the researcher's ability to conceptualize. How I attempted to overcome challenges of conceptualizing is discussed in section 2.2.1. Moreover, the researcher's theoretical sensitivity is another personal trait that needs to be assessed when evaluating the study. How my theoretical sensitivity was reached is also presented in section 2.2.1.

While these are the important quality criteria to consider, I have found that there are also other important aspects to consider when evaluating an orthodox GT study. *Generative capacity* was briefly brought up in chapter 1 and refers to the study's ability to create something new or ingenious in a certain context where "The results shall support the interplay of ideas" (Brytting, 1991, p. 113). I.e. there is a need for new terminology and new conceptualized categories that needs to be as close to the studied field as possible. The ambition I had with this dissertation was, in the same vein as Brytting (1991), to generate categories as close to the "everyday language" of the studied area as possible. This enables the categories to both "work" and "fit" for the substantive area, providing practitioners a better understanding of the studied field (Brytting, 1991). For this dissertation, as can be seen in chapter 4, a new conceptual theory was generated along with new connections and categories, all based on the actors' own descriptions.

Not surprisingly, there is also critique of the orthodox GT methodology among scholars, something I was made well aware of this during my time as a PhD candidate. The criticism not only comes in literature, but also from colleagues, who were most often not familiar with the orthodox GT methodology. They could criticize the procedures I conducted or met me with general skepticism towards the methodology itself. But as I came to realize, that critique usually stemmed from a discussion between two different paradigms of research, i.e., problems for how to interpret. Since the orthodox GT approach is mainly a qualitative and inductive methodology, questions often stem from positivistic researchers about objectivity. Discussing tabula rasa was one such example that was up for critique.

2.8.2 Respondents Honesty

I realized early on during the research process that ethics as a topic might be sensitive to discuss. Few, if any want to be perceived as an unethical person or would flat out confess to a stranger (in this case me) about their shortcomings. It was therefore assumed that there could be times when the respondents would not be completely honest or that it was possible that some respondents avoided answering or discussing certain questions.

It was therefore also possible that some interviewed individuals only told the politically correct story for how they thought they were expected to work and act in accordance with the societal norms. In hopes of overcoming this as much as possible, the following approach was undertaken:

1. All respondents was ensured before the interview that they were given full confidentiality, where published material could not be traced back to the individual nor their organization.
2. I believe that individuals can be biased toward his or her organization when discussing ethics. Therefore, the questions during the interviews were at times asked in a general context, where hypothetical scenarios were given in how they would act in a particular social setting, using past media reporting about scandals as examples.
3. There is also a belief of the author that it is easier to discuss the shortcomings of others than our own. Therefore, at times, the respondents were asked about competitors and their possible ethical breaches, something they were often happy to discuss. Usual follow-up questions could then be to ask how the respondent instead would have acted in that situation. For example, one question could be "Can you tell me about an instance of an ethical breach you have heard done by a competitor?" The follow-up questions would be "How would you act if you were put in such scenario?" (For more examples of questions asked during the interviews, see appendix 3)

2.9 Concluding and Summarizing

Since the aim of this study suggests that there was a need for new theoretical categories explaining the main concern of the actors along with their resolving of it – an exploratory research approach was required where the orthodox GT methodology was chosen. From Gustavsson (1998), orthodox GT as a research approach can be summarized and explained by the following bullet points as being:

- *Exploratory* – orthodox GT studies aims to discover new theories.
- *Inductive* – orthodox GT studies derive empirical data, comparing them with existing theories.
- *Empirical* – orthodox GT is a method which uses data from reality.
- *Qualitative* – orthodox GT as a method is suitable for analyzing qualitative data.
- *Explaining* & *Predicting* – One of the aims of orthodox GT is to explain and predict phenomena or a BSP. In orthodox GT explanation and prediction must be viewed in relation to the method's other approaches. The reason is that the method makes the researcher operate like a detective.

While there are several (often overlapping) steps and procedures included when conducting an orthodox GT study, the actual procedure can be summed up in five different steps:

1. To primarily (a) find the core category, and then (b) solely focus on issues that are only are related to it.
2. The inductive approach of orthodox GT is used at all times during the research process while the processes of theoretical sampling and the validation of the derived data are conducted in the later stages.
3. Another important procedure in orthodox GT is to constantly compare when conceptualizing (and coding). This step is normally conducted in conjunction with the second step (2).
4. Writing memos is a quintessential procedure in which the researcher needs to strongly emphasize constantly comparing the memos (s)he writes with each other.
5. The sorting procedure. As in step 4, the researcher also needs to put a strong emphasis on constantly comparing when sorting the data.

Due to my own personal preference for emergence and its coding procedures along with no pre-knowledge, orthodox GT was therefore chosen as a suitable approach for this study. In concluding this chapter I would like to highlight some of the most essential sources of literature focusing on orthodox GT used for this chapter. It was to a great extent thanks to this literature I managed to comprehend the procedures and other important aspects related to orthodox GT. While it exist more literature about orthodox GT, the reader can see in Appendix 7 literature I consider important when learning about the orthodox GT methodology. The substantive theory that is about to be unveiled in the subsequent chapter are revealed by the data, and not by me since I only act as an intermediary between the respondents and their knowledge. At the same time, I tried to the utmost of my abilities to temporarily suspend any pre-knowledge and preconceptions I might have had during the research process. In chapter 3, the reader is presented with how the substantive theory emerged.

3. How the Substantive Theory Emerged

This theory was conducted through continuous adjustments and modifications of categories as more empirical data was derived. Consequently, ideas and conceptualizations were reformulated, changed and re-conceptualized several times. Examples of the different conceptualized categories are found in appendices 5a–5e.

As can be read in this chapter, the path to what would become a theory for how to manage co-workers' ethical behavior in sales organizations was far from straightforward. This path will be summarized in six drafts for how the emergent theory was discovered and evolved.

3.1 The First Draft: The Beginning of an Emergent Theory

A first draft of the theory was constructed after having (1) attended a full day seminar for real estate students conducted by top management at one of Sweden's leading real estate agencies along (2) with three interviewed respondents. The focus of the seminar targeted ethical issues, the management of ethical issues and desired ethical behavior. Field notes were taken in conjunction with the several discussions throughout the seminar.

As for the respondents in the three conducted interviews, all three respondents operated in the real estate industry in managerial roles. In order to get as broad a perspective on ethics and managing ethics as possible, managers in differing positions within the same industry were approached. The targeted sales organization was real estate organizations. The first interview was conducted with an HR manager at the headquarters for a leading Swedish real estate agency. The second and third respondents both operated as franchisees in the same industry.

The collected data that came from the seminar and these interviews focused on ethics, management of ethics, proactive management of unethical behavior and customer care. After transcribing and writing memos, the process of open coding and writing more memos was undertaken. The seminar resulted in 12 different categories, while the first interview generated 27 categories and the second interview generated 19 categories, all with a number of sub-categories. As will be revealed in the subsequent text, these categories would be re-conceptualized further and then merged into eleven categories and several more sub-categories during this draft.

3.1.1 Findings after the First Draft

The first category was Ethical Termination. Ethics as a topic seemed to be a serious topic for all three respondents. They focused on discussing the consequences of acting unethically and what the manager actually did if they found out about co-workers acting unethically. Terminating the co-worker from their position (temporarily or permanently) was discussed if the ethical breach was too severe. As a result, this category was called Ethical Termination.

The culture of the sales organizations also seemed to be of importance, since the respondents often discussed core values, being a good role model and how this could affect the organization as a whole. Therefore, the second category was named Enterprise Culture.

Intuition was the third category discussed. The respondents discussed the complexity of ethics and how they often had to use a feeling when managing co-workers. Several respondents used the word "gut feeling" when describing this process. Other respondents described it as a finger-tip feeling they had. However, while the terms "gut feeling" and "finger-tip feeling" are distinct, it became apparent during the conceptualizing process that they were discussing the same thing – a feeling they had when managing. The term "Gut feeling" was therefore considered more appropriate when describing the social process.

Additionally, the respondents also discussed how they would have to manage complex ethical issues with no right or wrong answer, where sometimes the co-worker would be allowed to proceed with a certain work practice, whether or not the manager liked it. Because of this, the category of Intuition was formulated as it was deemed to encompass the social processes taking place when describing this sub-category.

The fourth category concerned taking care of co-workers. It was found to be of importance for the respondents to take care of their co-workers since it was argued that by doing this, the co-workers felt better and would therefore not only act better, but the likelihood of better conduct increased when working. The term "taking care of" is associated with the word nursing and therefore "nursing" was deemed as a suitable name for this category to describe the occurring processes taking place.

The fifth category concerns the importance of managers acting immediately upon encountering co-workers who act unethically. During the interviews, the respondents wanted to discuss unethical behavior, and I often replied by asking in the context of what they would do if they found out about ethical breaches. Their response was to immediately confront that individual since it was deemed that the unethical behavior otherwise could escalate and the negative consequences could be more damaging. This category was therefore named "Immediate Ethics Managing."

For category six, the three respondents discussed the importance of ethical conduct and as to why this would be a way to better protect their brand. It was important to manage the co-workers in such direction that their behavior would not damage the brand name. Therefore, the category of "Brand Protection" was conceptualized since it seemed to encompass a potential concern of the actors.

The next category was called "Ethical Calibration." It was discussed how co-workers did not always share the organization's ethical values or know how to ethically conduct business practices. The respondents discussed a desire to change these views and behaviors. A fitting word was calibration since it was suggested that the respondent wanted to change this to be in accordance with the organization's ethical practices.

Proposed category eight was difficult to name due to its complexity. It was at this stage called "Same-but-different Treatment" for lack of a better label. But I was certain that with more interviews, this category would be renamed or eliminated and therefore let the name remain. The focus for this category was that managers discussed the importance to treat and manage all co-workers the same, but at the same time still approach them differently due to their different needs, personalities and state of mind.

"Transboundary Information-Exchange" was the ninth category created in the first draft. Two respondents discussed approaching other managers if they found out that a co-worker operated unethically so that the other manager could better manage those ethical behaviors. The respondents deemed that other co-workers' unethical behavior could also have a negative impact on their organization as well.

The tenth category concerned co-workers and managers alike being controlled by external organs. The respondents expressed how they felt that their organization and ethical behavior was controlled by external organs like the FMI and auditing organizations. For example, the quality of their services could be checked randomly or if a customer complained. Also, if encountering complex ethical issues, co-workers and managers alike could contact external organs like FMI to seek counseling in ethical conduct. Because of the inherent social processes, this category was named "External Ethical Control."

The eleventh and final category for the first draft was called "Ethics, the Law and Bureaucracy" for lack of a better label for the time being. The respondents often discussed the law, written guidelines and lawyers which the main office had supplied for their co-workers to consult with in how to best act ethically if encountering complex ethical issues. I saw a connection between the presented sub-categories but could not at the time find an adequate term describing this category.

An illustration of the eleven potential categories along with 30 potential sub-categories that was conceptualized before the first draft is illustrated in Table 3.1

Table 3.1: Illustration of Potential Categories and Sub-categories

1. **Ethical Termination**
   - Resignation
   - Temporary Termination
   - Behavioral & Attitude Adjustment
   - Business Process Termination
2. **Enterprise Culture**
   - Role Modelling
   - Core Values
   - Additional Rule-Developing
   - Trust
   - Immediate Ethics Managing
   - Multidimensional Ethics
3. **Ethical Intuition**
   - Gut Feeling
   - Ethical Balancing
   - Ethical Flexibility
4. **Nursing**
   - Staff Welfare
   - Customer Caring
   - Brand Caring
   - Patencing/Clarity
5. **Immediate Ethics Managing**
   - Confrontation
   - Consulting
6. **Brand Protecting**
7. **Ethical Calibration**
   - Informal Calibration
   - Formal Calibration
8. **Same-but-different-Treatment**
   - Confrontation
   - Avoidance
9. **Transboundary Information-Exchange**
10. **External Ethical Controlling**
    - External quality Auditability
    - External Ethical Counseling
    - External Protection
11. **Ethics, the Law and Bureaucracy**
    - The Law
    - Advising Personnel
    - Written Guidelines
    - Protocols of Procedures

Due to the many categories found at such an early stage in the process, this indicates that I had possibly been exposed to many new impressions with a vast diversity. This means according to Gustavsson (1998) that I had not put any emphasis yet on a core category, and thereby had not blinded myself by pre-assumptions. Instead, fundamental basic patterns had been searched for.

3.1.2 Summarizing the Status after the First Draft

In the first draft, no core category was found whatsoever. Therefore, no basic social process was found explaining all the other processes. Thereby the fulfillment of Glaser's (1978) criteria for a core category was not reached. These criteria are:

1. The categories should be related to each other in an integrating way, where the categories are all linked together
2. The power to be explanatory
3. Describe a basic social process which can describe change
4. To be totally variable and pervasive when it comes to "type, degree and dimension" (Glaser, 1978)

The lack of a core category clearly indicated that more interviews were required. While the categories describe what the actors do, some categories were indeed related to each other. However, other categories had no relation whatsoever. Therefore, an integrated theory had not yet been discovered.

3.2 The Second Draft: The Emerging Theory after Nine Interviews

The second draft of the proposed theory included six additional interviews. The first four respondents were franchisee managers operating in the real estate industry while the second two respondents operated as sales managers in the car sales industry. Furthermore, after the nine interviews, I participated in an additional one-day seminar about ethics and ethical conduct in real estate organizations. For these interviews and seminar, notes were taken, memos were written and finally a sorting.

After the second sorting, the previous eleven categories had been reduced to ten potential categories along with 32 potential sub-categories. Four categories were new (written in bold in the list below) and one category was removed all together. The new derived data led to some changes from the previous interviews and a structure of the proposed substantive theory emerged. The structures and possible relationships of the substantive theory are depicted in figure 3.1:

Figure 3.1: A Second Draft of the Substantive Theory

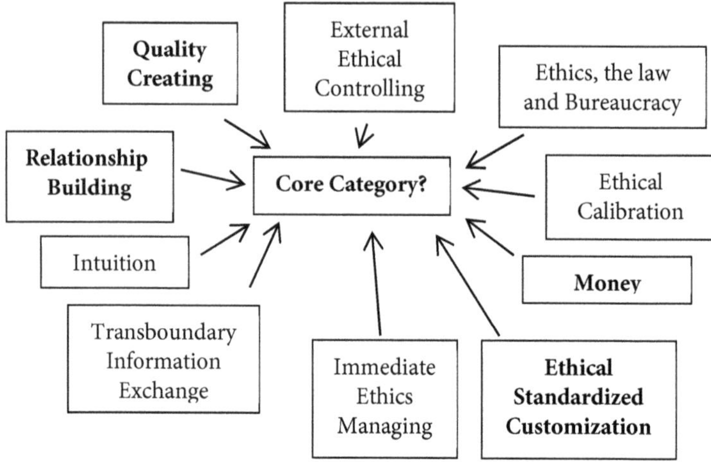

1. **Relationship Building**
   - Enterprise Culture-building
   - **Trust-building**
   - Nursing
   - **Chameleoning**
2. Intuition
   - Gut feeling
   - Ethical Balancing
   - Ethical Flexibility
   - **Multi-Dimensional Ethics**
3. **Money**
   - **Salary Managing**
   - **Business Transaction Management**
4. Immediate Ethics Managing
   - Direct Response
5. Ethical Calibration
   - Informal Calibration
   - Formal Calibration
   - Ethical termination
6. **Ethical Standardized Customization**
   - Confrontation
   - Avoidance
7. Transboundary Information-Exchange
8. External Ethical Controlling
   - External quality Auditability
   - External Ethical Counseling
   - External Protection
   - **External Staffing Procedures**
9. Ethics, the Law and Bureaucracy
   - The Law
   - Advising Personnel
   - Written Guidelines
   - **Protocols of Procedure**
10. **Quality Creating/Assuring**
    - **Patencing/Clarity**
    - **Recruiting**
    - **Researching/Troubleshooting**
    - **Follow-Up**
    - **Zero Tolerance**
    - **Anonymity**
    - **Neutrality**
    - **Role Awareness**

3.2.1 Major Changes

As for the newly emerged categories:

- The first new category for consideration was *Relationship Building.* It refers to those social processes that encompass building a relationship with the co-workers.
  This category were even considered as a core category at one point since it seemed like most of the interviewed managers seemingly wanted to discuss the importance of how to build relationships with their co-workers. The category encompassed discussions that concerned not only building a positive *enterprise culture* but also building *trust* between the manager and the co-workers. The category for consideration also included discussions of being a *nurse* and acting as a *chameleon* towards the co-workers to better build a relationship with them. "Nursing" refers to that managers take care of and look after their co-workers in hopes that the co-worker feels cared for, which in turn creates a stronger emotional bond, which ultimately has an effect on the co-workers' ethical behavior. In fact, one respondent who had previously worked as a nurse said that being a manager for a real estate organization and working as a nurse is like doing the same thing – taking care of people in a caring way. Being like a "chameleon" refers to a manager's ability to blend in to a particular social context with a co-worker. The respondents thought that people and social contexts vary. Different co-workers needs to be approached differently by the manager. Taking the suitable approach would have a greater effect on creating and maintain a relationship with their co-workers.
- *The* second new category for consideration concerned *Money.* It became obvious in the interviews that money was of great importance to the respondents when discussing ethical behavior and managing their co-workers. Topics like *salaries* and the *management of business transactions* were up for discussion since the respondents seemed to suggest they relate to ethical and unethical behavior.
- The third new category for consideration was *Quality Creating.* This category aimed at describing how managers use different tools in social settings and interactions to assure that the organization lives up to a certain ethical quality. Different topics (sub-categories) that were discussed during the interviews were seemingly related to this category. Examples of these are that managers display *zero tolerance* for unethical behavior, conducting *follow-ups* on ethical breaches, *recruiting* the

"right" co-workers and displaying *clarity* in order to avoid any confusion that can lead to unintentional unethical business practices.

- The fourth new category for consideration was Ethical Standardized Customization. This was originally the "Same-but-different Treatment" category but was re-conceptualized and reformulated, resulting in a more fitting name. This category encompassed managing co-workers differently but at the same time having a standardized approach in regards to ethical behavior, i.e., different co-workers require different types of management and approaches by the manager, but ethical issues must still be brought up. Managers must confront co-workers in the event of unethical behavior.

> Of course you need to manage differently, when it is an older person who might need a lot of information in order to understand everything, compared to say a younger person who has already done many housing businesses and know exactly how everything should proceed. (Respondent A:8)

The above quote from respondent A:8 illustrates how a manager could discuss the need to manage differently depending on the co-worker. Five changes were also made from the previous sorting.

- The Ethical Termination category was demoted from a category to a sub-category and was merged into the Ethical Calibration category due to a perceived better fit. Ethical Calibration was deemed a good fit since it encompassed different social activities which aimed at changing something already existing. In this case, it aimed at terminating a co-worker due to unethical behavior that was not deemed desirable.
- Both *Enterprise Culture* and *Nursing* were demoted from being categories to sub-categories respectively. They were both merged into a new category – *Relationship Building* along with two newly emerged sub-categories – *Trust Building* and *Chameleoning*. Both trust and to be able to be like a chameleon were deemed necessary when building relationships.
- The category of Brand Protecting was removed completely from the theory since no further respondents discussed this topic.
- *Bureaucratic documents* like keeping logs of sales were discussed by the respondents and how they were used to manage their co-workers'

ethical behavior. This sub-category was sorted into the *Ethics, the Law and Bureaucracy* category due to a perceived relationship.

- External Staffing procedures was a sub-category which fit under the External Ethical Control category. This sub-category encompassed external staffing procedures since these processes were conducted by an external actor. The purpose of this external actor is to ensure unbiased staffing procedures and staffing the best suitable candidate for the vacancy. As one respondent mentioned during the interviews:

  > If I want to recruit (new co-workers), I can get help from the central office, we have recruiters there. (Respondent A:5)

The above quote from respondent A:5 is an example that illustrates how a manager can get help from someone outside their office when in need of staffing new co-workers.

3.2.2 Summary of the Status after Nine Interviews

Still, no core category was found. The main differences between the first draft and the second draft were that some categories were merged into a category and some were created. Examples are Nursing and Enterprise Culture which are now are included in the new category of *Relationship Building*. The lack of a core category in managing co-workers' ethical behavior in sales organizations indicated that more interviews were required.

3.3. The Third Draft: The Substantive Theory after 19 Interviews

The third draft of the proposed theory included ten additional interviews. Four interviews were conducted in the cars sales industry, with three sales managers and one CEO. One interview was with a sales manager for a financial investing organization. Another respondent works as a sales manager operating in the pension broker industry. The seventh respondent works as a management coordinator for a financial investing organization. Another respondent used to work as a manager, but was no longer active in that position. The last two respondents both operate as managers in two franchises in the real estate industry.

In addition to the interviews, I had also participated in a complex sales process of windows for houses. This sales process also included meeting with the manager of the organization who was there to assist the salesperson if it was needed. As earlier, both notes and memos were written that were conceptualized.

In all, 19 interviews had been conducted and transcribed, two seminars about ethical conduct and one complex sales encounter had been attended (as an observer). After the third sorting, the previous ten potential categories were reduced to five. The number of sub-categories had been reduced from 31 to 29 along with several properties. Moreover, a potential core category was also up for consideration. The new derived data also led to some further changes in the structure of the proposed substantive theory.

A framework which was more densely constructed had emerged. The structures of the substantive theory are depicted in Figure 3.2.

Figure 3.2: A Third Draft of the Substantive Theory

– **Business Flourishing** (Alt. Business Thriving)

Relationship Investing

- Enterprise culture
    - o Role Modelling
    - o Key Values/Core Values
    - o Additional Rule-developing
    - o Fellowship building
    - o Openness
- Trust-building
- Nursing
    - o Staff Caring (well-faring)

Compassing

- Gut Feeling
- Ethical Balancing
- Flexibility
- Multi-Dimensional Ethics
- Ethical Calibration

Evolving Bureaucracy

- Law Adapting
- Advising Personnel
- Written Guidelines
- Documentation

Monetary Managing

- Salaries
- Incentives
- Goals

Quality Creating

- Clarity
- Recruiting
- Researching
- Follow-up
- Termination
    - o Dismissing/ Resignation
    - o Self-Termination
    - o Temporary Termination
    - o Attitude Adjustment
    - o Confrontation
    - o Business Process Termination
    - o Zero-Tolerance
- Anonymity
- Neutrality
- Role Awareness
- Immediate Management
- External Ethical Control
    - o External Quality Auditability/Inspection
    - o External Ethical Counseling
    - o External Staffing Procedures
- Proactive-work
- Transboundary Information Exchange
- Ethical Standardized Customization
    - o Confrontation
    - o Avoidance

3.3.1 Major and Minor Changes

By expanding into industries other than just the real estate industry, several categories re-emerged and were confirmed as crucial when managing co-workers' ethical behavior. There were seven notable findings and changes:

- The biggest finding in this sorting was the emergence of a potential core category – Business Flourishing. The name business flourishing was earlier suggested in a memo, but was eventually dropped due to not being sufficiently explanatory. The potentially emerged core category reflects an emphasis towards the field of management and to the actors' main concern: to in various degrees continuously conducting business and thus ultimately to be successful in what they do. The core category had a central role to dynamically connect the other five categories. The core category had some explanatory power related to the five categories. As a result, the core category was placed behind each category in order to highlight its central connection.
- Earlier no suitable name was previously found for the category of Money. However, after two new sub-categories emerged – *Rewards* and *Goals*, it became apparent that this process of managing co-workers' ethical behavior related to different monetary tools and influences a manager can use when managing. As a result, the category of *Money* was re-conceptualized as *Monetary Managing*. These two sub-categories were both placed in the Monetary Managing category due to their respective relationship to managers managing the organization's money. At the same time, the Business Transaction sub-category was removed altogether since it was deemed to not fit, and few respondents discussed it.
- The word "Intuition" was too close to the term gut feeling and the category of *Ethical Calibration* was reduced to a sub-category and placed in this category due to a better fit. Therefore, it needed to be reformulated and re-conceptualized. *Intuition* became *Compassing* since that word, seemingly at the time, better described the social processes taking place that the respondents discussed.
- Another major change was that the five categories of Ethical Standardized Customization, Immediate Ethics Management, Transboundary Information Exchange and External Ethical Controlling were all demoted to sub-categories and sorted into the Quality Creating category due to a perceived better fit.
- *Ethics, the Law and Bureaucracy* became *Evolving Bureaucracy*, since it became apparent that laws, ethics and bureaucracy are not static. They all can change with time and at the same time a proper word was needed which more adequately describes the occurring social process.

- *Relationship Building* became *Relationship Investing* since it became apparent that managers actually do not just build relationships, they also try to keep existing ones as well.

Smaller changes included renaming four out of five categories. The renaming and reconceptualization made the categories more inclusive towards the existing sub-categories. At the same time they also better describe the actual social process when managing ethical behavior.

3.3.2 Summary of the Status after Nineteen Interviews

Because of the several findings, the proposed theory was more nuanced than previously when it came to describing different social processes. The main differences between the second draft and the third draft were that the number of categories was reduced by half. The main reason for this was that further conceptualizations was conducted. This led to four of the existing categories being demoted to sub-categories and placed in other existing categories. More important however was the finding of a potential core category. A potential basic social process had emerged, which might possibly fulfill Glaser's (1978) criteria. However, due to the recent major changes, more interviews were required in order to see if saturation was reached.

3.4 The Fourth Draft: Major Discoveries after 20 Interviews

Due to a long time passing between interview number 19 and 20 another rigorous sorting and comparison was conducted. This analysis suggested that the proposed theory in section 3.3 was a bit fragmented. Several minor changes along with one major change and one major finding were made. As for the minor changes, the sub-categories were further reduced from 29 to 16.

The major change related to a name change of the proposed core category due to a more adequate fit. The major finding encompassed the discovery of three fundamental processes occurring when managing co-workers' ethical behavior.

Consequently, this major finding led to a further significant change in the existing structure of the proposed substantive theory. The current framework became more densely constructed due to these changes. The structures of the substantive theory are depicted in Figure 3.3:

Figure 3.3: A Fourth Draft of the Substantive Theory

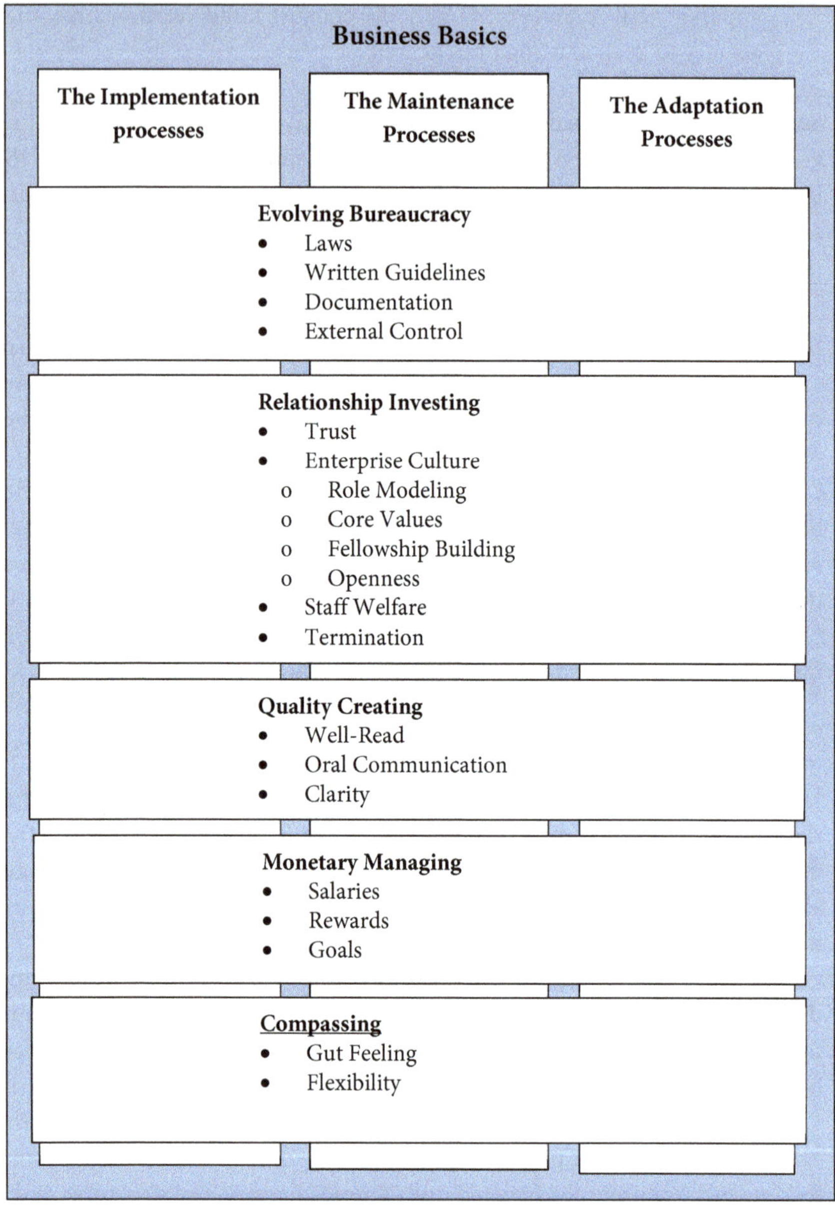

3.4.1 Major Changes and Findings

By conducting only one more interview, no major findings or changes were made in the categories. However, as mentioned one major change and one major finding were made:

- After additional reflections, discussions with the main supervisor and feedback from the respondents in regards to the proposed core category, the concept of Business Flourishing was not deemed suitable enough to fill the criteria of Glaser (1978). The name was reformulated to *Business Basics* to better reflect the BSP of what managers actually do to reach their main concern. The core category has a central role that dynamically connects the other five categories. The core category also has explanatory power related to the five categories. Additionally, the newly named core category not only encompasses the main concern of the actors, it is now both pervasive and variable as well. As a result, the core category is still placed behind all five categories in order to highlight its central connection.
- Moreover, as a result of further reflections and conceptualizations on both old and new material along with discussions with the main supervisor, it was discovered that when managing co-workers' ethical behavior, all five categories are expressed in three distinct processes: the implementation, maintenance and adaptation processes.
- In short, managers operate at all times in one of these three processes when managing co-workers' ethical behavior. This finding made the author go back to the earlier 19 transcriptions from the previous interviews. There it was confirmed that these processes also were expressed. For example, respondent B:7 expressed the need to implement a new salary system in order to reduce co-workers' stress and thereby better manage their ethical behavior:

> In order to not make (sales) people feel stressed about the performance-based salary… We now have a fixed salary system for all, both mechanics and sales people… But we are probably one of the few car sales companies which has (implemented) this, perhaps the only company. (Respondent B:7)

The above quote from respondent B:7 is from the discussion about implementing a new salary system. This finding led to some additional major restructuring in the proposed theory. The categories were now organized in such a way that they included all three processes and the core category, i.e., all three processes were placed behind each category in order to highlight their relationship, with the core category being in the back behind all categories and processes.

Except in the Monetary Managing category, several minor changes were also made in each category. These changes mainly concerned the elimination, merging or renaming of sub-categories:

- The sub-category of External Ethical Control was moved from the Quality Creating category to the Evolving Bureaucracy category. It was merged with Advising Personnel and renamed more adequately as External Control to describe the social processes.
- In the Relationship Investing category, two sub-categories were renamed. Nursing became Staff Welfare and Trust Building was renamed "Trust" in order to become more inclusive. The Sub-category of Chameleoning was eliminated altogether due to low levels of fit while the Termination sub-category was placed under to the Relationship Investing category.
- In the Quality Creating category, most sub-categories were eliminated due to low fit except Clarity. Two new sub-categories emerged (Oral Communication and Well-Read) due to re-conceptualizations. The category of Researching was merged with Well-Read while the sub-category of Transboundary Information Exchange was included under Oral Communication.
- In the Compassing category, the three sub-categories of Ethical Balancing, Multi-Dimensional Ethics and Ethical Flexibility were all merged and renamed more adequately as Compassing. This name change were deemed to better reflect the occurring social process.

3.4.2 Summary of the Status after 20 Interviews

Several changes occurred between the third and fourth draft. Minor changes included the reducing of sub-categories and sorting them somewhat differently. One major change related to the finding of three different processes, which in turn led to a major addition in the proposed model. Another major change related to the reformulation of the core category. This led to a better description of the actor's main concern; a core category had thus emerged. The concept of "Business Basics" seems to fulfill Glaser's (1978) four quality criteria for being a core category. Due to the major changes in the fourth sorting, more interviews were required as I was not sure whether or not saturation has been reached.

3.5. The Fifth Draft: The Substantive Theory after 24 and 25 Interviews

The fifth draft of the proposed theory consisted of an additional four interviews. One respondent operated as a CEO for a large pension insurance organization. The other three respondents operated all in managerial roles in the banking sector. The first of these three respondents operates as an office manager while the latter two operate as department managers. Focus for the banks besides operating with normal banking services also included focusing on advising in private and pension fund investing.

As per usual, field notes were taken during the interviews and memos were written.

Along with these four new interviews, combined with additional reflections, the only change after this draft was a reformulation of a category and thereby also the name. The name Quality Creating was considered to be too broad and too inclusive. It was reasoned that almost anything could fit in this category. This name was therefore considered too vague. After a reconceptualization, I realized that this category is about how managers educate their co-workers towards a more desirable ethical behavior, Eventually, a more adequate name emerged. Quality Creating became Educationing since the new name is better positioned to reflect the incurrent processes occurring.

The proposed substantive now consisted of the three processes, five categories and 16 subcategories – all related to the core category. Due to no major changes, this was a good indication that saturation could have been reached. To confirm this sentiment, an additional interview (no. 25) was conducted. The final respondent that was interviewed operated as a franchisee for a local real estate organization.

3.5.1 Minor Changes

By conducting one more interview, no major findings were made in the categories. However, after a discussion with two supervisors, one minor change was made: The category of Evolving Bureaucracy became Bureaucratization. The reasoning behind this is that using the gerund of Bureaucratization, this encompass the term evolving as well. The word evolving was deemed unnecessary to include in the name, since the new name could encompass changes in bureaucracy. No other changes or additional information were found or made. The current framework became further densely constructed due to these changes. The structures of the substantive theory are depicted below in Figure 3.4.

Figure 3.4: A Fifth Draft of the Substantive Theory

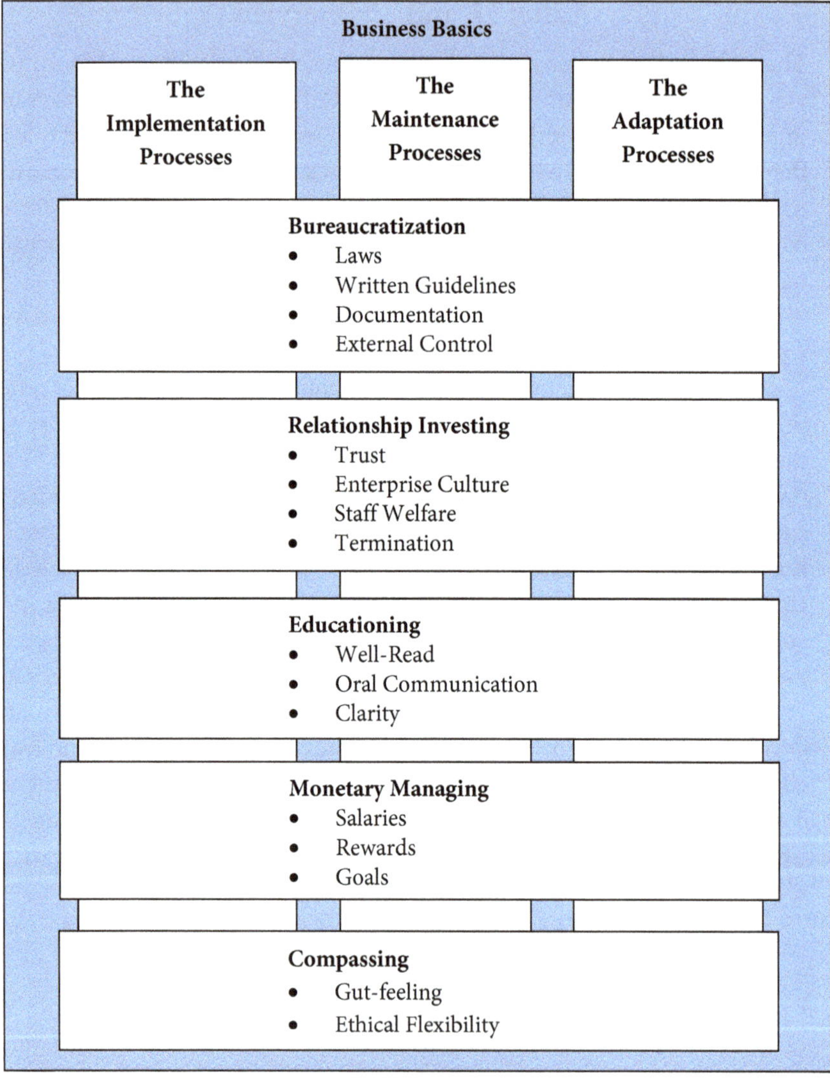

3.6. The Sixth Draft: Saturation Confirmed

While saturation had been reached, after the final seminar for this dissertation it became apparent that four more changes were deemed necessary to undertake:

1. The word "Compassing" was not deemed to be sufficiently appropriate to describe the Compassing category since metaphors should be avoided when conceptualizing (Gustavsson, 1998). After further conceptualizing, a more appropriate word (re)-emerged – Intuiting. This name change better reflects the social processes taking place and theoretically connects better to its sub-category. As a consequence of the re-naming, the Gut feeling sub-category was deemed as very similar in meaning to the Intuiting category. This led to the Gut feeling category being merged with the Intuiting category.
2. After discussing with my supervisor, a decision was made to remove the discussion about how role models help create organizational culture. It became apparent after going thru the empirical material again that when the respondents discussed the importance of being a role model, they discussed this in the context of setting examples to others for how to act, i.e., by acting as a role model, it was a way to (lead) teach their co-workers by example. Consequently, the discussions about being a role model became the Role Modeling sub-category, was placed in the Educating category due to a better fit.
3. Realizing that when the respondents talked about terminating a co-worker, they not only did this to prevent more unethical behavior from occurring again by that individual. It would also turn out that another important reason as to why managers terminate a co-worker who acts unethically is to set examples for other co-workers of what would happen if they also acted in a similar manner. Consequently the Termination sub-category was moved to the Educating category due to better fit.
4. It was deemed that the three processes (implementation, maintenance and adaptation) were not as distinct as initially thought since they had much less connection to the categories than initially thought. It was therefore decided that the three processes needed to be removed altogether in order to better describe what is happening.

   Due to the removal of the three processes, there was a need to restructure the proposed theory. The categories were re-organized in such a way that they were still all inside the core category, but without being displayed in any specific order.

In total 25 interviews had been conducted along with two full-day seminars. Moreover, the author had also appeared as an observer during a sales process, but not much came from that since the attending manager did not interact much with the sales person and the customers.

The structures of the substantive theory for this dissertation is illustrated in Figure 3.5.

Figure 3.5: A Sixth Draft of the Substantive Theory

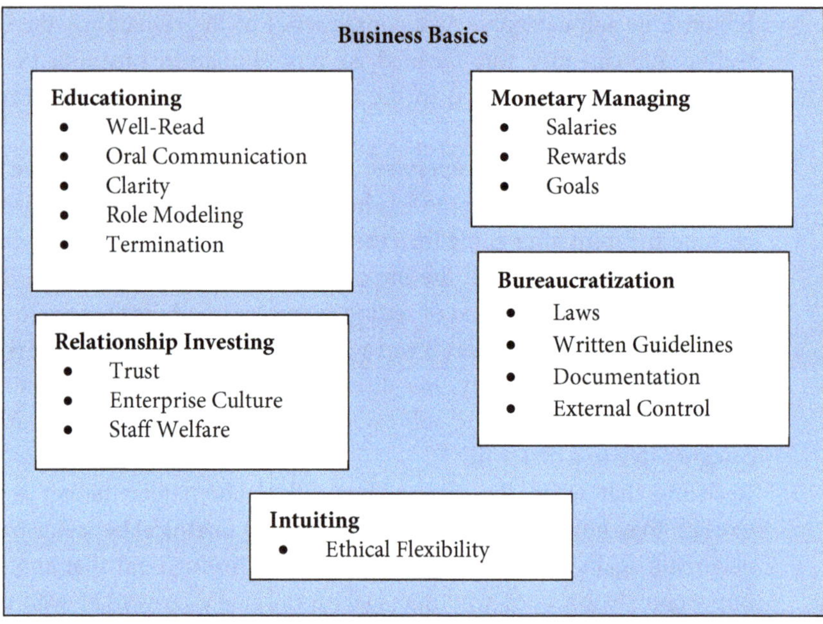

Initially I thought that the model in Figure 3.5 was the final draft for my theory. However, about a week later I came to the realization that it did not feel completely comfortable with the categories and the sub-category appearing as boxes as well as the positioning of the text for Business Basics. The boxes did not completely reflect the more dynamic aspects of the empirical data.

In an attempt to better accommodate those qualities in the data, I came to the conclusion that more circular and "round shaped" categories were more suitable. This makes them appear as being in a floating state, which in turn better illustrates the dynamism between the categories and the core category.

The sub-categories were also removed in order to put more focus on the actual processes.

Moreover, the text "*Business Basics*", while still placed behind the categories, it was moved to a more central position in order to better signal its importance as being the core category and its connection to each category. No other changes or additional information was added. The final version of the empirically derived substantive theory for this dissertation is illustrated in Figure 3.6.

Figure 3.6: The Final Draft of the Substantive Theory

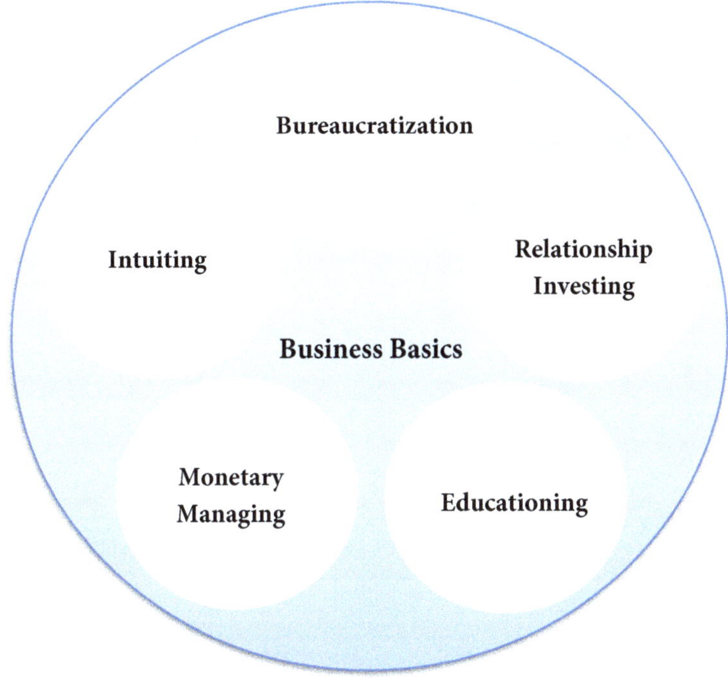

4. The Theory: Business Basics

In this chapter, the emerged theory is presented along with the core category, categories, sub-categories and empirical examples. In accordance with orthodox Grounded Theory, its procedures and this research's purpose – the creation of a new *substantial theory* along with a core category has emerged:

- Business Basics

Business Basics encompasses the main concern of managers in sales organizations – in this case, the basic social process to *continuously conduct business* by managing co-workers ethical behaviors. This can be achieved through five (often interrelated) social processes (see Figure 4.1). As for this dissertation, these social processes are called categories and named:

- Bureaucratization
- Relationship Building
- Educationing
- Monetary Managing
- Intuiting

Each category consists of a number of different but related sub-categories. When managing ethical behavior the manager can use one or more of the five categories along with their sub-categories. Each category can be expressed by itself or in conjunction with other categories - all related to the core category (see Figure 4.1).

Figure 4.1: The Business Basics Framework

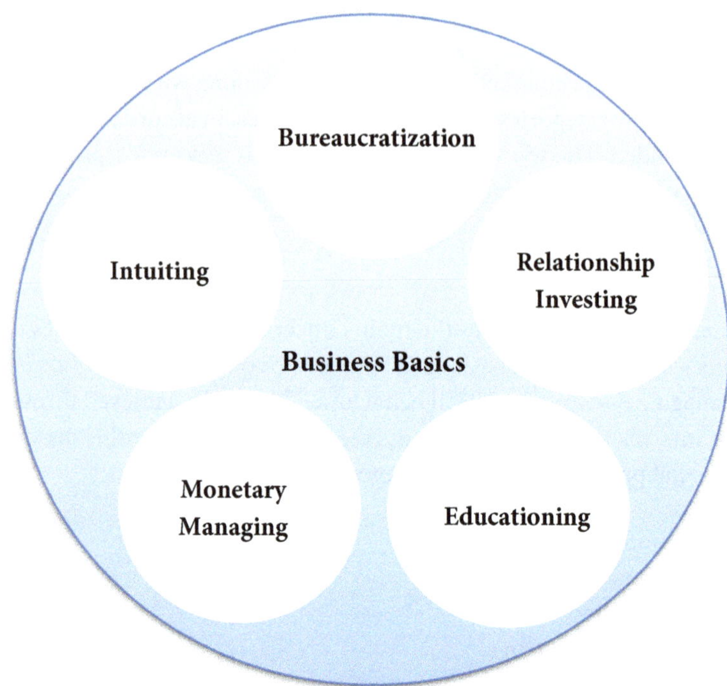

4.1 Business Basics

As presented in section 4.1, the core category for this dissertation is "*Business Basics.*" The lexical definition of "business" is "the activity of buying and selling goods and services, or an a particular company that does this, or work you to do earn money" (Cambridge Advanced Learners Dictionary, 2008b, p. 186) while the lexical definition for "basics" refers to the "simplest and most important fact, ideas or things connected to something" (Cambridge Advanced Learners Dictionary, 2008c, p. 109). These words were chosen in conjunction as it represents several aspects associated to the core category.

It was revealed in the empirical findings that the main concern of managers in sales organizations is to be able to continuously conduct business. For this, the organization needs to attract both new and returning customers. To be successful with this, managing ethical behavior is paramount and required at all times for any sales organizations which strives to continuously conduct business.

In fact, it was revealed that it did not matter what industry within the sales organizations the managers were operating in or what type of products or services they were selling. What they all have in common is that ethical behavior is paramount to such degree: Ethics was deemed by all managers as the fundamental basic when operating in their respective markets. This was a fundamental basic was expressed in several ways. For example, an office manager for a real estate organization (coded as Respondent A:7) clearly pinpointed the importance of ethics in their business:

> ...a basic foundation at work is to have ethics and morals. (Respondent A:7)

Another, similar anecdote was provided by respondent B:3 who discussed the importance of new and returning customers, and without ethics this was not feasible:

> First of all, you can never build a customer stock without ethics. Then you have to operate in a business where you are not selling to the same customer again and so on. (Respondent B:3)

Evidently, customer retention is important where ethics is perceived as an omnipresent, quintessential and pervasive tool to help the manager reach their main concern. In other words, working with ethics is perceived as a means to an end, it leads to both creating and retaining customers.

4.1.1. Differing goals

While the main concern and the importance of ethics remains the same, it was also revealed in the empirical data that the goals could differ between the respondents. Below, three examples of the expressed goals are provided to pinpoint how they differ, while their main concern stay unchanged:

- *Market Leadership* – Some managers aspire to gain or maintain market leadership – some want to be the market leader locally and some want to become market leader nationwide.

  For example, respondent A:3 revealed that they previously had the desire to merge with the second biggest actor on the market in order to become more dominant. This merger was stopped however by Swedish authorities in order to prevent them from gaining a monopoly. Despite having desires of becoming market leader, it was stressed that ethical conduct is a pivotal part for them as an organization and their strategy.

In the example given below, the respondent expresses a desire to become the market leader in their industry:

> My role here is to take us from here onwards and upwards… One concrete example for me in business… is to be the best… the way there for me is very simple, and that is for me to manage the whole group in regards to that we have a qualified majority of positive co-workers… (Respondent A:3)

In the same vein as respondent A:3, ethics is deemed to play a pivotal role according to respondent C:9 since it was reasoned that acting ethically in business will be an advantage:

> I believe from our basic task that you get what you focus on. If you focus of something that is not of virtue, but rather focuses, consciously or subconsciously on errors, then you will suffer (as a business). If you focus on striving to do what is right, both from your own perspective and from others as well, then you will end up right. (Respondent C:9)

- *Survival* – Due to different reasons, like fierce competition or being limited from accessing more market share, some managers have no goals or aspirations of becoming market leader. Instead, these focus on staying afloat to continue with their business in the current state. Respondent A:9 is one manager who expressed such a desire:

> (My goal) is to meet people (customers), facilitate for them to make it as good as possible for them. Of course we need to earn money. But I believe that the meeting with these people is our driving force. (Respondent A:9)

Yet, it was also stressed by the same respondent (Respondent A:9) that while they intended to rather stay afloat on the market in order to keep the business going, ethics still plays a pivotal role to achieve this in order to continuously conduct business by managing co-workers' ethical behavior:

> We can't make it without it (ethics). You can do a quick deal but you will destroy your reputation, so you don't get to do any more business. Then you are very short-lived. So ethics is extremely important. (Respondent A:9)

- *Development of their business* – Some managers can be happy with their organizations' market share and current affairs, despite position on the market. Instead, they want to develop their organization in other areas rather than just maximizing monetary profit and/or dominance on the market. To achieve this, ethical conduct is perceived as a fundamental basic. One example of this was provided by respondent C:3 who stressed that "the ethical regulations are very important. They are the backbone in everything we do." The same respondent later discussed how previous goals had come to change. Earlier the main objective was to gain market share, now it had all changed in favor of creating both better working-conditions and being able make co-workers feel better at work:

> I've changed a lot since back when I was 30 years old. Back then I had a stronger drive to get ahead. Nowadays, my drive is to have a job I am satisfied with, to have fair working conditions and a reasonable time at work – (in order to) to get some time with my partner… But I still want a job where I feel good about myself. (Respondent C:3)

Despite operating in different industries, despite what products or services they are selling and despite their different goals, what these managers have in common, and which requires managing their co-workers' ethical behavior, is that all managers want to be able to continuously conduct business. This highlights that their respective main concern are the same. Therefore, there should be no surprise that "Business Basics" for this dissertation is defined as:

> To create and be able to continuously conduct business by managing co-workers ethical behaviour (Author, 2020).

The purpose, which was introduced in chapter 1, proposed that the core category should describe the action in the substantive field. The core category for this dissertation should therefore describe how the main concern of the actors (the managers) is resolved, i.e., to be able to continuously conduct business by managing co-workers' ethical behavior in sales organizations via different social processes (five categories). Therefore, core category of Business Basics is on the pinnacle of the conceptual levels for this theory. Business Basics is pervasive in the social processes and transcends the boundaries of time, individuals and place.

Evidently, the core category describes a basic social process (BSP), The core category also have a central role that dynamically connect the other five categories as well as having explanatory power related to the five categories. Thus, the objective for a core category along with the criteria presented in section 2.8.3 for how to determine a core category is fulfilled.

Before going into a deeper presentation of the five different categories in subsequent sections (4.2–4.7), short descriptions on how the five different categories relate to the core category are here provided:

i. *Bureaucratization* – The first category refers to all forms of bureaucracy that managers encounter and can use to attempt to make co-workers act ethically.
ii. *Relationship Investing* – The second category focuses on how managers create closer and more personal relationships with their co-workers. The intention for this is to give the co-worker stronger emotional ties towards the manager and the organization whereby they are less likely to engage in unethical conduct
iii. *Educationing* – The third category relates to all forms of tools and influences the manager can use to educate their co-workers in correct, expected and desired ethical behavior.
iv. *Monetary Managing* – The fourth category refers to all monetary related activities a manager can use to manage their co-workers ethical behavior.
v. Intuiting – The fifth and final category refers to the managers own intuition, their inner ethical compass for how they can manage and solve complex issues that relates to the co-workers ethical behavior.

In short; the core category is a BSP which describes how managers can use bureaucratic documents to ensure that ethical proceedings occur during business deals; or how to maintain relationships with co-workers in order to better manage and influence their ethical behavior; or how to educate their co-workers via meetings in how to work towards desired ethical practices; as well as how managers can decrease sales goals in order to reduce co-workers' potential stress levels and thereby also reduce the risk of unethical behavior; or simply use their intuition to better manage complex ethical situations.

4.2 Bureaucratization

This category (see Figure 4.2) refers to all bureaucratic activities, tools and influences a manager can use to manage co-workers' ethical behavior.

The word "bureaucracy" refers to "a system for controlling or managing a country, company or organization… to follow rules carefully. It can involve long and difficult dealings with officials" (Cambridge Advanced Learners Dictionary, 2008d, p. 185). These bureaucratic activities, tools and influences are found to be the very foundation of any sales organization. One manager (Respondent B:4) who operates as a CEO for a car sales company clearly expressed the importance of the different bureaucratic activities, tools and influences needed when managing:

> You may think everything is easy and everything will be okay, you think you understand and know everything, and that all can be managed in the right way. No, it's not quite that simple. Everyone needs guidance, have a framework to work from… There must be guidelines in how you should act, in how you should conduct business, there must always be guidelines. (Respondent B:4)

The main objective for these guidelines is to ensure legal and ethical conduct when doing business. Respondent B:4 further elaborated on this by adding that if some of these guidelines are not managed properly, it can lead to co-workers engaging in both intentional and unintentional unethical practices. Ultimately this can lead to loss of customers, costly fines and ultimately not being able to conduct business continuously. In a similar vein, respondent C:9 also stressed this and on the need to protect the customers and other stakeholders from unethical behavior. As a consequence, ethics and bureaucratization need to be closely linked together and are therefore closely related to Business Basics.

The Bureaucratization category consists of four sub-categories: *Laws, Written Guidelines, Documentation* and *External Control.*

Figure 4.2: Bureaucratization

4.2.1 Laws

One of the most protruding sub-categories encountered in the empirical data is the *Law*. This sub-category was a frequently discussed bureaucratic tool by most respondents, including respondents A:3, A:11–12, B:3–4,6–7, C:3–6 and C:8. The law is bureaucratic due to its structure and complex setting of rules.

It was revealed in the empirical data that sales organizations are heavily regulated by laws. According to respondent A:9 who used to work as a nurse, regulations in the real estate business are so strict that they are more regulated than those at hospitals. Laws can also be specific to different industries. For example, the real estate business in Sweden has the Real Estate Brokers Law (Respondent A:4) while insurance organizations like banks have an authority called the Ethical Regulations Authority (Respondent C:3).

It was an underlying consensus among most respondents that the law is omnipresent and something the manager expects their co-workers to follow at all times. Respondent C:4 also discussed this and in the following quotation it becomes clear that the respondent is talking about the law as being omnipresent and controlling for the co-workers in their everyday work:

> According to the law, as soon as I sell something I have to tell about it, both written and orally.... All the time constantly... There are a lot of laws and rules, we can't do anything (even remotely unethical). (Respondent C:4)

To ensure legal conduct, the organization itself and external actors conduct regular, but often randomized controls and follow-ups (Respondent C:8). This can, among many things, consist of recording their co-workers' phone calls (during working hours) or include drug-testing since there is an increased risk of unethical behavior related to drug usage. Respondent C:8 discussed this as follows:

> We have internal controls. Every month we have a certain set of procedures, for example we record every phone call we make, just to ensure we are doing it right… Sometimes we discover before the customer that we have made an error, all thanks to our internal check-ups. So we have some procedures within our internal checkups where you as a manager can do randomized samples ensuring that co-workers actually (act within the law). (Respondent C:8)

According respondent C:3 new laws are implemented all the time in order to actively and proactively minimize unethical behavior. This can require a change in the ethical practices and routines at work. It is ultimately the managers' responsibility to ensure that new working routines are created that fit with the new law. For example, several respondents discussed the new GDPR law and its implementation (e.g. respondents A:11–12, C:6 and C:8). According to respondent C:6, this law was enforced and implemented in 2018 by the European Union in order to ensure better protection for individual integrity and to commit to appropriate behaviors.

> Take the GDPR for example. There we have a new bureaucratic law that we needed to implement… then you will have to find new ways conducting business in order to sell. (Respondent C:6)

With the new law also came new regulations, they dictate how work should be conducted. If the manager fails to communicate how to act in accordance with the new law, there was a risk of co-workers acting unethical, both intentionally and unintentionally. While there are new laws implemented, there are also times where existing laws need to be adapted to the current societal contexts. According respondent A:2, laws are therefore meant to be a bit indistinct since the lawmakers are never expected to foresee all potential unethical behavior that might occur. This statement goes hand in hand with the statement of respondent C:8, where the respondent claims that the laws are meant to be able to be adaptable, since changes occur with time. This was even further elaborated upon by respondent C:5 who in a similar vein suggested that laws are adaptable and evolve in order to better suit current ethical norms:

> There is a lot happening with laws in this business, and of course I am responsible to bring this (information) to our co-workers, so they can follow them. (Respondent C:5)

The Anti-Money Laundering Act was also discussed and how it had been updated four times since its initial implementation. According to respondent C:9, for every update, there is also a need to adapt behavior for the manager and the co-workers. Several respondents, among them respondent A:12, noted that it is usually the manager who communicates when new laws are enforced to the co-workers via meetings, presentations, brochures, etc. In short, laws come, go and evolve, they are there to ensure legal practices whereas the manager can always use it to manage the ethical behavior of the co-workers.

4.2.2 Written Guidelines

Another prominent sub-category frequently discussed in this category is *Written Guidelines* (e.g. respondents A:3–4, A:7–8, A:12 and B:5–6). "Written guidelines" is an umbrella concept for other closely related concepts like codes of ethics, mission statements, codes of conduct, ethical guidelines, etc. Due to their similarity in intent, they are defined as "statements that prescribe what the tourist and/or operator should do" (Malloy & Fennell, 1998, p. 453).

Although laws heavily regulate the sales organizations, all of these organizations have gone one step further by including written guidelines since they are most often written in greater detail regarding expected ethical conduct. This gets support from respondent A:12 who suggests that the written guidelines encompass how the organization and management want their co-workers to act ethically. Unlike the law, which is socially *enforced*, the guidelines are socially *desired* since the written guidelines better reflect the current societal expectations in how to behave.

Respondent B:4 reveal that managers, just like with the law, expects their co-workers to act within the framework of the written guidelines at all times, where random check-ups are conducted in order to ensure that the co-workers acts correctly. The same respondent stresses that it is paramount for co-workers to follow the written guidelines at all times. Otherwise there is a great risk of breaches in the expected ethical behavior, which in turn will detract customers:

> You just can't expect that things will be alright... It does not work that way... You need a tight framework (referring to written guidelines) on how you

should act and how to do things. That applies to the whole organization... you need to write a real manual (and give) to each and every one on how they should act. (Respondent B:4)

The respondent elaborates further upon this by stressing that if a co-worker follows the guidelines in how to ethically act during each business transaction, there will not only likely be fewer unethical activities but also fewer complaints from customers regarding unethical conduct.

The creation of written guidelines is also discussed in the empirical findings where they can be created in several ways. For example, written guidelines can be either created by the managers or with help from the co-workers. However, it is noted by several respondents (e.g. respondents A:4–5, 7–8) that it is most often the main office who creates and implements the base outline of the written guidelines for the rest of the organization to follow. According to respondent C:8, the written guidelines are often communicated by the managers to the co-workers via meetings and in written form when implemented. For example, respondent C:8 discussed about an earlier scenario regarding this:

When it (the new guidelines) came, we had a project within the organization where higher-ups who spent extremely many hours creating them. Then I received a finished package of information which I communicated to our co-workers... If we were a smaller company I would have had to do all this myself. (Respondent C:8)

In order to keep up with what is correct and expected ethical behavior at the time, just as ethics and laws, written guidelines are revised every so often (Respondents A:9 & B4). Respondent A:9 adds that when a change in the guidelines occurs, co-workers also have to adapt their behavior in accordance with them. (S)he described this as:

We have our guidelines on how we should work... they (the co-workers) got themselves a copy of the guidelines to bring with them. And they are revised every now and then. (Respondent A:9)

Several respondents operate as a franchisee, which means that they have a franchisor above them who dictates rules and regulations. It is however revealed that the franchisees and local offices often have the creative freedom to make additional rules to the written guidelines in order to better suit their local market (Respondent A:3–5, A:7 & C:8). Respondent A:5 said:

> Of course we have policies for co-workers within the brand as a whole regarding right and wrong, but then (my colleague) and I can make rules too for how we want co-workers to act. (Respondent A:5)

This was not just applied to one organization; another respondent (A:4) also operating in the same industry as respondent A:5 had the following to say:

> We have clear guidelines for both us as a franchisee and for those who are our subordinates. There we have a model, and it can be developed of course with your own ideas and so on. (Respondent A:4)

Sometimes these guidelines also differ internally within the organization in order to be better adapted to certain work positions. For example, one HR manager for a large franchisor (Respondent A:8) along with an office manager (Respondent A:7) both noted that managers can be provided with a specific manual from headquarters on how to manage different tasks. However, it is also stressed by respondent B:4 that the written guidelines should not be too rigid in order to better manage the situation in accordance with ethical practices:

> As I say, I believe the written guidelines we have are sufficient, but then you also have to use your head too, not becoming too rigid about rules. (Respondent B:4)

Just like the law, this indicates that while written guidelines are important, they can't cover all aspects in how to behave. There are certain times when a salesperson needs to think for themselves and possibly use their intuition of what is appropriate conduct at the time being, not just follow the rules.

4.2.3 Documentation

In regards to *Documentation* procedures, the third sub-category encompasses all procedures that require documentation when working and are strongly related to bureaucracy. The lexical definition of "documentation" is "collection and compilation of facts" (Allén, 1986, p. 222). As in any sales organization, documentation is an unavoidable tool managers have to work with (Respondent B:7 & C:6) where work and sales procedures often need to be heavily documented (Respondents A:12, B:4 & C:8). Respondent A:12, who works as a franchisee for a real estate agency talked about documentation and bureaucracy:

> The bureaucracy has become almost… well, the banks have more bureaucracy (than us), but we are not far behind. So after a sale, you have a huge pile of papers that are required to be documented, it is extremely controlled. But it is also a business where it is extremely important that everything is ethical. (Respondent, A:12)

To minimize the risk of unethical practices every sales process is documented, even the ones that do not come to fruition (Respondents A:4, A:11, B:4, C:4–6 & C:8). Therefore, sales people need to document their business procedures and different meetings in order to provide transparency and thus minimize the risk of being perceived as acting unethically. One example of this was provided by respondent C:4. (S)he spoke in general terms about the need for sales people to constantly document encounters with customers as follows:

> (According to the law) All the time constantly, one has to document everyone you meet and all advice you give… Those I met yesterday, I have to sit down and document… where the Financial Supervisory Authority will review this (business transaction). (Respondent C:4)

If a governmental organ like Allmänna Reklamationsnämnden (ARN) or Fastighetsmäklarinspektionen (FMI, translated to English as the Real Estate Brokers Inspection Authority) suspect unethical practices, they can have the manager or themselves start an investigation to attempt to discover possible breaches in business conduct (Respondent C:8).

When a new documentation process is implemented, it was discussed by respondent B:6 that local managers usually get the information from the headquarters. Respondent C:8 further elaborated on this by adding that the manager then communicates the new documentation procedures to the co-workers. The same respondent also discussed trying to involve the co-workers as much as possible in informing each other about how to document:

> When we implement (new protocols)... We are good at involving the co-workers and ask them how they want to do it. It is seldom we managers come with a complete "map." We have a kit of pictures we leave to the co-workers… When we have found the best way to do it, we try to spread (information) so

> that everyone does the same... We do this via meetings, and we have a responsible person in each team with different areas of responsibility. (Respondent C:8)

Documentation processes also change (Respondents A:4, C:5 & C:8–9). According to respondent C:8, one reason for making changes in the documentation processes can be to further limit unethical business practices. Respondent C:9 added that if there is a change in a law that was enforced, the organization may have to adapt their already existing documentation procedures to fit in accordance with the law:

> But if we take one example in regards to MIFID II... It is about a new law (being implemented from January 1st) which enforce consumer protection in regards to investment counseling. This means that on a certain day we have to work in a system which is compliant with MIFID II, so that we can show the supervisory organ that we act in accordance with the rules... And this is of course something that is not communicated on New Year's Eve. It has to be done way before that. (Respondent C:9)

Evidently, documentation processes are closely related to Bureaucratization, where these procedures evolve with time to fit the current societal expectations.

4.2.4 External Control

The fourth and final sub-category revealed in the Bureaucratization category is *External Control*. This sub-category refers to how a third party monitors business transactions. During the conducted interviews, it was noticed by several respondents (e.g. respondents A:4, A:6, A:9 & C:9) how they all expressed being monitored as a company by different external agencies, both governmental and non-governmental, in order to ensure that legal and ethical practices are complied with.

These agencies influence not just the co-workers' and the manager's ethical behavior, they also influence how the managers manage their co-workers' ethical behavior. Examples of these agencies discussed in the empirical findings were the IRS, auditing companies, FMI, the Competition Authority, ARN and the Financial Supervisory Authority. While agencies like these monitor sales organizations, it is the managers' responsibility to ensure that the co-workers act in accordance with the law, written guidelines and document their business transactions.

These organs fit the Bureaucratization category since they play a pivotal role in ensuring that the organizations act in accordance with the law, written guidelines and documentation processes and can be perceived as bureaucratic to deal with. It was discussed by several respondents (e.g. respondents A:1–4, A:6, A:8–9 & C:9) that if an agency unveils that a sales organization has engaged in unethical practices, remedies can be given. The remedies can consist of warnings, heavy fines or in a worst case scenario, revocation of the sales license. This puts an immediate and definite stop to conducting business. One respondent described this as:

> We have a governmental agency… that does check-ups to ensure we are doing our job properly. If you don't do it properly, you lose your registration. (Respondent A:4)

It was discovered that check-ups differ, where some look into customer complaints, while others look into the organization's annual financial statements. Another example was provided by Respondent A:2 who discussed that before 1994, the county administrative boards of Sweden were responsible for supervising that all real estate organizations in Sweden acted ethically. However, in 1995, FMI was implemented as a new governing agency to ensure that real estate organizations were acting within the law and following ethical standards. As a consequence of this, more case law was implemented, which helped managers to better guide their co-workers on how to work ethically in their work routines (Respondent A:2).

According to respondent C:9, all organizations are by law forced to have an auditing team which audits the organization's annual financial report. While auditing teams are not the only external monitoring entity, the Financial Supervisory Authority also conducts regular check-ups for organizations regarding their business transactions in order to ensure ethical behavior:

> We are a licensed business. An octroi is required to run a bank. Which means that were are under constant supervision, where the Financial Supervisory Authority has that task (to ensure ethical proceedings). (Respondent C:9)

Several respondents (e.g. respondents A:3–5 & A:8) also mention "Ombudsman" as an external unbiased counseling service for customers who are dissatisfied with business proceedings. For example, it can happen that customers feel they are exposed to unethical behavior by a salesperson. If that is the case, the customer can contact an ombudsman at the Association of Swedish Real Estate Agents.

4.2.5 Summary of Bureaucratization

To summarize this category, it was revealed and discussed how managers can through bureaucratic activities, tools and influences manage their co-workers' ethical behavior. It became clear from this section that these sub-categories are considered by the respondents to be part of a manager's every-day bureaucratic work when managing ethical behavior. Moreover, it was also presented how these activities and influences help managers to reach his or her main concern – to continuously conduct business by managing co-workers' ethical behavior.

Three important reveals were also made in this category. Respondents like respondent B:6 revealed that if a new law is implemented this can lead to two things. If a new law is enforced, it can also require that new written guidelines are necessary. I.e. One sub-category (Laws) can cause that the manager also manages via another sub-category (Written guidelines).

In similarity to the first reveal, the second reveal hints that this type of management does not just necessarily occur within the same category. Managing via one category can also lead to the manager also managing through another category. For example, it is revealed that implementing a new law can also lead to the manager having to educate their co-workers by informing them about it via meetings, email etc., i.e., the implementation of laws in the Bureaucratization category can lead to the manager managing ethical behavior via the Educating category (see section 4.4) too by educating his or her co-workers.

A final reveal shows that some sub-categories at times can be automatically linked together. For example, external control organs like FMI can look into the documentation processes in order to detect breaches in ethical behavior. No doubt, a dynamic process seems to have been unveiled in the empirical data since more than one category and sub-category can be used at the same time depending on the context.

4.3 Relationship Investing

The second category for consideration (see Figure 4.3) is the *Relationship Investing* category. This refers to the different tools, activities and influences a manager can use to invest in relationship with his or her co-workers.

For this dissertation, the word "relationship" refers to "the way in which two or more individuals are connected to each other" (Allén, 1986, p. 975). Investing is explained as a "bet with grounded hope for a later return of investment" (Allén, 1986, p. 525). By investing in relationships I refer to either creating, maintaining and re-establishing relationships to which the manager hopes that the relationship will positively affect the co-workers' ethical conduct. Several respondents discussed the need for them to invest in the relationships with their co-workers. For example, respondent C:4 described the necessity to have a good relationship with your co-workers since it leads to retaining your customers:

> I see myself as a friend to everyone (at work)... (and) the whole gang here... We are friendly (to each other) and then you keep your customers. (Respondent C:4)

By having a positive relationship with your co-workers, it is less likely that the co-workers will engage in unethical business practices. In turn, this leads to retention of customers. In a similar vein, respondent B:6 also described this category during an interview but in the following context:

> You invest in this person. It will take time (to create a positive relationship), but in the long run it will be better for us as a company. (Respondent B:6)

Ethics and Relationship Investing are closely linked together. The empirical data show that several managers (e.g. respondents A:4, A:9, A:10, B:1–2) expressed that focusing on creating closer relationships with the co-workers is a necessary strategy to be more successful in conducting business continuously. Having strong bonds with the co-workers leads to greater loyalty (e.g. respondents A:4, A:9, A:10, B:1–2). Respondent C:4 also noted that strong relationships between co-workers and managers can lead to higher loyalty, but adds that it ultimately leads to co-workers acting more ethically.

If some of these aspects are not managed properly, it facilitates an increase in demoralization and/or dissatisfied co-workers (Respondent B:2). In turn, this could lead to unethical behavior and business practices. As a result, there is a risk of repelling both current and possible future customers. Ultimately, the organization might no longer be able to continuously conduct business.

Relationship Investing consists of three sub-categories: *Trust*, *Organizational Culture* and *Staff Welfare* all revealed in the empirical findings.

The three emerged sub-categories reveal how managers can influence co-workers' ethical behavior in via Relationship Investing activities – the three sub-categories shown in Figure 4.3. If any of these sub-categories is managed wrongly, it can lead to unethical behavior.

Figure 4.3: Relationship Investing

4.3.1 Trust

Trust was a frequently discussed sub-category in this dissertation (e.g. by respondents A:4–9, B:1–3, C:1–4, and C:7–8). It was revealed that managers manage their co-workers' ethical behavior based on the relationship between the two with the help of trust. Without trust, the manager will not be able to continuously conduct business. There were several academic definitions for trust, where the one definition preferred by the author due to its appropriateness to the empirical findings was coined by Mayer, Davis and Schoorman (1995, p. 712) who explained it as:

> Trust is the willingness of a party to be vulnerable to the actions of another party based on the expectation that the other will perform a particular action important to the trustor, irrespective of the ability to monitor or control that other party.

Managers need to be able to trust their co-workers, and vice versa. Respondent A:9 said that without trust, having a positive relationship with the co-workers is a near impossible task for managers. Managing the co-workers' ethical behavior towards a desired destination will then be an even more difficult task. Respondent A:8 also noted the importance of trust and that created trust leads to a more desired level of ethical behavior and described this as:

> Trust is incredibly important… It is important to us that it (business transactions) is done correctly, you need people who do a good job and who you can trust. (Respondent A:8)

Respondent A:4 further elaborated upon trust and suggested that it leads to fewer conflicts within the group which means that the co-workers are less likely to engage in unethical behavior. The same respondent added that without trust, co-workers may not feel comfortable enough to discuss possible ethical dilemmas they encounter which can lead to unethical behavior. In other words, without trust, there are no relationships between the managers and the co-workers. Respondent C:7 discussed a strategy (s)he use in order to initiate trust:

> I don't have a program (to initiate trust), but what I can start with is when I have a new co-worker, I can have a conversation with them, including their expectations… and how I perceive things (ethical behavior at work), our ambitions… What direction we (the company) want to go. But also listen to the co-worker, their thoughts and ideas. (Respondent C:7)

Evidently, honest dialogue is important when wanting to initiate trust. Having an honest dialogue when starting to build trust is also seen as important by other respondents as well, including respondent A:9. Other contributing traits to implement trust were also provided by respondent A:9 who stressed the ability to display commitment while respondent C:7 stressed the ability to appear as a genuine person.

While *creating* trust seems to be of importance for managers, *retaining* and *maintaining* trust was shown in the empirical findings to be equally as important. For example, trust in this process is described as a phenomenon where research reveals that it is something that needs to be omnipresent and recurring in the everyday work in order to better manage the co-workers' ethical behavior. According to respondent A:5, one way for managers to try maintaining trust in the everyday work is for the management to always display commitment towards the co-workers. The importance of maintaining trust became even more apparent when interviewing respondent C:7 who pinpointed the need to constantly have good communication with your co-workers. It makes them feel included in different processes and thus feel they are able to influence:

> For this (trust), we need to constantly be good with communication so that the co-workers feel that they can be part of processes and have influence. It's not like I'm standing here every day pointing with my whole hand… things need to work despite the fact that I'm not here. (Respondent C:7)

The empirical findings also revealed that creating and maintaining trust is not a straightforward process that works in the same vein for everyone. One example was brought up by respondent C:7 who noted that all individuals are unique. Therefore, managers need to adapt to each and every co-worker in order to better create, maintain and/or strengthen the trust. This respondent suggested it often depends on how the manager communicates and expresses themselves. This can in turn get the manager a better individual understanding for each co-worker, which in turn can make it easier to manage their respective ethical behavior:

> In order to gain trust to one and another, a lot is about creating an understanding. Since all people are different, I need to adapt. I cannot break my own moral values, but I can adapt my way of communicating myself, expressing myself, and asking questions in order to reach results. (Respondent C:7)

There are also instances where trust is damaged and/or destroyed for a given reason. In order to re-establish the trust, respondent C:7 stressed that it is important for the manager adapt even more to the situation and work extra hard trying to repair it.

4.3.2 Organizational Culture

Organizational Culture is the second sub-category connected to the Relationship Building category. This sub-category was frequently discussed by several respondents across all sales industries (e.g. respondents A:3–4, A:6, A:8, A:12, B:1, B:5–6 & C:7–9). Early in the empirical findings, it was established that this sub-category is omnipresent and exists in all organizations – positive, negative or indifferent.

Despite several existing academic definitions, the most appropriate definition best describing this sub-category was coined by O'Reilly and Chatman. They defines organizational culture as "a set of norms and values that are widely shared and strongly held throughout the organization" (O'Reilly & Chatman, 1996; in Guiso, Sapienza, & Zingales, 2015, p. 62). **O**ther notable researchers like Treviño (1986) have a similar explanation and describe organizational culture as a guide on how to act in accordance with the ethical norms at a workplace. In similar fashion, respondent C:7 described the term as an important tool to influence and engage co-workers to act towards a certain desired ethical direction.

If a positive organizational culture is created at the work place, the co-workers will understand which behaviors are prioritized and will also develop a stronger emotional connection towards the organization. Thereby, the co-workers are more likely to comply with the existing ethical rules. A positive organizational culture makes it is easier for managers to create a positive relationship with their co-workers. Respondent C:9 discussed the importance of having a positive organizational culture and how to create it:

> What I can do to ensure (ethical behavior) is to have a (positive organizational) culture… My way of doing this is to act like a role model. (Respondent C:9)

A negative culture can facilitate unethical behavior among co-workers. For example, respondent (A:9) noted that if one don't like the work they are doing, it can lead to a negative culture at the workplace, culminating in unethical behavior. It was revealed by respondent C:8 that an inclusive organizational culture is paramount since it affects co-workers positively:

> It becomes a "We-feeling," and that comes from the culture, then everyone feels responsible. (Respondent A:8)

Respondent A:9 is familiar with dealing with a negative organizational culture and expressed the need to adapt to the situation by making an extra effort to change it into being positive:

> I fought hard trying to make a positive atmosphere and attitude (at the work-place), but each and every one has to take 100% own responsibility. You cannot just assume that someone else will solve it (negative organizational culture). One has to take 100% own responsibility for their own actions. (Respondent A:9)

Respondent C:8 discussed the need to adapt the organizational culture if the situation required such. The respondent discussed an instance where his/her co-workers disliked working Friday evenings and that they could lay out their own working schedule three months ahead of time. The organization need people working these shifts, resulting in management forcing some co-workers to work Fridays if too many had opted to not work that day. This created a negative atmosphere, but the manager (Respondent C:8) adapted to the situation and instead of letting co-workers always choose when to work, the manager distributed those Friday evenings evenly to their co-workers. Each person then knew far in advance when they have to work those Fridays. In addition to this, the manager added extra perks to those who worked these shifts, making it more attractive to work. This strategy made co-workers look forward to working those shifts, which led to a more positive organizational culture (Respondent C:8).

The empirical data also revealed two ways of creating organizational culture that need to be addressed:

i. Core Values (Respondent A:3–5, A:8–9 & B:1, B:5–6)
ii. Fellowship Building (Respondents A:3–4, A:6, A:8, A:12, C:4–5 & C:7)

It was established in the empirical findings that (I) *Core Values* is a way to create a sound organizational culture. Core values is created around the concept of improving relationships inside the organization. Core Values offer an opportunity for co-workers to become "part of the family," build a feeling of belonging. This can in turn create a stronger bond between the co-workers and the organization, ultimately helping them act more ethically. For example, respondent B:5 discussed core values for managers to incorporate as a mantra or a slogan encompassing desired ethical values and practices:

> We have our own core values that we live by (at work)… We work with these core values by having workshops. (Respondent B:5)

It was also established in the empirical findings that (II) *Fellowship Building* (see the main terminology section) is a way to build a sound organizational culture by attempting to make co-workers feel they are part of the group at work (and outside work) – a "we feeling". Another way to describe Fellowship Building is "a sense of togetherness between friends or individuals in a group."

This should not be confused with "Relationship Building" since the objective there is to have a positive relationship with the co-workers, but not necessarily be a group of friends. Creating a fellowship deepens the relationship. According to several respondents (e.g. A:6, C:7 & C:9), a fellowship can create a certain positive relationship based on a more positive collective organizational culture in the organization. This can make the co-workers more compliant and feel more responsible in terms of following ethical guidelines (Respondents A:6, C:7 & C:9). For example, respondent C:8 discussed Fellowship Building in the following context:

> We work a lot with team building, where you decide how personal you want to be. But you need to be a little bit private with them too, or else you won't build any relationship. (Respondent C:8)

In similar fashion to respondent C:8, Respondent C:3 also discussed Fellowship Building. A Fellowship Building activity can be to invite co-workers home to cook together in order to get to know each other as follows:

> I started to work here last August. Back then I put in a lot of time, all the way up to Christmas, getting to know the co-workers... Asking questions... (For example) Being at my place cooking together. (Respondent C:3)

Several examples of how managers can work with Fellowship Building activities in order to create a positive organizational culture were found in the empirical data, including:

- Arranging and inviting co-workers to *after*-work gatherings (Respondents A:2 & C:7)
- Attending football, ice hockey and golfing events (Respondent C:5)
- Meeting up in the managers home to cook food together (Respondent C:3)
- Include co-workers in different activities like creating written guidelines (Respondent A:4)
- Having education programs abroad in places like Ibiza (Respondent B:6), in order to make the co-workers create a fellowship (Respondents A:3, A:6 & C:5).

While all organizations seemingly have some form of Fellowship Building, it was unveiled in the empirical data that the amount of time spent on such activities varies greatly from organization to organization. For example, respondent C:5 admitted that they as an organization could be better at it, but said that they tried to do something at least once or twice per year, while others had it more frequently.

4.3.3 Staff Welfare

The third sub-category revealed in the empirical data is *Staff Welfare* (see the main terminology section). Staff Welfare for this category encompasses social, medical, cultural and other well-being measures for employees in a workplace (Allén, 1986, p. 905). This sub-category refers to the different Staff Welfare activities and -influences managers can use to establish and maintain relationships and thereby be able to better manage their co-worker's ethical behavior. Caring about their co-workers is of such great importance for many respondents that some even described themselves in the context of being a nurse (e.g. respondents A:2–3, A:6 & A:9). Staff Welfare facilitates a positive relationship between the co-worker and organization (Respondents A:2–3). Ultimately Staff Welfare can lead to co-workers acting more ethically and taking fewer shortcuts (Respondent A:2). Therefore this sub-category is closely related to the Relationship Building category.

The logic behind this is that people want to do a good job as long as they feel they are liked and feel they are being taken care of (Respondents A:3 & C:7). Respondent A:3 noted that if a person does not feel cared for, (s)he would most likely start caring less at work, resulting in a decrease in their ethical behavior:

> Everyone wants to be liked, it's not so damn difficult (to understand that). As a human being you want to be liked. You want to do a good job… It is because you want to do it, and want well and be part of a success. If you gets treated like crap, then you stop doing (a good job). (Respondent A:3)

A manager can for example implement different activities for the purpose of taking care of co-workers in order to establish a (positive) relationship. One such approach was mentioned by respondent A:12 who discussed having introduction plans and lunch for new recruits:

> Number one is that we have (implemented) an introduction plan we follow. Then we find a real estate agent who is responsible to educate all new recruits – This person does the things a real estate agent does in order to be successful. This real estate agent and I are both present when we introduce the new recruit. Also, the desk should be ready with a flower on it. A lunch should also always be included the first day for all new recruits. (Respondent A:12)

Another way to display Staff Welfare was discussed by Respondent (A:9). Managers display care for their co-workers by offering them to do regular health check-ups. One of many reasons behind this according to the respondent (A:9), is to detect potential stress or frustrations among the co-workers before it gets worse. Respondent C:7 also discussed how they have a wellness program where they provide their co-workers with the right to attend a gym or other similar health-related activities for up to one hour per week at full pay.

Several other examples were also found in the empirical data that concern Staff Welfare: Respondent A:8 noted that they have an adapted work schedule called "Child schedule" to make it easier for parents to plan their time. Respondents A:3 mentioned that their organization have added security alarms for their workers to make them feel safe when visiting unknown customers in their homes. Not all customers act ethically towards the sales-person either. A female salesperson can be in a vulnerable position if visiting an unknown person in his apartment. It was also revealed by respondent A:7 that most organizations tend to have different policies regarding taking care of co-workers with substance abuse issues (i.e., alcoholism, gambling, drugs, etc.) by offering different rehabilitation programs.

4.3.4 Summary to Relationship Investing

It became apparent from this section that this category is considered as an integral part of a manager's everyday process of both creating, maintaining and re-establishing relationships with his or her co-workers. By investing in a relationship with their co-workers, the managers get co-workers who are emotionally invested in the organization and are more loyal towards the manager. In turn, the likelihood of unethical practices decreases among these co-workers.

In addition to the summary, three important reveals were made. The first reveal concerns respondent C:7 who discussed that managers can invest in a relationship with a co-worker by establishing trust. One way to establish trust (Relationship Investing Category) is through communication (the Educa-tioning category), i.e., the investing in a relationship can go through the Educationing category (see section 4.4) by communicating with his or her co-workers.

The second prominent reveal is similar to the previous reveal but was described somewhat differently in the empirical findings (see section 4.3.2). Respondents A:3–4 and B:1 all revealed that there are instances a manager wants to include co-workers when creating the written guidelines (the Bureaucratization category). By including their co-workers in this process it is likely that it may lead to a more positive organizational culture (the Relationship Investing category) since there is possibility that they felt a stronger obligation to follow them due to their own personal involvement. This can in turn possibly lead to higher levels of ethical behavior. Respondent A:4 noted that the written guidelines can be adapted to better suit the local market as well as ethical practices and standards, where the co-workers often have better insight than the main office:

> We have clear guidelines for both, us as a franchisee and for those who are staffed. There we have a model, and it can of course be developed (adapted), where (employees) contributes their own ideas and so on. (Respondent A:4)

This suggests that using one sub-category in a category can cause the manager to use another sub-category in a different category. Two different sub-categories from two separate categories are here discussed and used as one when managing ethical behavior.

As for the third reveal, the empirical data reveal that organizational culture can also be built by being a role model. Like the second reveal, these are two sub-categories in two different categories, where one sub-category can have an effect on another sub-category. As a result of these reveals, a further unveiling of a dynamic process has occurred.

4.4 Educationing

The third category for consideration (See figure 4.4) is the *Educationing* category. The word "education" refers to the "ability convey the required knowledge and skills to an individual" (Allén, 1986, p. 1371). Synonyms to "educating" are teach, give instruction, train, practice, equip (with knowledge) and exercise (Strömberg, 1998a, p. 978).

This category encompasses all the educational activities, influences and tools managers can use to manage their co-workers' ethical behavior. For example, respondent B:6 discussed educating activities for co-workers regarding ethical issues in the following context:

> We often educate (our co-workers in ethical conduct). Next year we go to Ibiza. That will also give us a feeling of team building. (Respondent B:6)

The main purpose for them as a company was to attend a conference in Ibiza is to educate their co-workers in ethical conduct, among other things. As can also be read from the quote, a trip like this can also serve as an activity to create and/or strengthen relationships with the co-workers (Relationship Investing).

However, In order to educate others, most often managers first need to educate themselves. This category therefore not only encompasses educating co-workers, but also encompasses the managers as well. The empirical data show that in order to manage co-workers' ethical behavior, the manager can manage them via different education-related measures. This was for example discussed in the following context by respondent C:8:

> We work a lot with coaching and feedback. We talk about the values we have and the options we have.... A lot is about having the courage of to talk about these things (ethical and unethical behavior), and have the courage to give constructive feedback if you feel that the behavior are not in conjunction with our values. (Respondent C:8)

The empirical research also reveals that managers tend to favor educating their co-workers about appropriate ethical behavior that focuses on long-term business, i.e., what is best in the long run.

If managers fail to educate their co-workers appropriately, it can lead to unaware and/or uneducated co-workers in how to behave accurately. Both intentional and unintentional unethical behavior by the co-workers can have consequences for this mismanagement. This can in turn lead to customers and/or other stakeholders being exposed to this behavior. This, in turn, can put the organization at risk of losing customers, both current and potential new ones. As a result, the mismanagement of the co-workers' ethical behavior may lead to a failure to continuously conduct business. Therefore, ethics and Educating are closely linked together and are related directly with the core category.

Educationing consists of five related sub-categories: *Well-read*, *Communication*, *Clarity*, *Role Modeling* and *Termination* (see Figure 4.4). The sub-categories reveal how managers in different ways can manage co-workers' ethical behavior by educating them in accordance with expected ethical conduct that the organization, customers and other stakeholders require.

Figure 4.4: Educationing

4.4.1 Well-read

One of the most frequently discussed sub-categories encountered in the empirical data was *Well-read* (e.g. A:3–4, A:6 A:8–9, A:11). The term "Well-read" (from the Swedish "påläst") is synonymous with the word *Knowledgeable* (Strömberg, 1998b, p. 695), i.e., well-read and being knowledgeable are two closely related concepts. If the manager is not well-read about expected ethical conduct, written guidelines, laws, etc., miscommunication can occur. This can lead to both intentional and unintentional breaches in the expected ethical behavior by the co-worker. In turn, this can offend customers to such degree that it is no longer possible to continue to conduct business.

Therefore, managers need to be well-read about several aspects and areas in the organization in order to be able to correctly manage co-workers' ethical behavior. According to respondent A:11, there are several ways managers can become well-read about a topic. The most common approach is to start reading up on the topic. Respondent A:11 expressed this clearly in the empirical data:

> First and foremost I try to understand it myself… I read up on it quite simply. (Respondent A:11)

Respondent A:8 stressed that it is absolutely necessary for a manager to read up on the topic beforehand in order to get a better overall picture. For instance, if something new happens at work which requires change, like a change in routines, the manager need extra time to read up about it. The new GDPR-law is such an example which required adaptation in the work routines. When the respondent (A:8) was asked about what (s)he would do if (s)he encountered unethical behavior at the workplace, the response was as follows:

> I would probably get myself an overall picture to see what the biggest problems were, in order to locate the source to the problem. (Respondent A:8)

Respondent A:11 further elaborated on the necessity to read up. (S)he stressed that certain things are extra necessary to read up on a regular basis in order to know how to better manage co-workers' ethical behavior, where laws and written guidelines are such examples since they tend to change at times:

> In our case as a real estate agency, there is something called the Board of Supervision of Estate Agents (Fastighetsmäklarinspektionen) which sends out monthly or quarterly letters which I read-up on... (Sometimes) it could be that things that are legally correct are not ethically correct. But by reading these instructions, court rulings and praxis we become familiar with what is at least legally correct and not. (Respondent A:11)

Another example which several respondents (e.g. A:4, A:6 A:8–9) discussed was the usage and benefit of having lawyers to consult with when encountering complex social issues. Some sales organizations, usually larger organizations, have lawyers that the managers (and most often their co-workers) can use for consultation. By getting consulted, the mangers usually gets knowledgeable about how to better manage a particular issue. Thus, the risk of being sued or having other legal actions taken against them can decrease. Having lawyers to consult is perceived as an educational activity for the managers in order to help them become more well-read on how to better manage their co-workers' ethical behavior. Respondent A:3 also discussed this and said:

> We have six to seven lawyers who help support our brokers if something should go wrong. (Respondent A:3)

Another frequently discussed topic by several respondents (e.g. respondents A:9, B:4 & C:7) in regards to being well-read, managers to look at customer surveys in order to detect unethical behavior and thereby get an overall better picture at the workplace. By looking at the customer surveys, the managers collect knowledge and evidence on if some co-workers act unethically and how they did it. Thus, the manager becomes well-read about current mishaps. If it for example is discovered that a co-worker have broken the written guidelines for ethical conduct, the manager can take further action in order to hopefully prevent unethical behavior in the future and thereby better coach the co-workers in the future. As respondent C:7 explained:

> We (often) measure customer satisfaction and we coach our co-workers towards better customer satisfaction. (Respondent C:7)

This suggests that when the manager detect unethical behavior, they can more easily rectify this behavior for the future based on that knowledge they get from this instance. In conclusion, the importance for managers to be well-read was clearly highlighted in this section, where several examples are provided as to why being well-read is important and how it can be used to better manage ethical conduct.

4.4.2 Communication

There are several definitions for "communication" where the most suitable for this dissertation are made by Albanese (1981; in Axley, 1984, p. 430) who explains communication as an "information flow that transfers meaning and understanding from an information source to an information receiver." André (2008, p. 178) defines communication as "exchange of thoughts, opinions, or information by speaking, writing or other means." In order to educate others, communications is needed. As a result, communication clearly fits in the Educating category.

In each interviewed sales organization, communicating with their co-workers through different activities is seen as a central part of getting out information regarding desired ethical conduct. Meetings, education programs, seminars, sales training, workshops and performance appraisals are different activities managers can use to communicate desired ethical behavior – hence the word "communication." Failing to communicate can lead to unethical behavior, which in turn can offend customers. Revenue is then likely to be lower and it might no longer be possible to continue their business.

Some respondents that discussed different activities to communicate are Respondent B:6 and C:9 who both used the same anecdote when discussing. They noted that there can be a new law or a new documentation process that affects the work routines in such way that a different ethical approach is needed. Respondent C:9 noted that the manager can initiate meetings or hold an educational seminars focusing on this in order to better communicate to their co-workers how to work and act ethically:

> After a certain date the new law applies. This means that there is going to be theoretical learning… at least you can see pictures of what it will look like… When you had training, you have to ensure that all has participated. (Respondent C:9)

Respondent C:9 expressed a firm belief that having regular and recurring meetings (or parts of meetings) dedicated to ethical conduct like organizational values is a necessity. The meetings help educate the co-workers in how to solve complex ethical issues. In other words, regular meetings about ethical conduct is perceived as a way to manage, educate and influence ethical behavior.

While having regular and recurring meetings was discussed by several respondents as being imperative when educating and managing ethical behavior, two other types of meetings were also discussed. The first is having follow-up meetings about previous issues. According to several respondents including respondent A:7 and respondent A:9, during the follow-up meetings, managers can more easily detect if there is any improvement in behavior or if more education are needed.

Respondent B:4 adds that these follow-up meetings are a forum for managers to educate themselves and co-workers about what works and what does not. The same respondent added that it is sometimes a necessity to provide individual follow-up meetings with a co-worker in order to ensure that he or she comprehends what the organization's desired ethical work routines are:

> In order to do follow-up (on an ethical breach), I sit in individual coaching meetings with each co-worker. I also have distinctive meetings with the whole group, but I put more time with each individual. (Respondent B:4)

The second type of meetings outside the recurring and regular meetings are workshops for co-workers. Workshops can also be a way for sales organizations to communicate desired ethical behavior. Respondent C:8 talked about a new workshop their organization held which concerned the importance of inclusion, diversity and how it can affect co-workers' ethical behavior:

> We have started three days with workshops we call inclusion and diversity – It's about value dialogues. For 2.5 hours, six co-workers sits around a table and get a case (to discuss). Thanks to this, we dare to talk about these things, because we all know how it feels. You have been the last person to be picked at gym class. And we don't want that anyone should feel that here ever. (Respondent C:8)

Respondent C:9 further discussed the necessity for workshops as a means to direct their co-workers towards a desired ethical approach:

> We start with Codes of Conduct… we have certain values which works as our (moral) compass at work… We start with defining in our work group what the (values) mean to us… There we work in workshops… An ordinary day I have my meetings so that they start directly in the morning… Once a week we have an informational meeting, which is for the whole office – the classic meeting hour so to speak… On page two in the material (for upcoming meetings), there it is written exactly how the work group has been involved and how our values translate into our everyday workdays. Every time I have a meeting and come to page two, I stop there and go through some of these definitions and work with it in the group. (Respondent C:9)

Many sales organizations also send their new recruits on introduction and sales training where expected ethical conduct and business practices are communicated. For example, one notable respondent (C:7) stressed the need to train their salespeople correctly. Sales training is a good example of how to educate co-workers in how to behave when conducting business. However, since individuals differ, it was discussed that some recruits need more introduction than others. According to the same respondent (C:7), managers usually take this into consideration and often adapt the introduction time to the individual recruit if needed in order to ensure that as many co-workers as possible understand and get educated properly:

> If we look at our introduction plan (at work), it is six to eight weeks long. We have been testing different variants. The longest we have done is eight weeks, and the least amount of weeks is six… (It depends) on how fast a co-worker learns so to speak… If something is difficult to learn or if we progress too fast, we are different as people. If some feel it is easy we may hurry up, while others may need more time, then we may have to adapt. (Respondent C:7)

If the manager does not adapt to the individual co-worker, that individual can misunderstand ethical expectations, and ultimately cause unintentional unethical behavior.

4.4.3 Clarity

The third sub-category expressed in the Educationing category is *Clarity*. The most suitable definition in current literature describes clarity as "a cluster of teacher behaviors that contributes to the fidelity of instructional messages" (Chesebro & Wanzer, 2006, p. 95; in Schrodt et al., 2009). According to Suchan and Dulek (1990), "Clarity is business communication's most sacrosanct topic" and explained that the biggest problem in communication is (the lack of) clarity.

Several respondents (A:5, A:9 & C:7) stressed that when a manager displays clarity about rules, expectations, etc., the risk of misunderstanding in how to behave is reduced. The ability to display clarity in order to avoid misunderstandings that can lead to unethical behavior is therefore perceived as quintessential by many respondents (e.g. respondents A:11 & B:6). Evidently, Clarity needs to be closely related to the Educationing category in order to better manage ethical behavior.

It can be argued that by having meetings, seminars and workshops are a way for managers to display clarity on a particular matter. However, for this dissertation the sub-category of clarity refer to when managers make an extra effort to convey their message to the receiver. This means that the managers clarify their message in order to ensure that a person or group understands it, in this case, to understand how to act and behave ethically. A common approach to discuss the context of clarity by several respondents in the empirical data is here provided by respondent B:6 who discussed it as:

> We should be high on morals and in everything we do, ethics should permeate it all. But it is a very floating area, so I try to get everything down so it becomes more clear (to the co-workers). (Respondent A:3)

Thus, it is clear that the respondent makes an extra effort to make his or her co-workers understand expected ethical behavior. Two respondents (A:8 & A:3) stressed that sometimes the manager needs to be extra clear about a particular issue with one co-worker, while another co-worker needs extra clarity about another issue. Respondent A:3 explained this in the following context:

> Of course you need to manage people differently in different ways, an older person may need extra information in order to understand a certain thing. (Respondent A:3)

Respondent C:7 discussed clarity in the following context:

> We show (new co-workers) from the start what our (business) model looks like, what we do quite simply… so that the seller gets complete insight in the whole process. (Respondent C:7)

In a similar vein, respondent C:8 discussed about a time when it was found out that a co-worker dressed inappropriately at work and the manager had to clarify what the acceptable organizational dress code is:

> I think it is important that we behave as professionals… For the summer, a girl (co-worker) came wearing almost no clothes – almost like she was going to the beach. It was very hot outside, and I get that. But at work, you can't wear a minimal top. That's not okay, what impression does that make on the customers. This is an integrity issue, so I deal with it as follows. I don't talk to her in front of the whole work force. I rather take her to the side (and tell). You can say a lot of tough stuff, but in way that still is received positively, you do it with a big heart and respect. It's not about putting her to shame, it's about teaching insight. (Respondent C:8)

For this instance the manager needed to clarify to the co-worker about dress codes, and that certain clothes can detract customers since certain clothes can be perceived as inappropriate.

Another example of clarity was provided by several respondents (e.g. respondents A:8–9 & C:9) who all discussed strict zero-tolerance policies for certain unethical behaviors. Having zero-tolerance policies sends clear messages to the co-workers of what is tolerated and not. Breaching these can lead to termination (see section 4.4.5). For example, respondents A:3 and A:7 both expressed that racism and discrimination are such examples that are not tolerated by any organization under any circumstances.

4.4.4 Role Modeling

The fourth sub-category expressed in the Educationing category is *Role Modeling*. It was stressed throughout the majority of the interviews that managers needs to act as a paragon of virtue (role model) in sales organizations (e.g. respondents A:1–9, B:1, C:3 & C:7–8). Role models set examples for others to follow in how they act themselves. As a result, being a role model is a way to educate others in how to behave. Therefore, this sub-category clearly relates to the Educationing category. Respondent C:7 exemplified the importance of being a role model by stating:

> To me, being a leader is about getting co-workers to follow me and the organization towards a certain direction… The boss's behavior sets the (organizational) culture. If I say we should be in the office at 8:00 sharp (tomorrow), and I come in at quarter past, it does not work. Then they (the co-workers) will start coming in late too. (Respondent C:7)

The manager is usually the person who sets the standard in the company of what is to be tolerated, which also affects the organizational culture. In order to manage co-workers' ethical behavior, the manager must act as teaching others to act, where the behavior of the manager rubs off on the rest of the co-workers (Respondent A:8). One respondent explained the importance and the impact that comes with being a positive role model as the following:

> It is all about showing them (the co-workers) a right set of behavior and amplify it. That is how you get people to act the way you want. (Respondent A:3)

Being a positive role model for the co-workers is something that cannot just be whenever the manager chooses to. According to respondent A:3, managers need to adopt this behavior into their everyday work routine in order to better affect others' ethical behavior:

> A manager should always act as if he or she were constantly being filmed by a hidden camera. (Respondent A:3)

In other words, to be successful in managing co-workers' ethical behavior in sales organizations, a manager cannot stop acting ethically just because others might not be watching. Being caught breaching ethical guidelines might send a wrong signal to the co-workers that unethical behavior is acceptable as long as no one is watching. In turn, these unethical practices can offend customers.

According to respondent A:3, it is not always the manager in the organization who needs to be a role model; a co-worker can also be a role model for the others. Respondent A:3 also suggested that if there is a moral decay within the organization, the root of it can often be traced back to poor management and leadership. The respondent thought that the managers has acted in such a way that others started to perceive him/her as a negative role model, i.e., this moral decay seldom occurs if the company is managed in a proper way.

4.4.5 Termination

Termination is closely related where the empirical findings presented in this section reveal this relationship. To start, several respondents discussed the necessity to terminate (see the main terminology section) a co-worker from his or her employment within the organization due to unethical conduct (e.g. respondent A:3 & C:9). While termination of an employee can occur due to several reasons other than just ethical breaches, the respondents in this study tended to discuss termination in the context of terminating employees due to unethical practices.

While termination leads to stopping unethical practices in the organization from that individual since that person no longer work there, termination also serves another purpose. Terminating a co-worker due to unethical practices is a way for managers to signal to the other employees what behavior is expected and not tolerated. If the manager should decide not to terminate unethical co-workers, there is risk that other co-workers adopt the same behavior, ultimately driving many customers away from the organization. Driving away customers can, as stressed several times earlier in this chapter, be harmful for the managers' desire to continuously conduct business.

It was revealed that it is usually the severity of the ethical breaches that determines whether a co-worker get terminated or not. The more severe the ethical breach is, the greater the likelihood for the co-worker to face termination. Racism and discrimination towards a customer or a colleague is usually a reason for being terminated:

> Under certain instances you have to be extra strict, have zero tolerance against certain behaviors in order to set an example. (Respondent A:3)

Respondent C:9 also discussed termination to set examples. (S)he terminated a co-worker who had acted unethically, which in turn led to enhanced ethical practices by the remaining co-workers:

> I've ended up in some conflicts of interest... I ended up in a situation where everyone around you thought, what's happening, how come that the one who was always celebrated gets fired? (Respondent C:9)

However, while terminating an employee for major ethical breaches often occurs, it was also revealed in the empirical data that several minor breaches can also result in termination. However, the manager first needs to take all these minor breaches into account, in order to get a holistic perspective, before deciding whether termination is an option or not.

4.4.6 Summary of Educationing

Managers can through educational activities, tools and influences better manage their co-workers' ethical behavior. Moreover, it is also presented how these activities and influences help managers to reach their main concern – to continuously conduct business by managing their co-workers' ethical behavior by educating their co-workers in ethical conduct. Three reveals were also made. First, respondent C:7 revealed that informing (the Educationing category) about written guidelines (the Bureaucratization category) can be part of meetings. This suggests that using one sub-category in one category can mean that the manager also manages via another sub-category in a different category. Two different sub-categories from two separate categories are here discussed and used as one, displaying a dynamic process for how to manage ethical behavior.

The second reveal concern being a role model (the Educationing category). While being a role model is perceived as a way to educate by action others in how to act ethically, being a role model can also affect the organizational culture (the Relationship Investing category). Again, two different sub-categories from two separate categories are discussed. This further solidifies the existence of a dynamic process when managing co-workers ethical behavior in sales organizations. The third reveal is similar to the previous two reveals but encompasses a dynamic relationship between two sub-categories within the same category, displaying Clarity by having zero-tolerance (the Educationing category) and terminating (also the Educationing Category) co-workers due to certain unethical practices. As a result, an inter-dynamic process has been revealed between two sub-categories since more than one sub-category are used in this instance.

4.5 Monetary Managing

The fourth category for consideration (see Figure 4.5) is the *Monetary Managing* category. This category encompass different *monetary related* activities, tools and influences a manager can use to manage their co-workers' ethical behavior, hence the naming of this category.

If Monetary Managing is not managed properly, it can lead to stressed, demoralized and/or dissatisfied co-workers. Consequently, there is an increased likelihood that co-workers start taking short cuts and acting unethically which may escalate to the extent that the organization gets negative publicity or worse. This will not only drive away new customers, but also offend current customers as well. Ultimately, this can lead to reduced turnover to the extent that the sales organizations will not be able to continue their business. It is therefore in the managers' best interest to manage this category appropriately. Most respondents discussed this category but to different degrees. One way to exemplify how the respondents discussed the Monetary Managing category comes from respondent C:7:

> One can control co-workers (ethical) behavior via monetary systems. Especially if you use it in the everyday work as some sort of bonus system and things like that. (Respondent C:7)

The respondent (C:7) suggests that demoralization can lead to demoralized co-workers acting unethically, which will affect the organization in a negative way since it detract customers. Respondent B:4 explained that in a worst case scenario, unethical behavior can ultimately lead to heavy costs or that the organization goes out of business. Respondent C:4 also addressed this by saying:

> If we do something wrong, like Company X did earlier a few months ago, it was some minor thing (they did), they were fined to pay 50 million Swedish kroners. So it is a lot of money if you do something wrong. (Respondent C:4)

The empirical findings reveal that Monetary Managing consists of three sub-categories: *Salaries Systems, Rewards*, and *Goals* (see Figure 4.5). The three sub-categories reveal how managers in different ways can manage their co-workers' ethical behavior.

Figure 4.5: Monetary Managing

4.5.1 Salary Systems

The first sub-category, *Salary systems*, is directly related to Monetary Managing since managers can manage their co-workers' ethical behavior through their salaries. Salary systems refer to a pay structure employers use to pay their co-workers for their labor on weekly, biweekly or monthly paychecks (Mayhew, 2019).

To start, there are strong implications in the empirical data and an underlying consensus among the respondents that organizations need to pay their co-workers salary on a pre-set date – whether it is performance-based or a fixed salary. If the sales organizations for some reason fail to pay salary to the co-workers on the expected day, this can potentially create frustration. If irregular salary pay continues there is a high risk that it might not only create a temporary set-back in morale and frustration – it can also be a potential driver for co-workers to become demoralized and thereby start acting unethically which in turn can detracts customers.

Respondent A:5 explained that *performance-based* salary is the norm in most sales organizations there the pay is based on the salesperson's sales performance. For example, it is common practice that brokers in the real estate business receive a percentage based on how much (s)he sell a house or an apartment for. Similarly, in the car industry it is not uncommon that the more cars a salesperson sells, the more their salary increases for that month. In contrast to performance-based salary, having a fixed salary means having the same salary paid to the employer on a weekly, biweekly or monthly basis. The benefits of a fixed salary compared to a performance-based salary is that the worker knows beforehand how much he or she will be paid. With performance-based salary, the worker never knows how much he or she will receive each pay day where there is an opportunity to earn much more than regular work would pay.

Potential drivers to unethical behavior related to performance-based salary were widely discussed by several respondents, including by respondents A:5, A:7–8, B:7 and C:5. They reveal the following three drivers to unethical behavior:

- Uncertainty of getting paid
- Salespeople acting in their own best interest, not the customer's
- Increased levels of stress

Respondent C:5 further elaborated upon this by stating that there can be a strong correlation between performance-based salary and unethical behavior:

> If one has high performance-based salary, this attracts unethical behavior. It is not unique to (this) business. It's the same everywhere. (Respondent C:5)

This suggest that if there is an opportunity to earn extra money, it was suggested that it is possible that the salesperson can breach the ethical guidelines in order to sell. In contrast to both the real estate and car sales industries, a new law to prevent unethical behavior was implemented for the financial advising, private investing and pension fund industries. According to respondent C:4, this law forces these organizations to implement a fixed salary system for all co-workers:

> We are not allowed to have this (performance-based salary) anymore... It is a new law against performance-based pay in Sweden. (Respondent C:4)

While discussing performance-based salary, respondent A:8 noted that a fixed salary tends to reduce the level of stress, and thereby also the risk of engaging in unethical behavior. Several respondents in both the real estate industry and the car sales industry have noticed the correlation between stress and performance-based salary. While the norm in these two industries are a performance-based salary, having a fixed salary system is not exclusive to the financial advising, private investing and pension fund industries. For example, one CEO for a car sales organization (Respondent B:7) noted that they had implemented fixed salary for their salespeople in order to reduce potential stress levels:

> In order to not make (sales) people feel stressed about the performance-based salary... We now have a fixed salary system for all, both mechanics and salespeople... But we are probably one of the few car sales companies which has (implemented) this, perhaps the only company. (Respondent B:7)

Conversely, several respondents (e.g. respondents A:3–10 & B:3) revealed another approach to reduce potential stress levels linked to performance-based salary. A fixed salary is paid to all new co-workers for their first six months in the company before going over to performance-based salary:

> During the first six months they (the salespeople) do not have performance-based pay. (Respondent B:3)

According to respondent B:3, six months is usually perceived as sufficient time for the salesperson to get acclimatized to the sales environment, build their own customer base and get experience without the stress of performance-based salary. While a six-month fixed salary is usually applied to all new salespeople, it was also revealed that the length of the fixed salary can be adapted to the individual and their performance during these first months (Respondents A:8, A:12 & B:1–2). If the salesperson is already well-seasoned, he or she might need less than six months with a fixed salary (Respondents A:7 & A:8), while inexperienced salespeople might need longer than six months (Respondent A:12). Evidently, the manager can adapt the length of the fixed salary so that it best fits the individual person and their performance.

It was also revealed in the empirical data by respondent A:5 and respondent B:6 that managers allow their salespeople to adapt prices. By allowing the salesperson to adapt the price to the customer's financial situation, the manager can indirectly help reduce a salesperson's stress levels. For example, respondent B:6 discussed in regards to if a sales person does not reach any progress in sales deals for some time, it can lead to the salesperson starting to feel stressed due to lack of sufficient future income. In order to avoid this stress, the manager can provide the salesperson with the right to adjust the price in order to become more affordable for the customer. While this in turn might lead to lower earnings than initially intended, the manager reasoned that the salesperson is least more likely to sell and make some money.

4.5.2 Rewards

The second sub-category related to the Monetary Managing category is *Rewards*. **R**ewards in this dissertation refers to monetary and non-monetary incentives an organization can provide their co-workers due to achievement, effort or recognition of a high work performance. This sub-category are directly related to Monetary Managing since managers can manage their co-workers' ethical behavior by rewarding them if performing well at work. Providing co-workers with rewards was discussed by several respondents (e.g. respondents A:5, A:11 & C:6–7).

According to respondent C:6, reward systems are not only meant to increase sales, they can also be perceived as a means to influence their co-workers to act more ethically. Respondent C:7 suggested that rewarding well-performing co-workers is seen as a desirable activity to manage ethical behavior.

When the respondents referred to the word "well" in well-performing, they do not solely refer to making "well" monetary-wise for the organization. According to respondent C:4, "well" can also refer to how well the co-worker complies with ethical standards and procedures as well as the amount of satisfied customers they have. An example of how respondents in the empirical findings discussed Rewards is provided in the following context:

> A bonus I recall is that we tried to increase our housing sales. The winner would get a hotel weekend… It was new and we did it locally at our office. (Respondent A:11)

It was noted in the empirical data that for those organizations which only have fixed salary, rewards were more discussed during the interviews. For example, respondents C:3, C:4 and C:6 all discussed rewarding their well-performing co-workers since they could not affect their own pay like those having a performance-based salary. To exemplify, respondent C:6 discussed recurring monetary rewards as an encouragement of positively engaging people:

> It is boring to just get your monthly pay. They should have a bonus once a year or every six months… Then you get them positively engaged at work. (Respondent C:6)

Respondent C:4 also discussed rewards, but in the context of having "seller-of-the-month" rewards for their co-workers. The reasoning is not only to get their co-workers to be more productive in selling, but they also reason that it is usually the most honest salespeople who are the ones who perform the best (Respondents A:5 6 C:4). According to respondent A:5, one evidence of this is that high levels of honesty at the workplace often positively correlates with both high customer satisfaction and high sales performance. In a similar example to seller-of-the-month rewards, both respondents C:8 and C:9 have innovator-of-the-month awards. The intention of this reward is to reward those co-workers who provide good solutions to improve work-related tasks.

However, the empirical data also revealed that managers at times not only reward individuals for their single effort, they can also reward for well-performed group efforts by paying out extra money collectively to their respective pension funds (Respondent C:4).

Another and final example concerning rewards was brought by respondent A:11. The respondent had to adapt their reward system since it was only their top broker that was rewarded each month and it was usually the same broker who became the top seller. This resulted in the other brokers becoming more negative in their mindset, losing their ambition to sell. In order to motivate the other brokers, the respondent revealed that those who sold the second most and third most were also rewarded:

> We made a mistake since we only had a prize to the winner... So those who were behind … felt early that there was no point… We won't catch up. So there were no rewards selling extra houses. We talked about it and decided to have a prize for the second and third as well. (Respondent A:11)

4.5.3 Goals

The third and final sub-category revealed in the Monetary Managing category is *Goals*. This sub-category is directly related to the Monetary Managing category since unrealistic set goals by the manager can result in co-workers taking short-cuts to achieve them due to stress. This topic was discussed by several respondents, including respondents A:4, A:11, B:4, C:4–5 and C:7.

Research defines "goals" in this context as "a standard for appraising organizational performance" (Thompson, & McEwen, 1958, p. 23). The empirical findings reveal that goals can include a range of different things, including setting financial numbers, reaching ratios, staying within a budget or selling a certain amount of a specific product or service in a set period of time.

There was a general consensus among several respondents (e.g. respondents C:6–7) that goals are important for sales organizations in order to continuously conduct business. For example, respondent C:7 revealed that setting sales goals too high for the salespeople can have a negative effect on their ethical behavior due to stress. Respondent B:1 also noted that unreasonable goals could be linked to unethical behavior:

> We are trying to set reasonable goals. We get our goals from the main office on how many units we have to sell… If they (the goals) are not reasonable, they (the co-workers) might start taking short cuts. But, if there are reasonable goals, the risk of unethical behavior decreases. So there we can affect them (the co-workers ethical behavior). (Respondent B:1)

In a similar vein, respondent C:7 stated that if financial goals are set too high, it can lead to different types of unethical behavior due to that the salespeople strives to reach these goals. As a remedy for this, the goals can be revised and adapted in order to become more realistic:

> The co-workers could feel very stressed by them (high financial goals)… so they are driven towards higher sales where the consequence can be that they are selling other types of products to the customer than initially intended… So yes, we could say that we adapt our sales goals… we are more for working towards customer satisfaction. (Respondent C:7)

Respondent C:4 further elaborated on this and stated that sometimes unforeseen things happen, co-workers become sick for an extended amount of time, relatives die and so on. (S)he said that this might lead to the sales organization being unable to meet those financial goals and budgets that have previously been set (Respondent C:4). Consequently, the manager can adapt to the situation by accepting reduced goals:

> Her little daughter eighteen months old died, got an apple stuck in her throat… then you have to turn a blind eye since you cannot demand that they should meet the budget for some time. (Respondent C:4)

The empirical data clearly reveal that goals are not static. Sometimes the managers need to revise them due to a range of different reasons in order to better manage their salespeople's ethical behavior.

In addition to setting too high goals leading to unethical behavior, respondent C:5 mentioned a previous scandal involving their organization where the financial goals led to too high monetary rewards. In turn, this benefitted some co-workers within the organization to the extent that they started to act unethically in order to receive higher monetary rewards than were originally intended (Respondent C:5).

> Even now, this (scandal) can be read about in the newspapers today, the (financial) goals were adjusted down. (Respondent C:5)

Respondent C:5 continued and noted that when this came to the attention of top management, the organization immediately adjusted the goals and the rewards. Additionally, respondent A:7 reported how they have regular meetings with the franchisor to report whether or not they as an organization have met their pre-set financial goals:

> Even if they (the franchisor) are not here, they visit me locally. I report the numbers, and they have a couple of meetings per year for this. (Respondent A:7)

Respondent C:7 further elaborated on this by noting that if the numbers were not met, one explanatory factor behind this could be that the co-workers experience stress. As a consequence, they are not able to perform as desired. Respondent C:7 further revealed that implementing new goals, and thereby moving away from old goals, can be perceived as a way to decrease stress. Reaching high customer satisfaction over the more traditional "selling a certain amount of services or products goals" were examples of new goals that managers can implement:

> If you steer (co-workers) with sales goals, this can mess with their heads, meaning that if I sell this much, I'll get this much money. Then there is a risk for that it (The business transaction) does not become in the best interest of the customer... We don't have that (Sales goals) anymore... (Instead) We are now rewarding for high customer satisfaction. (Respondent C:7)

Evidently goals are important in the management process of co-workers' ethical behavior, where goals can either be adapted or new goals implemented if they are perceived as too stressful by the co-workers.

4.5.4 Summary of Monetary Managing

As a conclusion to this chapter, it was revealed how managers can use *Salary systems, Rewards* and *Goals* to manage co-workers' ethical behavior. Moreover, it was also presented how these activities and influences can help managers to reach their main concern – to continuously conduct business by managing their co-workers' ethical behavior.

Two notable reveals were made: (1) It was addressed how one sub-category (highly set goals) can affect another sub-category (Rewards), which consequently can negatively affect the co-workers' ethical behavior. (2) The final reveal concerns how one category can force change in another category. It was revealed how a Law (Bureaucratization category) can force sales organizations to change their the Salary Systems (Monetary Managing) in order to decrease potential unethical behavior.

4.6 Intuiting

The fifth and final category for consideration (see figure 4.6) is the *Intuiting* category. It was discussed in the empirical findings that the lines between what is considered right and wrong are often blurred due to complex social contexts and processes. Many respondents agree that managing ethical behavior in sales organizations consists of complex social contexts and processes. They often require more actions than just following the law, communicating, educating and acting ethical. Rational decisions are not always made. To manage these social processes, it was revealed that intuition can be needed.

Intuition is a *feeling*, an instinct something that is required to manage co-workers' ethical behavior sufficiently. Using intuition when managing is akin to management without any proof that supports the matter of context; the management process can be based on a particular "feeling" the individual has. Based on the empirical findings, the explanations of this category are well aligned with how literature definitions appropriately describe this category.

According to the dictionary, the word "intuition" refers to an individual's "ability to form an instant opinion or make an instant judgment without (consciously) having access to all the facts, and is often contrasted with reasoning and understanding logically" (Allén, 1986, p. 534). Intuition can be further explained as a "feeling for how to react or act in a certain situation based on a certain context" (Strömberg, 1998c, p. 398). While this "feeling" was frequently discussed by several respondents, I realized they all discussed the very same phenomenon but used different words when describing it. Some respondents discussed gut feeling, some mentioned a "feeling," others referred to their own "inner ethical compass" during the interviews while some even discussed Fingertip-feeling when managing. The confirmation of their relationship to intuition can be found in current literature having several synonyms to it. This includes words like instinct, a feeling, a gut feeling, a nose for, a sixth sense, etc. (Strömberg, 1998c, p.398) and having an inner compass (Khandelwal & Taneja, 2010).

The importance of intuition when managing ethical behavior seems to be so significant that several managers across different sales industries (e.g. respondents A:5–6, A:11, B:1, B:5–6 & C:6) all discussed its importance. Without it, there is a risk of mismanaging their co-workers causing them to misunderstand a situation. In turn, this can lead to having dissatisfied customers due to unintentional unethical business practices. As a result, it is generally agreed by the respondents that intuition and ethics need to be closely linked together. Respondent C:6 discussed its importance in the following context:

> Gut feeling is very important. It goes together with honesty and transparency. It is so easy to cut corners, but it will create a backlash that bites you in the butt. (Respondent C:6)

Some respondents (e.g. respondents A:5 & A:10) discussed intuition in terms of being an individual's inner ethical compass. They contested that all individuals have intuition – their own inner ethical compass, a sense of justice for separating right from wrong when managing ethical conduct.

Respondents A:3, A:11 and B:4 further elaborated on this and argued that having a sound intuition is essential when managing co-workers' ethical behavior due to all the involved complexities invthis process. Like respondents A:5 and A:10, they also referred to intuition as a correctly set ethical compass. A compass can be described as a tool which individuals can use when navigating in social settings. In this case, navigating in an ethically desired direction with the aim to continuously conduct business by managing their co-workers' ethical behavior. Respondent A:3 explains the importance of having an ethical compass:

> But in the end, (one must ask himself) if this (behavior) is fair, and the person (manager) must always base this situation on his or her judgement, (and ask themselves) what type of ethical compass do I have? (Respondent A:3)

It was noted by respondent C:9 that if a manager does not have such a compass, or is making decisions solely based on the written guidelines, it can lead to less successful decisions. It can for example culminate in stringent decisions being made, making the whole company to be perceived as unethical by different stakeholders.

Another example of when intuition was discussed during the interviews came with respondent C:9. The respondent explained that (s)he wants to get a "feel" during regular meetings in order to discover if there is any underlying friction or what the general vibe is among co-workers.

> I want to capture the feeling… is it a positive (atmosphere)? Or will they be grinding their teeth when going out to meet customers. (Respondent C:9)

Clearly, intuition can be used by managers in order to detect potential friction. If friction is noted, the manager can then take preventative action to avoid unethical behavior affecting customers. An example of this is to talk to the employee to see if there are any issues that need resolving (Respondent C:9).

Intuition was also clearly expressed by respondents A:6 and A:8 who discussed that staffing new co-workers requires good intuition by the manager. Respondent A:6 described the staffing process as one that can require a subjective evaluation through intuition regarding the applicant's personality. According to respondent A:5, by staffing an individual with a more desired "ethical character," the manager can indirectly steer other co-workers due to minimizing the risk of them being influenced and exposed to unethical behavior from an unethical individual. Another similar example was provided by respondent A:11:

> If you look beyond the merits where two candidates are exactly the same on paper, the bottom line is that I would pick the individual I felt I have the best chemistry with… (for that I) use my gut-feeling. (Respondent A:11)

Clearly, when a manager is faced with two (or more) individuals who are equally qualified on paper, the manager will use his/her intuition to select who is deemed the better fit for the job.

Another scenario related to intuition was discussed by respondent C:9. It concerns a time when the respondent found out that a co-worker had attempted to commit suicide. The respondent had to rely on his/her intuition in order to hopefully approach that person in such a way that will not cause further damage to his/her mental health. Hopefully, this would help avoiding irrational and unethical behavior by the co-worker. Otherwise, this can not only cause harm to the co-worker, but customers can also be exposed to behavior they would not be comfortable with.

Similar anecdotes were also provided by respondent A:9 and respondent B:7. Respondent B:7 noted that managers need to act differently depending on the context. Intuition can be necessary to have in order to be able to meet a co-worker and his/her present mindset. Managers can have to manage a situation differently by using their intuition. Depending on the person that individual's mental state and other individual characteristics and traits like age and gender, sometimes a manager can joke more with a co-worker while at other times they need to be more formal when approaching:

> You need to know when you can step forward or take a step back – How are you going to manage them. You manage them very differently. Are you going to be aggressive, raise your voice, talk fast, or take a step backwards, work in a more analyzing way? I think your body language is very important, that you are present in the mind and listens to the person, manage them differently… (Respondent B:7)

In short, the manager's intuition can be used as a tool to manage, influence and hopefully create a more desirable ethical behavior among co-workers. In turn, this will hopefully be more favorable for business. In turn this will hopefully facilitate so that the manager can be able to continuously conduct business. As a result, the management of ethical behavior and intuition needs to be closely linked together. Thereby, a direct relationship between this category and the core category exists.

It was also revealed in the empirical findings that a manager's intuition consists of a related sub-category – *Ethical Flexibility*. The sub-category further reveal how managers can manage co-workers ethical behavior by using their own intuition. The Intuiting category along with its sub-category is depicted below in figure 4.6.

Figure: 4.6: Intuiting

4.6.1 Ethical Flexibility

The one sub-category emerging from the empirical data relating to the Intuiting category is Ethical Flexibility. This sub-category was discussed by several respondents across all industries included in this study (e.g. respondents A:3, A:12, B:6-7, C:3-4 & C:9). According to the dictionary "flexibility" means "the ability to adapt" (Allén, 1986, p. 304). Therefore, for this dissertation, Ethical Flexibility refers to the managers' ability and willingness to adapt to the situation and co-workers' ethical behavior based in his or her intuition. One respondent expressed this as:

> If I have ten co-workers, I (might) have ten different needs, thoughts and ideas of what is right and not. I (sometimes need to adapt. (Respondent C:7)

Several more respondents, including a real estate franchisee (Respondent A:12), also agree that there are scenarios where a manager needs to be flexible enough to put his or her own ethical compass aside in favor of their co-worker's ethical behavior, i.e. let that co-worker act the way (s)he act despite not agreeing with such behavior:

> I have a *gut feeling*... and sometimes I have to make some sacrifices (on what to accept). I'm the one who decides, but I will not go to war with just anyone for anything. The important ones, yes, those battles I'll take (Since they otherwise be harmful to the company). (Respondent A:12)

Respondent C:9 provided interesting information where (s)he discussed the necessity for being ethically flexible. Daily conflicts of interest can be potential drivers for unethical behavior. While a manager for example does not agree with a certain behavior a co-worker displays on a daily basis, the manager can still be flexible enough to allow that particular behavior, even though it goes against his or her own ethical compass (Respondent C:9). Just because that one person does not like certain behavior does not mean that it is wrong. In a similar vein as respondent C:9, respondent A:11 discussed a scenario where (s)he turns a blind eye in favor of a co-worker's ethical behavior solely because it is legal and due to its complex nature:

> I've seen brokers throughout the years who act *legally* correct, but (they) still know that this behavior might not be considered as *ethically* correct… The problems is that as long as it is correct in accordance with the law… if the real broker does this for his own gain, I can't just ask the broker do it differently. (Respondent A:11)

Clearly, there are instances where managers overlook certain behaviors. At times it is considered by managers to be more important to keep co-workers satisfied and let them proceed with their conduct rather than trying to manage their behavior towards a different direction. Respondent A:3 discussed a hypothetical scenario on how (s)he would react if it was discovered that a co-worker is a well-known and frequent "swingers club visitor" in town. The respondent argues that such behavior can hurt the organization's brand and reputation. The reason being that the co-worker risks being associated with such ethically challenging activities by others and that the manager might feel it is ethically wrong to engage in such activities as well. Still, the manager has to balance his or her own moral compass against that behavior in order to make a decision if it is okay or not:

> Is this (information) relevant? For example, is it relevant that this co-worker spends his or her weekends at a swingers club? What should I (as a manager) do with this information? Of course, I don't give a crap about it, you can do whatever you want as a private person, while we still have brand to manage… We (also) have to be flexible. (Respondent A:3)

Evidently, there are instances the manager ignores certain behavior since it is legal and does not directly concern their work even though some might consider it to be unethical. In a similar example provided by respondent B:6 it becomes even more apparent that ethical flexibility can be important when managing co-workers' ethical behavior. Perceived racism is the sort of topic the respondents seem to take seriously. As for those issues, managers really need to balance their own ethical compass against a co-worker's behavior. Respondent B:6 addressed this:

> If a co-worker votes for a certain political party it does not mean that they are racist… if one is a (racist) on their spare time, and at the same time are nice to all customers and help all customers… then it is… (okay). (Respondent B:6)

However there are also instances where managers need to be inflexible, when they can't turn a blind eye (Respondents A:3, A:5, A:12 & B:6). One such example was provided by respondent A:5. It can come to the manager's attention that a co-worker posts racist material online on his or her free time to the extent that it can be harmful for the sales organization and its reputation due to being associated with that person. According to this respondent, while managers generally try not to interfere with co-workers' behavior in their spare time, there are still limits to what the manager can tolerate. Respondent A:3 discussed discrimination and provided an anecdote of when there was a need for managers to be inflexible:

> There is one thing we are not flexible with, and that is that we treat all people equally, regardless of sexual preference, gender, color, religion, etc. If you're not up for this, you can go look for work somewhere else, I don't want you here. (Respondent A:3)

This was also brought up by respondent C:9 who noted that managers can feel that a co-worker's behavior is unacceptable and that if the behavior is not changed, it can lead to termination for the co-worker. Respondent C:9 continued and discussed an instance when there was no room for flexibility, where termination was the only option even though this salesperson was a high revenue generator:

> I've ended up in some conflicts of interest… there I ended up in a situation where everyone around you (thought), what's happening, how come the one who was always celebrated gets let go. It is a very fine line for me to walk. I would want nothing than to explain that everything is not about hunting for revenue. It also has to be done the right way. (Respondent C:9)

Clearly, in the above given scenario, certain unethical behavior by co-workers can be directly harmful for the company, even though the behavior occurs during a co-worker's spare time. Some of these behaviors are not tolerated while others are. It is up the manager's intuition to make a decision on whether he or she should be flexible with that particular situation and behavior. To sum up this sub-category, I will provide a quote from respondent C:4:

> I dislike those (managers) who always think they are right. I think everyone should be able to have their say, and then it does not always mean I'm right, despite me thinking so. (Respondent C:4)

This means that there are more ways than the manager's preferred way to act ethically correct. Managers can be flawed and need to take this into consideration when managing. Their intuition may suggest one thing, while it might be necessary to go in another direction and thus accept the behavior of the co-worker since it may be acceptable enough to allow it to continue for the time being.

4.6.2 Summary of Intuiting

As a summary to this category, it was revealed and discussed how managers, through an intuitive feeling, can better manage co-workers' ethical behavior to reach their main concern. Due to co-workers being different as individuals and differing in mental state at times, it was revealed that managers need to use their intuition when managing their ethical behavior and be able to adapt not only to the individual, but also to the social context.

It was also revealed that there are times a manager does not agree with a co-worker's ethical behavior but still is flexible enough to allow them to continue the way they behave – deviating from their own ethical compass. But there are also those scenarios where the manager cannot compromise, strictly following their own ethical compass.

One major reveal was made in this category. Respondents A:3 and C:9 both revealed that there are instances when a manager needs to be inflexible (the Intuiting category) about a certain behavior and thus Terminate (the Educationing category) that individual. This suggests that using one sub-category in one category can cause the manager to also manage via another sub-category in a different category. A dynamic process between two different sub-categories from two separate categories has once again been revealed, i.e., more than one category can be used at the same time depending on the context when managing ethical behavior.

4.7 Concluding and Summarizing Business Basics

An integrated framework along with a core category (named Business Basics) has been revealed. The core category explains the actors' (respondents') main concern: a basic social process (BSP). This BSP explains how managers attempt to continuously conduct business by managing their co-workers' ethical behavior. Thus, the objective for a core category are fulfilled.

Managers want to be able to conduct business continuously and Business Basics is the common denominator to achieve this, regardless of industry, products or services. Conducting business continuously can be about managers wanting to reach different levels of success, survival on the market due to fierce competition, reach market leadership, personal development, etc. However, all those require ethical conduct by the co-workers in those organizations if the manager wants to be able to continuously conduct business.

The managers main concern is resolved through five distinct categories; Bureaucratization, Relationship Investing, Educationing, Monetary Managing and Intuiting. These five categories facilitate tools, influences and activities for managers to manage their co-workers' ethical behavior. Each of the categories can be used to various degrees each time.

It was revealed that there are times managers use one of these categories when managing, while there are other times two categories (or perhaps more) at the same time by the manager. The empirical data also reveal that the categories works in conjunction with each other or where one category can lead to another category when attempting to manage co-workers' ethical behavior. Therefore, the conceptually presented framework of Business Basics (the substantive theory) is to be seen as a dynamic process for how the managers resolve their main concern, not as a linear or sequential process.

A dynamic process for this dissertation is the interaction between two or more seemingly opposite tendencies. Examples of dynamism between two opposite tendencies related to the empirical findings can be of how managers educate (the Educating category) co-workers on the organization's written guidelines (the Bureaucratization category). Another example are that laws (the Bureaucratization category) can dictate for managers to change their salary system (the Monetary Managing category).

It should also be noted that during the conducted interviews with the respondents, the importance of the five different categories seemed to differ. Some respondents tended to put more emphasis on certain categories and sub-categories when discussing, while others were more keen on discussing other categories and sub-categories. For example, some managers tended to be more empowering than others, focusing on discussing Relationship Building activities like creating Trust (e.g. respondent C:8). Other managers like respondent C:6 tended to favor Monetary Managing activities since the respondent seemed to express a preference to look at numbers in order to see that everything was progressing as planned.

Nota bene: Despite possible preferences, all categories are used to different extents when managing co-workers ethical behaviour. All respondents discussed almost all categories at least once during the interviews.

Despite the reveal of the core category, its sub-categories and how managers resolve their main concern, the commitment of the manager plays a pivotal role. If the manager doesn't put any emphasis on managing their co-workers' ethical behavior, it is not likely that the co-workers will automatically engage in expected ethical conduct. The manager must actively focus on managing their ethical behavior.

In conclusion, while a substantive theory has emerged, one important step is missing when working from an orthodox Grounded Theory approach – to validate the empirical findings in existing research. This procedure is undertaken in the next chapter.

5. Validating the Theory and Further Discussions

The main objective for this chapter is to present and synthesize a limited amount of literature to validate the empirical findings regarding the management process of co-workers' ethical behavior. The literature presented is by no means comprehensive or meant to be exhaustive. Instead, this body of work should rather be perceived as examples and supportive arguments that validate and contribute to the understanding of the theory of Business Basics. For how relevant literature was derived, see Appendix 8.

Hopefully, this chapter will also constitute new information that can clarify, provide more angles and strengthen the theory. As a result, a second objective for this chapter is to highlight interesting discoveries, thoughts and possible gaps that in current literature have not been sufficiently covered.

One issue need to be addressed. The reader might encounter literature in this chapter that is not directly related to sales organizations and ethical behavior. However, as stated in section 2.7 regarding the usage of literature from other disciplines, if key conceptual relatedness in other disciplines or contexts fits and supports the empirical findings in this study, they are included in the discussion (Glaser, 1998). Additionally, it should also be noted that literature with a specific focus on sales organizations is often borrowed from other disciplines due to current lack of literature (McClaren, 2015).

5.1 Business Basics

As written in chapter 4 regarding the Business Basics theory, managers may have differing goals. Some managers can have the goal of wanting to become the market leader in their industry. Others managers can have the goal of surviving on the market while some managers' may desire personal development in their job. To achieve any of their goals, they need to be able continuously conduct business. In order to succeed with this, the empirical findings clearly suggest that an ethical basis is paramount where the co-workers ethical behavior needs to be managed. That is the meaning of Business Basics.

In more detail, this core category describes a social process and consists of five distinct categories. These categories represent different activities, tools and influences a manager can use when managing their co-workers.

How does the Business Basics theory relates to existing literature? As it turns out, most of what is encompassed in the Business Basics theory also exist the current literature, although often formulated differently. For example, the core category is in line with what the literature shows. Those organizations that act ethically tend to be more successful due to better long-term customer retention (Pettijohn, Pettijohn & Taylor, 2008; Crane & Matten, 2010; Ferrell et al., 2015). Evidently, the respondents included in this dissertation are well aware of the importance of ethical conduct and its consequences if breaches occur. Gaining and retaining customers in sales organizations are important for the long-term survival.

While the literature to different degrees attempts to cover the process of managing co-workers' ethical behavior, there are still distinctive differences compared to the aim of this study. For example, some studies focus on the process of supervising unethical sales behavior while (e.g Bellizzi & Bristol, 2005) while other studies present ways for how managers in large corporations can institutionalize ethics (José & Thibodeaux, 1999). While the literature to different degrees attempts to comprehensively cover the process of managing ethical behavior in organizations, the respective focus and aim differs as well as the fact that most studies seemingly use quantitative methods.

Unlike Business Basics which divides the management process into five dynamic categories, existing literature tends to divide area into three distinctive theoretical themes for influencing ethical behavior. The three themes can be described as follows:

- **Organizational influencing factors** (e.g. communication channels, rewards & disciplinary systems, ethical leadership, ethical climate, written guidelines, monitoring systems, organizational culture)
- **Individual influencing factors** (e.g. communication abilities, moral awareness, state of mind, ethical leadership, being a role model, age, gender, background, education level)
- **External influencing factors** (e.g. social institutions, economic conditions, political conditions, bureaucratic conditions, national culture, situational factors)

As can be seen, within each of these three themes, many of the influencing factors can be deduced to my own research. For example, Bolander et al. (2017) and Trevino et al. (2006) both discuss reward systems as an organizational influencing factor for influencing employees' ethical behavior. Gellerman (1989) and Lee and Cheng (2012) both stress the importance of codes of ethics and their influence on organizations. In Business Basics, reward systems are part of the Monetary Managing category while codes of ethics are described as written guidelines and are part of the Bureaucratization category.

Much of existing literature also tend to cover one or two themes, but not all three. However, one explanation can be that most of the respective objectives and aims of these studies never were to holistically explaining the whole process of managing ethical behavior. Instead, some researchers tend to focus on a certain range of influencing factors. For example, Hawes and Rich's (1998) main focus is managing salespeople's ethical behavior through role modeling, trust, supervision and feedback. This leaves out other important aspects like economic conditions. In a similar vein, Murphy (1988) solely puts focus on the implementation process of business ethics in sales organizations, not as an ongoing process.

Some of the literature which cover all three themes are literature reviews (e.g. Treviño et al. 2006) while others are comprehensive academic books (e.g. Treviño & Nelson, 2016). The most prominent research that covers all themes and is closest to the aim of this dissertation is the study conducted by Stead et al. (1990). Their purpose was to develop a comprehensive model by reviewing and compiling earlier research so businesses can more effectively improve their ethical conduct. However, not only does Stead et al. (1990) not discuss or include the law and legal compliance in their model, they focus on business organizations in general – not exclusively sales organizations.

The same discussion can be applied on McDonald and Nijhof (1999). While their focus is to create an integrated model for stimulating ethically responsible behavior, their focus is on organizations, not sales organizations. Like Stead et al. (1990), their presented model also consists of previous research. By using previous research compiled by others, it is possible that the current researcher fail to recognize important information and little nuances that might have been included otherwise.

The respective studies of Stead et al. (1990) and McDonald and Nijhof (1999) also have other differences compared to Business Basics. Their respective models and frameworks describe sequential and linear processes where at times, more than one possible outcome depending on the context can occur. Business Basics on the other hand, nothing is linear. Instead, it describes a dynamic process where the interaction of two (or more) seemingly opposite tendencies (categories) are used when managing.

Other notable authors attempting to comprehensively cover this management process are Wotruba (1990) and Schwepker and Good (2007). Unlike Stead et al. (1990) and McDonald and Nijhof (1999), their respective focus is on sales organizations, making them seemingly closer to the focus of this dissertation. Yet they differ to Business Basics due to their respective aims. While much of Wotruba's (1990) focus is on the ethical decision-making process, he expands beyond that and aims to present a framework for analyzing ethical behavior in sales organizations. Schwepker and Good (2007) on the other hand aim to provide a hypothesized model for how sales managers can influence employees and train them into becoming an ethical sales force.

Additionally, while both Wotruba (1990) and Schwepker and Good (2007) presents frameworks that explain relationships, they display a more linear process between influencing factors than displaying dynamic processes – something that not Stead et al. (1990) nor McDonald and Nijhof (1999) does in their respective frameworks. In contrast to these four frameworks, Business Basics presents how two distinct categories can affect one another in a dynamic process, while for example Wotruba's (1990) model only displays how individual and situational factors affect the moral reasoning of the individual. I.e. external influencing factors portrayed as a separate influencing factor.

But it must be noted that it does exist comprehensive frameworks for managing ethical behavior in different organizations and how relationships between different influencing factors therein are described. However, it is also clear that it seems like none describes the management process as a dynamic processes.

Moreover, it should also be clear that the objective for this dissertation is to identify and conceptualize a social process, which is in accordance with orthodox GT studies (Glaser, 1978). The respective objectives in the literature presented in this section differ compared to this dissertation and can thus be perceived as a strong potential explanation as to why they do not describe social processes. For example, literature like Schwepker and Good (2007), Stead et al. (1990), Treviño and Nelson (2016), Vardi and Wiener (1996) and Wotruba (1990) does not sufficiently describe this social process where the reason is threefold. They base their models either (1) on quantitative research, (2) on previous research or (3) is a comprehensive academic book. Additionally, the existing models tend to present a linear (e.g. Schwepker & Good, 2007) or a sequential (e.g. Wotruba, 1990) process.

However, obviously it exists literature which describes social processes within the studied field. But this literature seems to only focus on one or a few factors – not the whole process. Notable examples are Treviño, Brown and Hartman (2003), whose focus is on ethical leadership, and Victor and Cullen (1988), whose focus is on the ethical work climate. While these studies describe social processes, it is not sufficient to comprehensively explain the whole process of managing co-workers' ethical behavior in sales organizations.

As a result, the most notable finding in this section concerns how the integrated framework in Business Basics describes the ongoing social processes for how to manage co-workers' ethical behavior in sales organizations while other related literature does not. A social process is something that is ongoing and floating rather displaying than a "frozen" picture. One way for me to show something is ongoing was to put a 'gerund' to the categories I conceptualized. For example, adding an -ing to Monetary Management, better describes it as an ongoing process. Another way for me to attempt describing this social process was to construct the integrated framework without arrows pointing toward different relationships, placing each category in a "floating state" within the core category.

To sum up, two important findings have been revealed in this section:

1. Unlike Business Basics, there is seemingly no integrated frameworks which describe and conceptualize the social processes for managing co-workers' ethical behavior in sales organizations.
2. The second finding suggests the absence of describing dynamic processes. Existing integrated frameworks and models do not sufficiently describe the dynamic processes between categories when managing co-workers' ethical behavior. In contrast, these dynamic processes are a highly prominent feature in the Business Basics framework.

5.1.1 Further Findings

A third finding is also revealed. None of the literature which attempt to present a comprehensive framework except Trevino et al. (2006), discusses the importance of a manager's intuition when managing co-workers' ethical behavior. However, Trevino et al.'s (2006) article is a literature review attempting to present a coherent portrait of the current state of the field. In other words, it is not an empirical study presenting a comprehensive theory which includes the importance of intuition when managing co-workers' ethical behavior in sales organizations.

One possibility to this finding may be attributed to the tools orthodox GT provides. Conducting open interviews with the respondents allowed me to reach a certain depth and attain information that normally can be missed when conducting quantitative studies. Since the relevant literature is mainly conducted through quantitative data or uses existing research, it is possible that the authors have missed the impact intuition has on the whole management process.

While there is a great body of research regarding intuition and its importance when managing ethical behavior, this discussion is further discussed in section 5.6.

5.2 Bureaucratization

The first category in the validation chapter is Bureaucratization. There is a great body of research related to bureaucracy where the father of bureaucracy in literature is often attributed to Max Weber (1864–1920) from which research within the field has since expanded. This category was defined in section 4.2 as "the bureaucratic activities, tools and influences a manager can use when managing co-workers ethical behavior."

A clear link can be drawn from the empirical findings to the existing literature. Existing literature explain bureaucracy as "adherence to rules and regulations and a formal, impersonal administration of control systems" (Hit, Black & Porter, 2005, p. 586). Other researchers describes bureaucracy as instrumental for organizations when there is a need to manage the activities of several co-workers in order to carry out products or services to customers (Kwok, 2014).

Ferrell and Skinner (1988) found that bureaucracy can not only affect ethical behavior but also that the more individuals perceive bureaucratic structuring as positive in their respective organizations, "the higher the level of reported ethical behavior will occur." This is a strong indication that bureaucracy is a prerequisite for managing ethical behavior and is thereby directly related to Business Basics.

As presented in chapter 4, this category consists of four sub-categories: *Laws*, *Written Guidelines*, *Documentation* and *External Control.* These will each be validated with existing literature.

5.2.1 Laws

The first sub-category related to the Bureaucratization category is the *Law*. It was established in section 4.2.1 that the law is bureaucratic due to its structure and complex setting of rules. Several respondents discussed these legal measures as a means to manage ethical behavior. This sub-category comprises of the enforced legal responsibility of the organization, demanding all actors in the industry to comply.

In the introduction (section 1.5) it was established that there are conflicting academic voices in regards to the relationship of ethics to the law. Scholars like Carroll (1991) argue that there is a distinction, while others like Crane and Matten (2010) problematize it, having a contrasting perception.

Despite the differences, there is a large body of research focusing on how managers can make co-workers better comply with legal frameworks and how the law can affect one's ethical behavior. To start with, current research reveals that more than any other area of management, the dimension of law affects co-workers' ethical behavior the most (Hitt, Black & Porter, 2005). In supporting arguments, scholars like Treviño et al., (2006) stress that the dimension of law has an important impact on an individual's ethical decision-making process. Most adult individuals are largely influenced by the law at a conventional level, meaning that what they think is right and wrong is influenced by the law (Treviño et al., 2006). Research shows that due to the pressures from legal aspects, many organizations have implemented different approaches such as policies and programs to manage ethical behavior (Weaver et al., 1999; Treviño et al., 2006). This is a notable finding since it confirms the findings in Business Basics of dynamic processes occurring between two sub-categories within the same category – Laws and Written Guidelines.

In other related literature to this sub-category, Bodecker, Morgan and Stoltman (1991) discuss that if a salesperson is deemed to behave improperly by the aggravated customer, there is a risk of facing litigation for the co-worker and the organization. The authors mention several measures a manager can make to minimize legal breaches. Working proactively by conducting a self-test of current supervisory and selling practices along with training salespeople in current laws, will help co-workers to take greater ethical responsibility. This is yet another notable finding of dynamic processes occurring between two categories – Laws and Educating (Sales Training).

In more recent research related to Bodecker et al. (1991), Ferrell, Ingram and LaForge (2000) developed a seven-step process to guide legal (and ethical) compliance among salespeople in sales organizations. Their seven-step process is based on how governmental support for self-regulation and incentives for proactive involvement can help minimize legal misconduct. Researchers Treviño, Weaver, Gibson and Toffler (1999) on the other hand investigated what works and what hurts in legal (and ethical) compliance for co-workers. In contrast to previous research, Treviño et al. (1999) found that having a value-based culture within the organization is an effective way to foster co-workers' legal behavior. For this, sincere leadership is needed where the leader needs to be able to reward them and show consistency between word and action. Research also shows that in order to enhance the probability for salespeople to better comply in legal sales behavior, leadership, compensation, training and evaluation are suggested to work best (Boedecker et al. 1991).

Notable implications were made from the text above where existing literature confirm the existence of dynamic processes between different categories. For example, it was found in the literature that an ethical culture (Relationship Investing) can strengthen an individuals' legal behavior (Bureaucratization). Furthermore, dynamic processes between sub-categories within the same category are also noted in existing literature. To exemplify, supervising co-workers' (External Control) ethical behavior can have an effect on the individuals' willingness to comply with legal requirements (Laws).

Moreover, in order for laws to have greater influence on the co-workers' ethical behavior, research also shows that the laws need to be enforced actively by the manager and the organization (Dickson, 1978). One major factor for co-workers breaking the law is the possibility of not being detected. According to research an increased likelihood of being detected of breaking the law is a greater deterrent than a severe punishment (Gels & Stotland, 1980; in Bommer et al., 1987, p. 269). If the risk of getting prosecuted for the crime is low, the same research shows that an individual's ethical behavior tends to decrease. Clear parallels can be drawn to the empirical findings where some respondents notes that working as a salesperson can be a solitary job, with few colleagues or managers to interact with. The empirical findings reveal that managers have little insight in those business transactions. Instead, it was revealed that managers have other measures to affect their salespeople's ethical behavior. Implementing a channel for customer complaints and having strict documentation procedures are such examples.

5.2.2 Written Guidelines

The second sub-category related to the Bureaucracy category is *Written Guidelines*. As explained in section 4.2.2, written guidelines for this dissertation are perceived as an umbrella concept for other closely related concepts. It should be noted that there are academic voices which have contrasting ideas as compared to my simplification of the name. For example, Brandl and Maguire (2002) make the distinction between codes of ethics and codes of conduct, explaining that "Codes of ethics are general guides to operational values and decisions, while codes of conduct are more specific or formal statements of the values and practices of a business." However, due to their similarity in intent, I choose to perceive them as "statements that prescribe what the tourist and/or operator should do" (Malloy & Fennell, 1998, p. 453). This simplification was made due to the conceptualization process and hopefully makes this section more comprehensible.

One of the first individuals to cover written guidelines in research was Edgar Heermance (1924), describing them as a standard definite enough to serve as a basis for moral pressure. Today, there is a substantial amount of academic literature related to the topic, confirming the empirical findings that written guidelines can work as a means for managers to manage their co-workers' ethical behavior. To exemplify, several researchers, including Murphy (1988), McDonald and Nijhof (1999) and Stevens (2008) all argue that an organization's written guidelines work as a formal control mechanism that managers can use as a guiding tool to improve co-workers' ethical behavior. Madhani (2015) provided three strong reasons as to why written guidelines are important for organizations:

1. They demonstrate an organization's commitment to ethics
2. They help employees to recognize the existence of moral issues
3. They provide clear-cut guidelines regarding the organization's expectations of ethical decisions and behaviors. (Madhani, 2015, p. 9)

However, research suggests that managers cannot simply create the written guidelines and pass them down to employees in hopes for them to be successful. The co-workers themselves need to feel they are part of that creation process. This provides the co-workers a sense of ownership, thereby making them more committed to act in accordance (Stevens, 2008). This was something that was also discussed by several respondents. Furthermore, Brown et al. (2005) note that it is important for managers to establish and implement written guidelines that enable the manager to be able to both reward and discipline co-workers. This notable finding further confirms that a dynamic process between two or more categories exists. Since Written Guidelines is a sub-category in the Bureaucratization category and Rewards is a sub-category in the Monetary Managing category, a dynamic relationship seems to exist between these categories.

Moreover, several other researchers (e.g. DeConinck, 1992; Weeks & Nantel, 1992) pinpoint the importance of the managerial role for the written guidelines to be successful. They suggest that since managers usually have a great influence on the behavior of their co-workers, the managers must also follow and embrace these written guidelines rigorously, otherwise they will not be effective. This is yet another finding which confirms the dynamic relationship between two categories. In section 4.3.2. the importance of the manager to act as a role model was brought up since it could affect the organization's culture. The manager must also act as a role model when it comes to complying with written guidelines.

While there is a substantial amount of literature dedicated to written guidelines, far from all are free from criticism. For example, Lawton (2004) suggests that the written guidelines cannot guide co-workers in specific situations since they usually only provide general statements of values and therefore have little operational value. Sometimes the written guidelines may also be difficult to enforce for an organization as not all of the co-workers might agree on the content and its principles (Lawton, 2004). Additionally, researchers also discuss the importance of leaving room for flexibility. Weeks and Nantels (1992) stress that the written guidelines should not always be set in stone. They should be flexible due to the different contexts in social interactions and situations, otherwise they can be counterproductive. Again, the discussion above can clearly be applied to the empirical findings in section 4.2.2.

5.2.3 Documentation

The third sub-category – *Documentation* – is also a bureaucratic tool to manage ethical behavior which was revealed in the empirical findings. This sub-category is very similar to management theorist Henri Fayol's (1841–1925) school of Administrative Management Theory (AMT). In contrast with Weber's school of bureaucracy, AMT focuses more on fundamental functions for managers and how an organization is run. AMT perceives organizations as rational systems that need to run both efficiently and consistently where documentation plays an integral part to ensure co-workers engage correctly in business procedures.

As discussed in section 5.1.1, according to the empirical findings supervising salespeople's ethical behavior can be difficult. This is confirmed in current literature where it is revealed that salespeople's work independence is a contributing factor to the difficulty for managers to supervise them (Challagalla, Shervani & Huber, 2000). However, supervising is still needed in order to ensure that organizational polices are being carried out properly. To problematize this, Stathakopoulos (1996) noted that if a co-worker is too closely supervised, it can create role conflict. However, too little supervision can lead to unethical behavior amongst salespeople. In order to solve this, managers/sales organizations have implemented different documentation processes (e.g. logbooks) where the sales-people are required to write down all of their encounters with customers, document the history of a bidding process of a sale, etc. (Hummels, 1994). Research further reveals that by implementing these administrative procedures an increase in the efficiency of the organization occurs and thereby also is likely to improve the ethical behavior amongst the co-workers (Hummels, 1994).

In related research, Brodhead and Higbee (2012) discuss the benefits for organizations to archive written documentations about previous unethical breaches. They argue that the organization can benefit from this since the manager and the organization can incorporate past ethical breaches into future training sessions for co-workers on how to act. This statement is supported by Uduji and Onwumere (2013), who argue that the manager needs to make it clear that unethical behavior is unacceptable and that each breach in ethical behavior needs to be documented.

These findings solidify the empirical data provided in section 4.2.3. Documentation procedures are needed to better manage co-workers' ethical behavior where managers are well aware of its benefits.

5.2.4 External Control

The fourth and final sub-category related to the Bureaucratization category is *External Control.* This sub-category was explained by the respondents as how co-workers and managers alike felt monitored by different external entities, both governmental and non-governmental, in order to ensure that legal and ethical practices were followed. To trust that co-workers act within the legal and ethical boundaries is not enough. External Control fits into the category of Bureaucratization since it plays a pivotal role in ensuring that the organizations act in accordance with other sub-categories.

This sub-category is similar to a concept called Panopticon, a control system for behavior created by Jeremy Bentham (1748–1832). Foucault (1977) further developed the Panopticon concept and explained it as a design to control individuals by observing them randomly, where the individual never knows if he or she is being monitored. Since the individual does not know if they are being monitored, there is an incentive to act at all times in accordance with the expected ethical and legal practices (Foucault, 1977). The individual feels a need to adapt their behavior due to feeling monitored. This is similar to how respondents described that both governmental and non-governmental agencies made them feel.

The concept of Panopticon has been further applied in several research areas. Among them are sales organizations where Hawes and Rich (1998) and later Uduji and Onwumere (2013) are both notable examples of covering the impact of supervising salespeople. Much of the existing research seems to focus on how managers monitor co-workers' ethical behavior by hiring supervisors.

Current research confirms the empirical findings in section 4.2.4 in regards that there is a great chance that salespeople develop unethical behavior if not being monitored (Hawes & Rich, 1998). However, researchers also argue that there is a limit to how much a salesperson can be monitored before turning resentful and unproductive (Uduji & Onwumere, 2013). Uduji and Onwumere (2013) came to the conclusion that monitoring should not only be to ensure that ethical and legal practices are complied, but also as a means for continuous training. While there are a number of measures to monitor salespeople, research suggests that the most effective method of supervising is to conduct personal observations by the sales manager (Dubinsky, Yammarino & Jolson, 1994).

However, this is not always feasible since it would take too much time from the sales manager when salespeople's work is solitary and not always at the same location. This example was not encountered in the empirical findings. No respondents ever mentioned personal observation. It could be an example of managers not wanting to interfere with their colleagues too much, since their presence might affect the business deal. A more feasible way of monitoring is implementing customer complaint channels, which was already discussed earlier in this chapter and in the empirical findings.

However, current research not only encompasses monitoring co-workers as a way to manage others' ethical behavior. Current research also encompasses how managers can contact external agencies to seek guidance for how to better manage others' ethical behavior. For example, if a co-worker acts unethically, the manager might feel the need to first seek advice from an external consultant who is an expert in the field before taking action against that co-worker. André (2008) suggests that it is a prerequisite to get a good legal counsel in order to better manage ethical behavior. This statement goes hand-in-hand with the empirical findings in section 4.2.4, where several respondents discussed the option they had to seek guidance from experts.

5.3 Relationship Investing

The second category for consideration is the *Relationship Investing* category. It was revealed in the empirical findings in section 4.3 that managers can better manage their co-workers' ethical behavior by investing in a relationship with them. This category was there explained as those activities and influences managers can use to create, maintain, enforce and rebuild relationships with employees in order to better manage their ethical behavior.

There is a large body of research concerning how relationships affect co-workers' ethical behavior. In a study as recent as 2017, Schwepker and Good found empirical evidence that confirms the empirical findings in section 4.3. By creating close relationships with co-workers, the manager can more easily reduce unethical behavior and unethical intent. For example, a manager who is seen as loyal, likable and competent can more easily create positive relationships with co-workers. In turn, this can create greater loyalty towards the manager from the co-workers. This has proven to reduce unethical behavior.

There are several other empirical studies with a specific focus on sales organizations investigating the importance for managers to invest in relationships with their co-workers to better manage their ethical behavior (e.g. Paparoidamis, & Guenzi, 2009; Ahearne et al. 2013). What is seemingly a notable theme across these studies is that they all agree that it is important for managers to have a positive relationship with the co-workers in order to more effectively manage their ethical behavior.

As presented in chapter 4, the Relationship Investing category consists of three sub-categories: *Trust*, *Organizational Culture* and *Staff Welfare*. These sub-categories are validated with existing literature in the subsequent sections.

5.3.1 Trust

The first sub-category related to the Relationship Investing category is *Trust*. Several respondents discussed this topic as a cornerstone to both build and maintain a relationship with co-workers to better affect their ethical behavior.

As will be seen in this section, existing research focusing on the effects of trust confirms the empirical findings in section 4.3.1. Researchers seem to agree that it is essential to establish trust for managers since it is a core factor for good leadership and establishing relationships which in turn affects the ethical behavior of their co-workers (e.g. Bennis & Manus, 1997; Martin, 1999; Treviño & Brown, 2004). Research also seems to suggest that trust is the cornerstone for not only developing but also maintaining sturdy work relationships (e.g. Flaherty & Pappas, 2000). If a manager has the reputation of being trustworthy, he or she can more easily affect their co-workers' confidence as well as their ethical decision-making (Yukl, 2012).

Research also shows that co-workers tend to trust their managers more and thereby tend to act more ethically when the managers display personal integrity in the organization (De Pree, 1997). Several researchers have found strong indications that managers who treat employees in an ethically correct way more easily gain their trust (e.g., Dwyer, Shurr & Oh 1987). In other words, if a co-worker feels they are treated fairly at work, the manager will gain their trust, creating a positive relationship between them, reducing the likelihood of unethical behavior.

Lewicki and Bunker (1996) discussed the development of trust and how it can evolve over time. In their article, trust was divided into three levels:

1. *Calculous-Based Trust*: In the first level of trust, the authors stated that people will do what they say and promise due to fear of consequences and repercussions. This type of trust can be seen as an incentive to act ethically.
2. *Knowledge-Based Trust*: This type of trust is grounded in the other person's predictability to act in a certain way. It relies on information, and develops over time as we learn more. This type of trust can be seen as a predisposition to act ethically.
3. *Identification-Based Trust*: The third and last level of trust is when people learn to understand and appreciate the other persons' needs and wants. This type of trust can also be seen as a predisposition to act ethically.

The last level of trust is the most important level of trust in order to manage ethical behavior more effectively since when an individual understands and appreciates others' needs, a stronger relationship is created (Lewicki & Bunker, 1996). From the empirical findings, it is clear that most managers, except perhaps top managers at large sales organizations due to the large number of employees, attempt to create identification-based trust with their co-workers in sales organizations, i.e., being close to their co-workers is of great importance.

Moreover, researchers have also presented several factors that create trust, factors like expertise, candor, compatibility, customer orientation and dependability (Wood et al., 2008). Others points out competence, communication, commitment, conflict handling and satisfaction as trust-builders (Ruppel & Harrington, 2000). Green (2006) presented a five-step sequential model for creating trust, which includes the following five steps: engage, listen, frame, envision and commitment.

While the respondents in this dissertation never discussed creating trust in such a sequential process, isolated elements from the process was discussed. For example, one respondent discussed how (s)he would sit down with newly hired employees attempting to initiate a relationship and trust by having a conversation about expectations, ambitions and listen to the co-worker's needs and wants.

Evidently, trust is important and goes both ways. Employees need to be able to trust the manager. Managers also need to be able to trust that their employees behave within the boundaries of what is expected from them. However, this does not suggest that they should not ensure that expected business practices are being followed by controlling them. Examples of controlling measures were provided in section 5.2.4, where customer complaint channels and stricter documentation procedures were given as examples managers can use.

5.3.2 Organizational Culture

The second sub-category to the Relationship Investing category is *Organizational Culture*. As described in section 4.3.2, organizational culture for this dissertation is defined as "a set of norms and values that are widely shared and strongly held throughout the organization" (O'Reilly & Chatman, 1996; in Guiso, Sapienza, & Zingales, 2015, p. 62). It was with this definition in mind, I based the validation process in this sub-category.

Existing literature confirms the empirical findings that organizational culture can have a significant impact on the ethical behavior of individuals within an organization (e.g. Jose & Thibodeaux 1999; Treviño & Brown, 2004; Treviño, Weaver, Gibson & Toffler 1999). There are also several academic voices suggesting that to maintain a positive relationship with co-workers within the organization, the manager needs to have a positive organizational culture. For example, Treviño (1986) explains that organizational culture can help employees evaluate how to act best in a given situation. With a positive culture, ethical conduct is more likely to occur. Treviño (1986) also notes that having an ethically weak organizational culture can lead to an increase in unethical practices.

Other related literature further confirms the empirical data that organizational culture can help motivate ethical behavior. For example, André (1995) suggests that organizational culture can encourage an appreciation for human diversity. Hochwarter et al. (1999) points out how organizational culture can facilitate individuals to better express their moral values at work.

In other related research, Treviño et al. (1999) aimed to identify both what works and what damages ethical management and ethical compliance by approaching over ten thousand employees in different business organizations. Along with several other notable researchers within the field like Stead et al. (1990), José and Thibodeaux (1999) and Treviño and Brown (2004), all stressed that a value-based organizational culture is a key component for managing ethical behavior. Treviño et al. (1999) suggested that implementing both reward and disciplinary systems as well as including a value-based ethics program better facilitates the creation of a positive ethical culture. This is another notable reveal confirming the empirical data of the existence of a dynamic process between categories when managing co-workers' ethical behavior. To affect co-workers' ethical behavior through organizational culture (the Relationship Investing category), reward systems (the Monetary Managing category) can help, as well as implementing an ethics program to educate their co-workers (the Educating category).

However, this is not the only notable finding in existing literature that confirms the empirical findings in chapter 4 of a dynamic process when managing co-workers' ethical behavior. In research presented in 2016, Treviño and Nelson presents an integrated framework where they discuss how managers can use the organizational culture to help foster their co-workers' ethical behavior. They reveal that maintaining an ethical organizational culture is best achieved through the interplay of both formal systems (e.g. written guidelines and ethical training) and informal systems (e.g. ethical leadership like being a role model). Here is yet more evidence of the existing dynamism when managing since written guidelines is a sub-category in the Bureaucratization category, ethical training and being a role model related to the Educating category.

These are needed to create an ethical organizational culture. Moreover, while I am convinced that many of the respondents are aware of such terminology like formal and informal systems, they never discussed them using such words. Evidently, current literature not only subtly confirms the dynamic relationship between categories and sub-categories, it is also evident that current literature explains the process of managing co-workers' ethical behavior differently compared to how it is described in Business Basics. This can be a result of using orthodox GT as a methodology, helping me to conceptualize categories in a different light than has been previously presented in academic literature.

Another example found in research to create organizational culture is through an organization's *core values*. Core values in an organizational culture have an impact on the ethical behavior of employees and are explained as a system of norms and values that are held by most workers in the organization (André, 2008). Current literature therefore validates the empirical findings in section 4.3.2 that core values can also have an impact on co-workers' ethical behavior.

5.3.3 Staff Welfare

The third sub-category related to the Relationship Investing category is Staff Welfare since it can be used to manage co-workers' ethical behavior. As described in section 4.3.3, this subcategory encompasses activities such as social, medical, cultural and other well-being measures for employees in a workplace. As a consequence, I feel that it is closely related to the field of Human Resource Management (HRM) and Human Resource practices (HR) since their common denominator is to take care of the employees.

One of the most prominent theorists in this field is Mayo (1880–1949) who managed to turn focus from both individual and psychological consideration to focus on the group with his humans relations theory in management (Mayo, 2004). As for ethical concerns, it took a central place in the earlier history of HRM where staff welfare dates back to when the Welfare Workers Association was formed in 1913 (Winstanley & Woodall, 2000). Researchers like Adeyemi (2013) have pointed out that the lack of welfare for co-workers aggravates unethical behavior, which is clearly discussed at great length in the empirical findings.

Thus, there is a clear link between the empirical findings of this dissertation and the existing body of current research. For example, Elarabi and Johari (2014) explain HRM as a vital management task which plays a vital role in organizations. HRM concerns the development of both the individuals as well as the organization in which they work.

Empirical findings reveal that the welfare of employees also helps increase job satisfaction. Several researchers confirm this and present empirical evidence that sound HR practices positively affect a co-worker's performance (e.g. Ferris et al. 1998). Empirical evidence also suggest that HRM practices which emphasize promoting ethical behavior also attract individuals to seek employment there since it can not only increase job satisfaction but also increase organizational commitment (Treviño & Nelson, 2016). Thereby, a clear link can be made between the empirical findings and current research that Staff Welfare can be used as a means to positively affect co-workers' ethical behavior.

In conjunction to managing ethical behavior through Staff Welfare, Buckley et al. (2001) argue that HR systems can promote an ethical culture. As a consequence, the researchers suggest that HR systems should be considered as a partner with the organizational culture when wanting to create a competitive advantage for the organization. As with other sub-categories in this chapter, a dynamic relationship between categories and sub-categories are revealed in existing literature on how to manage co-workers' ethical behavior. Here, a dynamic relationship between Staff Welfare and Organizational Culture was discovered.

As can be seen above, academic literature confirms the impact Staff Welfare has on co-workers' ethical behavior that was encountered in the empirical data. Staff Welfare is instrumental in investing in a positive relationship with the co-workers to better manage their ethical behavior.

5.4 Educationing

The third category for consideration is Educationing was explained in section 4.4 as 'those educating activities and influences managers can use to manage co-workers' ethical behavior' in sales organizations. The word "education" was there defined as the "ability to convey the required knowledge and skills to an individual" (Allén, 1986, p. 1371), and is synonymous with words like teach, give instruction, train, practice, equip (with knowledge) and exercise.

As in previous two categories, there is also a large body of research validating the empirical findings for Educationing. First and foremost, this category reminds me of learning theories like Weber (1990). He constructed a preliminary review of different programs on how to best educate others in ethical behavior. He arrived at the conclusion that while ethical awareness and moral reasoning improve after being educated, it is usually short-lived. Consequently, educating in ethics is something that needs to be conducted on a regular basis, not as a one-off session for individuals. This correlates with the empirical findings in section 4.4 where it is discussed that some managers tend to conduct plenty of educating opportunities for co-workers on recurring basis where they discuss organizational values and desired ethical behavior. If the co-workers are not educated sufficiently, unethical behavior may occur. In turn, this can have a negative impact on customers. As a result, this can lead to a decrease in revenue and ultimately make the manager unable to reach his/her main concern – to continuously conduct business.

According to Bontis, Crossnan and Hulland (2002), educating co-workers can culminate in two different types of learning:

- Feedback learning – This type of learning occurs when the manager provides their co-workers with information that is both necessary and useful for their work. For example, to communicate ethical regulations can support the feedback learning flow.
- Feed-forward learning – This type of learning occurs when the experiences and knowledge of the manager are used to inform co-workers about different decisions taken.

This further confirms the empirical findings in section 4.4 where it was revealed that managers pass on information to their co-workers that is given to them from higher-ups in the organization. The empirical findings also reveal that the managers pass on information based on their own experiences and knowledge. Despite Bontis et al.'s (2002) discussion about the two types of learning, as will be shown in this chapter, thanks to the conceptualization process, the empirical findings express learning differently, where sub-categories are instead presented.

This category encompasses not only how managers educate co-workers, but also how they can educate themselves and consists of five sub-categories: *Well-read*, *Communication*, *Clarity*, *Role-Modeling* and *Termination*.

5.4.1 Well-read

The first sub-category is Well-read. The respondents discussed its importance to properly educate co-workers on how to act ethically. Being Well-read in this dissertation refers to the need for managers to read-up on relevant issues so they become sufficiently knowledgeable to educate others properly. It was established in section 4.4.1 that Well-read and being knowledgeable are two closely related concepts and are thereby used interchangeably. For this sub-category there is a large body of research focusing on the importance of being knowledgeable in order to better educate others. For example, Ugurlu (2013, p. 908) stressed the importance of managers being knowledgeable and that it also requires that the manager to "aware of the performance increaser characteristic of the knowledge." Researchers also point out that in order to effectively impact co-workers' ethical behavior in accordance with current written ethical guidelines, managers must not only be aware of them but also need to be knowledgeable about their content (Wotruba, Chonko & Loe, 2011).

It was found in the empirical data on more than one occasion that in order to educate others in desired ethical conduct in the organization, the manager must have knowledge of the ethical content. According to Lee and Cheng

(2012), ethical knowledge can take many forms, one of them being well-versed in the organization's codes of ethics and its stipulations. The same authors stress that there is a difference between ethical knowledge and actual ethical conduct since individuals do not always act in accordance with what they say others should do (Lee & Cheng, 2012). According to Lee and Cheng (2012), McPhail's (2009) theoretical framework of knowledge management "views individuals' knowledge of ethical values as tacit rather than explicit." Tacit knowledge can be difficult to both verbalize and write down to pass on to others. Instead it is crucial to act ethically (the Role Modelling sub-category), something that is also revealed in section 4.4.4.

The discussion above gives support to Davenport, Long and Beers' (1998) notion that transferring tacit knowledge successfully from on individual to another is a difficult process. The assumption is therefore that just because an individual has tacit knowledge about ethics does not automatically mean it can easily be passed on to others. However, Davenport et al. (1998) found several successful factors that contribute to a more effective transfer of tacit knowledge. This includes that organizations:

1. Have a knowledge-friendly culture (Organizational Culture in the Relationship Investing category)
2. Have a clear purpose and language when passing on knowledge (the Clarity sub-category)
3. Have multiple channels for the transfer (the Communication sub-category).

Several examples of dynamic relationships are thus revealed in the text above, further validating the empirical data.

5.4.2 Communication

The second subcategory is Communication. Several respondents discussed communication as being a focal point to educate their co-workers in ethical behavior.

As will be seen in this chapter, the existing body of literature confirms the empirical findings regarding the importance of communication to manage others. To start, Dainty, Moore and Murray (2007, p. 61) stress the importance of communication and ethical behavior by explaining that "The importance of effective communication to individuals, teams and organizations cannot be overstated. Virtually every text on how to manage people contains important principles of how to communicate effectively with the workforce." For example, researchers like Stevens (1999) stress that communicating written guidelines (the Bureaucratization category) is imperative in order to inspire co-workers to act ethically. The written guidelines cannot just exist, they also need to be articulated and reflected upon, something that is achieved through communication. Again, a dynamic relationship is revealed, this time between the Communication sub-category and Written Guidelines in the Bureaucratization category.

Current literature like Stevens (1999) covers several communication channels organizations can use to reach their co-workers with their message. Among them are: face-to-face communication, telephones, writing letters, sending memos, sending e-mail messages, Skype sessions and faxes to name a few commonly used communication channels. How the communication proceeds within these channels will differ. For example, communicating new implemented written guidelines can require face-to-face communication in a formal meeting of having a lecture or a seminar about it for co-workers. Several of these communication channels were discussed in the empirical findings (section 4.4.2). There it became clear that depending on the message, different communication channels were used.

One focus of Steven's (1999) study was to determine how managers best communicate desired ethical behavior to their co-workers. She found that the co-workers tend to favor communication channels such as training programs and coaching, something that was also brought up on several occasions in the empirical data. There is also literature confirming the empirical findings in section 4.4.2 suggesting that there is a need for managers to "proactively communicate with employees about ethical conduct which is normatively appropriate for the organization" (Xu, Loi & Ngo, 2016, p. 495).

Current research also tends to divide the communication into *formal* and *informal* communication channels (e.g. Rouiezs et al., 2005), something also discussed to a certain degree during the interviews. Depending on the severity of an ethical breach, a manager could talk to a co-worker briefly in passing if the breach is considered small, making the conversation informal. Other times, a manager can send a co-worker to participate in a seminar regarding how to sell ethically, here using a more formal communication channel to communicate desired ethical sales conduct. Research suggests that frequently exchanged and strategic information is best suited for formal channels while unstructured problems are better suited for informal channels (Rouiezs et al., 2005). While this was never spoken directly about by the respondents, it was hinted at when some respondents referred to "unstructured" problems as "watercooler talk."

On the other side of the spectrum of effective communication is ineffective communication. Ineffective communication may lead to damages in the manager's performance and counterproductive behavior by the receivers of the message. Research has identified several reasons communication problems can damage the performance of managers when delivering an ethical message (Longenecker & Yonker, 2013). Those managers who are not listening to their co-workers and managers who do not share information are two examples of why problems can arise when managers fail to communicate adequately. This claim further validates the empirical findings regarding failure in communicating.

5.4.3 Clarity

The third sub-category in the empirical findings in the Educationing category is Clarity. Clarity for this dissertation is explained as "*a cluster of teacher behaviors that contributes to the fidelity of instructional messages*" (Chesebro & Wanzer, 2006, p. 95; in Schrodt et al., 2009).

There is a clear link between the empirical findings and the existing body of research. It was emphasized in the empirical findings that displaying clarity is of importance when managing co-workers' ethical behavior. Several researchers like Bischoff and Eppler (2011) confirm this notion by stating that the most serious communication problem in businesses is lack of clarity. This suggests that if managers are not clear in their message regarding desired ethical conduct, it may lead to ethical breaches.

Bischoff and Eppler (2011) also discuss that due to differences in culture, communications habits and styles can vary, which may lead to misunderstandings. Misunderstandings and conflicts can also arise due to vagueness in different roles and responsibilities of an organization. In order for the communications to be more effective, research also stresses that repeating messages can be necessary (Williams & Dewett, 2005), something also discussed by the respondents. However, too much repetition can be counterproductive, leading to co-workers developing both a negative attitude and negative behavior (Ilgen et al., 2005).

Literature like Williams (1995) list several specific examples a manager can do to be perceived as more clear. This includes avoiding using the passive voice, complex nouns, foreign terminology, jargon and unstructured texts. Existing literature also reveals several other approaches managers can adopt to better clarify to their co-workers about expected ethical conduct, which include:

- Clarification of the organization's norms (Grojean et al., 2004; Treviño et al., 2003),
- Discussing the moral consequences of different decisions (Grojean et al., 2004;),
- Discussing the different expectations of the different roles (Treviño et al., 2003),
- Openly discussing both organizational and personal values (Grojean et al., 2004; Treviño et al., 2003)
- Providing guidance with suitable remedies for complex ethical problems (Grojean et al., 2004).

What is notable is that these are not discussed in the empirical findings. The empirical findings rather focus on how managers can make an extra effort to convey their message to the receiver. Depending on the person, this suggests that the way the information is articulated needs to be adapted to the individual co-worker.

5.4.4 Role Modeling

The fourth sub-category in the Educationing category is Role Modeling. Academic literature defines a role model as a "person you respect, follow, look up to or want to be like" (Sargent, 2001, p.177). As a result, I see a close relationship between Role Modeling and paternalism, since the behavior of that person may express an attitude of superiority.

However, since this sub-category deals with how managers, as role models, can manage co-workers' ethical behavior it therefore reminds me more of the Social Learning Theory (SLT). SLT concerns observational learning, i.e., experiencing through another individual (Manz & Sims, 1981). Being a role model was a topic frequently discussed by the respondents where some even noted that they attempt to act ethically as if they were under constant surveillance since their behavior had a direct effect on their co-workers' ethical behavior.

Existing research further confirms the empirical findings for this sub-category. For example, it was found that the top managers' ethical behavior indeed has an impact on co-workers' behavior (Ferrell & Weaver, 1978). Other researchers like Neubert et al. (2009) and Schwepker and Good (2017) stress that being a role model is the single most important factor for influencing co-workers' ethical behavior. These influences can occur either via observing by learning, identification and by imitation. For a manager to be perceived as a credible leader, it is imperative that the manager conveys and encourages certain behaviors that are deemed to be in accordance with current norms and ethical standards (Brown et al., 2005). One prominent trait role models need to have is to lead by example, the individual needs to act as he or she teaches, be a paragon of virtue (Neubert et al., 2009).

This suggest that the manager should know best how to act ethically in a paternalistic way, by promoting their own ethical behavior into a group. However, as was revealed in the empirical findings, I too believe that managers do not always know what is best, even when it comes managing ethical behavior. Therefore this should be taken to the equation when discussing the topic for this dissertation.

For example, research shows that role models can contribute to negative behavior as well. Brown and Treviño (2006) found that if a manager has Machiavellian or neurotic characteristics it can be directly harmful to the ethical behavior of the co-workers. Norms are of little or no value for the co-workers if the manager does not follow them. Evidently, this sub-category is closely related to the SLT since co-workers tend to act as ethically as their managers act.

Moreover, one of the first studies focusing on the effects of role models related to sales management was conducted by Rich (1997). He found that the managers who act as a role model increased the levels of overall performance of the co-workers as well as trust toward the manager, where higher levels of trust in turn also lead to an increased overall performance.

Figure 5.1: Rich's Hypothesized Model (Rich, 1997, p. 321)

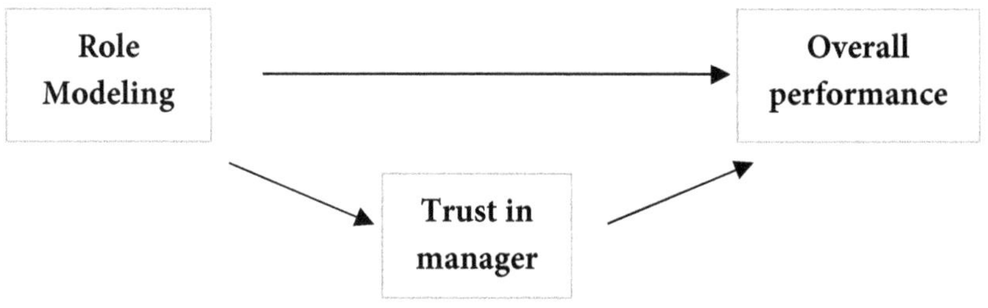

Rich (1997) noted that it was surprising to find that trust has such a pivotal part in affecting overall work performance. In sections 4.3.1 and 5.3.1 it was established that trust does indeed have an effect on overall performance. This further suggests that being a role model and trust both have an effect on the main concern of the respondents. Rich's (1997) hypothesized model also presents yet another notable finding further confirming the reveal of a dynamic process between categories in Business Basics. Since role modeling is a sub-category in the Educating category and Trust is a sub-category in the Relationship Investing category, a dynamic process seems to exist between these categories.

5.4.5 Termination

The fifth and final sub-category in the Educationing Category is *Termination*. This sub-category was explained in section 4.4.5. as a manager's necessity to be able to terminate the position of a co-worker due to unethical practices. Terminating the employment of a co-worker due to unethical practices send signals to the remaining co-workers of what practices are expected and tolerated and what happens if they are not met.

Current research is well aligned with the empirical findings: Terminating a co-worker for acting unethically can discourage other co-workers from engaging in such behavior (Laczniak & Inderrieden, 1986). As a consequence to this reasoning, as with Role Modeling, this sub-category can also be linked to the Social Learning Theory since it concerns observational learning (Manz & Sims, 1981). Research suggests that an individual's observation of a negative (or positive) outcome can alter that individual's behavior in the future – it becomes an "outcome expectancy." An individual who observes and remembers other people's punishments often expect a similar management response to them if they were to act in a similar manner (Treviño & Ball, 1992). However, if the punishment is moderate, research has found that it does not influence the outcome expectancy of the individual. Severe punishment on the other hand, like termination, was found to be salient enough to alter the behavior of an individual (Treviño & Ball, 1992).

Moreover, in regards to terminating co-workers for unethical practices, existing research also reveals that not all co-workers are terminated for the same ethical breaches (Bellizi & Hite, 1989). It was found that "sales managers can be willing to overlook certain unethical practices by the best salespeople due to the negative financial consequences involved with a decision to terminate the top performers" (Bellizi & Hite, 1989). It was also found by the same researchers that harsher disciplinary action, like termination, was more often applied only if the organization itself faced negative consequences. Additionally, while upper management on the one hand expects sales managers to take disciplinary action like termination against co-workers who act unethically, they also expect their sales managers to reach sales ratios. This creates a more stressful and complex situation for the managers to handle (Beliizi & Hite, 1989). However, as revealed in the empirical findings sales managers have at times the option to alter the sales ratios depending on the situation.

To problematize further, research also shows that shareholders tend not to care about the ethical behavior of the sales people to any great extent, depending on the context. For example, if the severity of unethical behavior is not specified, 94% of the shareholders do not favor terminating a successful salesperson, while only 6% of shareholders were in favor of this (Epstein, McEwen & Spindle, 1994). It was also found that 81% of shareholders were not in favor of terminating a top salesperson despite acting illegally, as long as that activity is considered a common business practice (Epstein et al., 1994). In fact, 5% of the shareholders considered providing a reward to that co-worker, encouraging a continuation of this behavior (Epstein et al., 1994). In short, the results of Epstein et al. (1994) indicate that shareholders are more interested in profit and not as concerned about co-workers' ethical behavior when conducting business.

It is notable that the shareholders to some extent question the relevance of ethics in a cynical way. It can be because they are detached from the business processes and the everyday work. As a result, they have little insight and do not fully realize the potential dire consequences unethical behavior might lead to as those who are closer to the business. Consequently, regarding the cynical view of the shareholders, this can in turn culminate in higher pressures being put on the managers to reach higher sales ratios which is why managers at times may overlook certain practices from a top seller.

The previous discussion reveals two notable findings. As for the first notable finding, it was not brought up for discussion during the interviews that some managers may overlook certain unethical practices depending on who is doing it due to pressures to reach sales targets. I believe it could simply be that this was considered a sensitive topic by the respondents to discuss since I feel no manager wants to publicly admit treating employees differently and was therefore not discussed.

As for the second notable finding, Bellizi and Hite (1989) found that some unethical behaviors can be overlooked by managers depending on how well the salesperson performs. Epstein et al. (1994) found that shareholders may have little concern for ethical behavior, favoring sales over ethical practices. This finding in existing literature challenges the importance of Business Basics as a theory, suggesting that ethics is perhaps not as important as the respondents suggest.

However, while it might be true that shareholders may favor a quick sale over ethical behavior, there are strong contradicting indications in the empirical data suggesting that managers in sales organizations do indeed emphasize ethics. One example relates to the fact that the upper management in one of Sweden's leading real estate organizations holds full-day seminars for real estate students at universities. If ethics was not of importance, why bother having these seminars? Additionally, the way Bellizi and Hite (1989) define sales organizations differ from this study's more narrow definition. This may suggest that while there are organizations where managers may overlook certain behaviors, this does not necessarily suggest that it applies as much to the managers in sales organizations as defined in this study.

The empirical research revealed in chapter 4 suggests that sales organizations, as defined in this study, are sensitive to unethical behavior. In turn, this strongly implies that managers needs to emphasize ethical behavior in order to be able to continuously conduct business. Moreover, this study focuses on revealing the main concern for the managers in sales organizations, not the main concern of the shareholders. But the lack of interest of ethical conduct can still be something that is experienced as problematic for managers due to pressures from shareholders.

5.5 Monetary Managing

The fourth category for consideration is the *Monetary Managing* category. It was defined in section 4.5 as "those monetary and monetary-related activities and influences managers can use to manage co-workers ethical behavior."

As in the previous three categories, there is also a large body of research validating the empirical findings for Monetary Managing. This category reminds me of Herzberg's (1987) motivational theory. Herzberg (1987) found that extrinsic values such as pay and rewards can have a positive or negative impact on the employees' job motivation depending on the size of extrinsic values. For example, higher salary and rewards tends to lead to higher job satisfaction and vice versa.

The link between job satisfaction and ethical behavior is discussed in Viswesvaran et al.'s (1998) organizational justice and cognitive dissonance theories. Their findings suggest that managers can favorably influence organizational outcomes by supporting and rewarding ethical behavior. If the motivation of the employees decrease due to the fact that a manager has mismanaged monetary management activities, it is likely that the risk of unethical behavior increases. In turn, customers and potential customers can be exposed to unethical behavior by the salespeople, driving away customers from the sales organization in favor of searching for substitutes. Eventually this will lead to the manager not being able to reach her or his main concern.

This category consists of three subcategories: *Salary Systems, Rewards* and *Goals.*

5.5.1 Salary Systems

The first sub-category related to Monetary Managing is *Salary Systems.* Several respondents discussed their co-workers' salaries (both performance-based and fixed) as a means to manage ethical behavior. Existing research confirms that salary can to different degrees affect the ethical behavior of co-workers (Wiley, 1997). However, researchers are conflicted in regards to the effect commission-based salary can have on an individuals' conduct. Researchers like Wiley (1997) also claim that performance-based salary can contribute to greater happiness and thus has a positive effect on ethical behavior. Research shows that high performing co-workers more often than not feel a sense of ethical justice by getting paid more than lower performing co-workers (Adom, 2018).

However, there are also those who contend that from a long-term perspective, high salary is not sufficient for people wanting to work. Instead, it is rather how much the co-worker values his or her position at work (Chen & Hseih, 2006). Moreover, in 2003 Kalra, Shi and Srinivasan provided empirical evidence that the higher the performance-based salary is per sale, the higher the incentive to act in an unethical manner. This suggests that having a commission-based salary can be a potential factor for a salesperson to breach ethical conduct in order to achieve a higher result. If an opportunity were to present itself, the likelihood of a co-worker acting unethically increases. An example is keeping certain information away from a potential buyer in order to be able to make the most of a sale (Román & Munuera, 2005).

Commission-based salary can be perceived as demanding, stressful and risky in the sense that the co-workers never know beforehand how much they will earn each month. The empirical findings found that stress is one of several factors which may lead to unethical behavior when having a commission-based salary. According to Honeycut, Glassman, Zugelder and Karande (2001), implementing a fixed salary system leads to a decrease in unethical behavior. Consequently, research reveals that implementing a fixed salary system is a way for managers to encourage long-term perspectives with the customers (Román and Munuera 2005). Reducing the stress leads to reducing the risk of the salesperson acting unethically (Robertson & Anderson, 1993).

As found in existing research, the respondents in this study's empirical findings also discuss the problems with commission-based salary contributing to unethical behavior. Attempts to minimize ethical breaches have been made by implementing a more bureaucratic workload where the purpose is to better monitor business transactions.

While commission-based salary is the norm in the real estate and car sales industries, sales organizations operating in the pension insurance advising and private investing industries recently had laws implemented, banning them from having commission-based salary. It was revealed that this would have an effect on co-workers' ethical behavior.

The empirical data also revealed one notable exception in the car sales industry. As a means to reduce stress for the co-workers, one manager had implemented a fixed salary for all co-workers. However, that respondent claimed to be unique in the industry in Sweden for having this. What is important to note is that managers themselves have noted the risks with commission-based salary leading to unethical behavior. But there are also studies which suggest that salary satisfaction has a significant effect on co-workers' work enthusiasm. With commission-based salary, employees have the potential to make significantly more money than with a fixed salary. Managers want to have motivated salespeople. Consequently, this becomes a dilemma. A commission-based salary can lead to higher job motivation, but it can also increase the incentives to engage in unethical business practices.

5.5.2 Rewards

The second sub-category related to Monetary Managing is *Rewards*. Rewards for this dissertation refers to monetary and non-monetary incentives an organization can give to their co-workers for achievements, effort or recognition of a high work performance, often in order to positively affect their ethical behavior.

In the empirical findings, rewards were often discussed in the context of "seller-of-the-month" rewards and "innovator-of-the-month" rewards, etc. While rewards can differ from organization to organization, Porter and Lawler (1968) divided rewards into two categories: extrinsic and intrinsic. They defined extrinsic rewards as "tangible benefits obtained as a result of doing the job, such as pay and promotions while defining intrinsic rewards as the satisfaction that a person derives from doing the job." However, Anderson and Oliver (1987) divided rewards differently than Porter and

Lawler (1968). They divide rewards into behavioral and outcome-based rewards, where the researchers state that both types can be used to positively affect ethical conduct. As can be noted when comparing with the empirical findings, rewards discussed by the respondents differ compared to existing literature where it is presented on a more academic level. Perhaps one reason can be attributed to GT. It allowed me to capture data from the "real world," not from academic books.

The importance of rewards revealed in the empirical chapter is also confirmed by Meyer and Nujjoo (2012) who describe them as critical incentives to attract and retain employees. Existing research further confirms the empirical findings that rewards systems can be a catalyst for both ethical and unethical practices (Hegarty & Sims, 1978). Treviño and Brown (2005, p. 83) specifically stress its importance, saying "Leaders influence followers by demonstrating high ethical standards in their own conduct and by using the reward system to teach employees vicariously about the outcomes of ethical and unethical behavior in the organization."

There are several more studies validating the relationship between rewards systems and ethical behavior in the empirical findings. For example, researchers like Hegarty and Sims (1978) found that providing rewards to one co-worker can also affect other co-workers as well, i.e., to see a co-worker receiving rewards for a certain behavior can reinforce the behavior of the observer, something that was subtly hinted at during an interview.

However, research also indicate that rewards do not always have positive effects; they can at times also have detrimental effect. Eisenberger and Cameron (1996, p. 1153) found that detrimental effects can occur under "highly restricted and easily avoidable conditions." For example, if a reward is presented independently from an individual's performance, the individual can realize that they cannot influence the rewarding. Thus, Eisenberger and Cameron (1996) suggest that this can lead to reduced work motivation. For sales organizations, salespeople are most often able to influence their rewards. Therefore, this is probably why rewards are quite common as a motivator in sales organizations.

In regards to motivation, what is also noteworthy from the empirical findings is that rewards tended to be more frequently discussed by managers in those sales organizations who had stopped commission-based salary. I found it interesting as to why they discussed this more, and I realized that motivating their co-workers is most likely important. These managers had to focus on finding other ways to motivate their co-workers than just salaries. As a result they tended to discuss rewards more than the other respondents.

5.5.3 Goals

Goals is the third and final sub-category in the Monetary Management category. In the empirical findings (section 4.5.3) it was revealed that goals can be used as a tool for managers to influence and manage their co-workers' behavior. Goals for this dissertation encompass tools like setting financial targets, reaching ratios, budgeting or selling certain amounts of a product or service.

As can be seen in this section, the existing body of research supports the empirical findings for goals and its impact on an individual's ethical behavior. However, current research not only tends to use different terms at times than the ones used in this study, existing literature also expands on the concept, explaining that an organization's goals can include: high productivity, industry leadership, organizational stability, profit maximization, organizational efficiency and growth (England, 1967).

McClelland's (1967) work on "achievement motivation" indicated a strong relationship to goals. It was found that that an organization's goals can make co-workers work more efficiently. This notion is further confirmed by Locke and Latham (1990; in Schweitzer, Ordóñez & Dourma, 2004) suggesting that one of the most effective tools a manager can use is to set goals when wanting to motivate co-workers. Consequently, the importance of goal-setting in organizations has become an integral part for both management and motivational theories (Ambrose & Kulik, 1999). It is clear from the empirical findings that some respondents put more emphasis on discussing goals than others for how they manage ethical behavior. The assumption is that there are differences in preference for the managers to manage the organization and what is most efficient.

However, being "efficient" does not equate to acting ethical. In recent years, despite being used to improve co-workers' performance, goal-setting as an organizational strategy has been questioned by scholars. While Hegarty and Sims (1978) came to the conclusion that goals did not significantly affect a co-worker's ethical behavior, several other researchers have since presented contradictory findings.

One of the first studies to empirically prove that goals can lead to unethical behavior was conducted by Schweitzer et al. (2004). They found that if a goal was not met by a co-worker, that individual was more likely to engage in unethical practices instead of doing their best to reach them. In 2014, empirical evidence indicated that the likelihood of poorly performing individuals acting unethically increased if that individual believed beforehand that the goal was easy to reach (Moore, Wakeman & Gino, 2014). If that individual anticipated a more difficult goal, the likelihood of acting unethically was not as high.

Ordóñez and Welsh (2015) provided further empirical evidence that goals like sales, targets, quotas, expectations and reference points can have a negative impact on a co-worker's ethical behavior. The quality of personal interrelationships can be diminished, which in turn can lead to stress and/or increased tension (Ordóñez & Welsh, 2015). However, the authors suggested that the probability of one individual acting unethically is not solely tied to the financial incentives in the goal. It was argued that the goal itself can be the source of the problem since research shows that an individual's behavior is affected by the proximity toward meeting the specific goal.

Moreover, if a goal is deemed too difficult by the co-worker to reach, this can lead to several negative effects. Current research points out several types of negative effects directly related to goals. For example, goals can lead to individuals concealing information that might have a negative impact on the outcome of the situation (Lee, Keil & Wong, 2015). Other negative consequences related to goals are acting, lying, taking excessive risks and reduced co-operation in order to reach these set goals. As a consequence, researchers warn that goal-setting as a strategy must be conducted with great caution by management (Schweitzer et al., 2004). As a remedy to this, managers need to be flexible and consistent when it comes to goals (Kane-Urrbazo, 2006). Research shows that managers who display inflexibility can cause erratic behavior in terms of unethical behavior (Kane-Urrbazo, 2006).

Evidently, existing literature coincides with the empirical findings that goals can have a negative impact on the co-workers' ethical behavior. In order to reduce stress and thereby hopefully better avoid unethical practices, it was revealed in the empirical data that managers at times altered the goals to better fit the situation.

5.6 Intuiting

The fifth and final category for consideration is Intuiting. Much of the literature presented in this chapter presents different rational models for how to manage ethical behavior. However, there are researchers who question the privileged status of ethical reasoning in these rationalist models. Sonenshein (2007) suggests that managing ethical issues is not always based on broad and conscious ethical reasoning, but is also based on intuition. The concept of intuition in management was up for discussion in research as far back as in

1938 where Chester Barnard discussed the functions of the executive manager (Sadler-Smith & Shefy, 2004).

Researchers like Sadler-Smith and Shefy (2004) suggest that while intuition can be easy to recognize, describing it can be difficult. This is something I can directly relate back to when interviewing certain respondents who at times had difficulties explaining why they managed as they did during certain scenarios. The respondents also used different words for describing managing through intuition, words like gut feeling and just "having a feeling." As in many academic fields of research, several definitions for a concept exists. "Intuition" is no different, where several good definitions exist. While two fitting definitions were presented in section 4.6, the definition provided by Shapiro and Spence (1997) also sufficiently fits the concept of managing co-workers' ethical behavior through intuition. They explain it as a "non-conscious, holistic processing mode in which judgments are made with no awareness of the rules or knowledge used for inference and can feel right despite one's inability to articulate the reason" Shapiro & Spence, 1997, p. 64).

Since this category concerns the managers' intuition and how they use it to manage ethical behavior in social settings, it reminds me of a study conducted by Simon (1987). He investigated the role of managerial intuition when making managerial decisions. It was there suggested that empirical evidence supports the notion that the intuitive skills of a manager are important when managing other individuals. In more recent studies related to this, Provis (2010) notes that if managers have low intuitive skills, it is more likely that they makes poor intuitive decisions, which in turn may result in unethical practices. That is, if the situation is mismanaged, it can create further problems with unethical behavior for the sales organization which may prevent the management from reaching their main concern.

Researchers like Shapiro and Spence (1997) also share this opinion. While operating in the field of psychology they stress that intuition is central when it comes to the survival of the individual. The reason for this is that individuals need to learn different essential co-variations in the environment. To suggest that intuition is central when it comes to the survival of the individual is a bold statement. However, clear parallels can be drawn to the empirical findings where the empirical findings frequently stress the importance of intuition. Having an intuitive feeling is of the utmost importance when managing co-workers' ethical behavior. If ethical behavior is mismanaged due to lack of intuition, this can eventually negatively affect customers, which in turn may lead to decrease in customer revenue. The manager will then not be able to continuously conduct business. Therefore, the statement by Shapiro and Spence (1997) may not be so bold after all.

Several other researchers within the intuition field have discussed and conducted studies with focus on intuition's impact on the management process, further validating the importance of intuition revealed in the empirical data. For example, as early as 1981, Chakravarti et al. (1981) found empirical evidence that model-based estimates were secondary to the judgment of the manager's intuition when making decisions in complex social settings. Later, Agor (1986) found that intuition is frequently used by managers when making strategic decisions. Today, existing research also indicates that when encountering complex social situations with short time constraints to make decisions, intuition can enable the manager to handle the situation better (Dane & Pratt, 2007). As presented as early as chapter 1, sales organizations includes complex social settings where many strategic decisions need to be executed. Perhaps is to no surprise why many of the respondents chose to discuss intuition.

One respondent discussed using his/her gut feeling when deciding who to hire between two individuals when all other credentials were almost identical. However, this reasoning is not completely unproblematic. Research show that by using intuition can lead to biases (Miles & Sadler-Smith, 2014). Bias was not discussed by any of the respondents. The reason might be that they did not think about addressing it or felt uncomfortable discussing it since it might be perceived as a sensitive topic.

Moreover, the empirical findings in chapter 4 reveal Intuiting as an important category. It is further revealed in section 5.1 that its importance is not explored or included in existing literature that presents comprehensive frameworks and models that are closely related to the studied field.

On the other hand, in this section it is revealed that there is much literature that recognizes the importance of intuition in the management process and ethics, validating the empirical findings.

One possible explanation can be that the existing literature use quantitative data or on findings based on earlier studies. It is therefore a possibility that these researchers have missed to include the importance of intuition, where benefits of conducting in-depth interviews can more easily detect hidden information.

However, a second possible contributing explanation can be that recent academic literature suggest that the importance of intuition may be dependent on the organizational context and its setting (Ashkanasy, Zerbe &

Härtel, 2016). In other words, intuition is more prominent in the management process in some organizations while being less prominent in others.

As was noted in chapter 1, McClaren (2015) stresses that studies and literature with a focus on sales organizations often borrow data and literature from other disciplines. In contrast to the literature in section 5.1 which does not solely focus on such organizations, it is revealed in this section that the existing literature indeed suggest that intuition has an important effect on the management process.

As a result, one can therefore argue that it seems like the importance of intuition when managing is contextually dependent on the organization, where both existing literature and the empirical data reveal that intuition is indeed important for sales organizations. Subsequently, two important indications are noted:

1. Intuition is important for this management process in sales organizations.
2. Intuition tends to be more prominent in sales organizations than in other organizations.

To summarize, while important and possibly more prominent in sales organizations than in other organizations, it seems like intuition is not included in any existing comprehensive framework or models of the studied field.

The Intuiting category also consists of a sub-category: *Ethical Flexibility.*

5.6.1 Ethical Flexibility

This sub-category is explained in section 4.6.1 as the managers' ability and willingness to adapt to the situation and to their co-workers' ethical behavior. This sub-category addresses issues like if the manager is willing to deviate from his or her own intuition in regards to what (s)he considers to be correct ethical behavior in favor of a co-worker's ethical behavior.

There also exists a great body of research related to this sub-category. For example, Haidt's (2001) social-intuitionist model approach to ethical judgment is the kind of research that blurs the distinction between an individual's motivation and judgment. This model coincides with the empirical findings of this dissertation that a manager does not always act in accordance with his or her own moral compass. There are times when the importance of the manager's ethical judgement depends on the consequences.

Ethical Flexibility reminds me to some degrees of transformational leadership. For example, according to Yasir and Azmi (2016), the managers' ability to be a flexible leader can be associated with transformational leadership. Existing research indicates that transformational leaders are more likely to promote ethical traits like justice, equality and fairness than other types of leadership (Carey, 1992). This validates the empirical findings that managers need to be flexible as it can help them to better manage their co-workers' ethical behavior. Bass and Steidlmeier (1999) further confirm this analogy by stressing that transformational manager's need to focus on not only promoting ethical policies and procedures, but also focusing on enforcing both ethical conduct and an organizational culture which encourages ethical practices. This is a notable finding, further validating the reveal in the empirical findings of a dynamic process existing between categories when managing co-workers' ethical behavior.

In addition to transformational leadership, Ethical Flexibility seems even more related to *Flexible Leadership*. In the literature, several terms describe this topic, including flexible, versatile, agile and adaptable (Yukl & Mahsud, 2010). According to Kaiser, Lindberg and Craig (2007), a strong indication of being a flexible leader relates to an individuals' ability to balance others' behaviors and values in such a way that it becomes most suitable for that given situation. Mintzberg (1973) suggests that managers have a wide range of tasks and responsibilities to which there is often a need to shift quickly from one activity to another.

This can require different types of behavioral changes by the manager. The skills, mood, mindset, values and needs of the co-worker can also vary, and due to this, the manager needs to be flexible (Yukl & Mahsud, 2010). According to Yukl and Mahsud (2010, p. 82), to be an effective manager, the individual needs to "find an appropriate balance for objectives that involve difficult tradeoffs, such as reliability and efficiency versus the need for innovative adaptation of emerging threats and opportunities." Different competing trade-offs and values can involve behaviors that are polar opposites. An example of this is empowering behavior versus controlling behavior.

Moreover, researchers Yukl and Mahsud (2010) also suggest that due to an increased pace of change that affects enterprises, flexible leadership has become a more important characteristic for managers in recent years. Examples of changes which require the manager to be flexible include an increased concern for acting ethically within the organizations (Yukl & Mahsud, 2010). Sales organizations face high paces of change and a high demand for ethical behavior. Consequently, the statement of Yukl and Mahsud (2010) is of little surprise, suggesting that flexible leadership is a prominent characteristic for managers in sales organizations.

From the above discussion, it is evident that the academic description of both transformational leadership and flexible leadership are well aligned with how this sub-category is explained. In turn, this validates the empirical findings of the importance of flexible leadership.

5.7 Summary and Conclusion on Validating the Emerged Data

In conclusion, as a summary to this chapter the main objective of this chapter was reached. All five categories of Business Basics and their respective sub-categories were validated with existing literature to which several theories and other related research were linked (sections 5.2–5.6).

In addition to this, three notable findings were also made:

1. It seems that there is no comprehensive framework which sufficiently describes the social processes for managing co-workers' ethical behavior in sales organization (section 5.1.1).
2. In contrast to Business Basics, the dynamism existing between categories (factors) is not as sufficiently expressed in existing comprehensive literature of the field (section 5.1.1).

   Yet, other related existing literature which covers certain parts of the studied field reveals and hints at dynamic relationships between different categories (factors) (sections 5.2 – 5.6).
3. While being a prominent category in the Business Basics theory (section 5.1.2), existing frameworks and more comprehensive studies related to the studied field do not include intuition. Yet, later presented research (section 5.6) stresses the importance of intuition when managing. In contrast to the research in 5.1, that research has specific focus on intuition, not the whole management process. Consequently, there are seemingly no frameworks or more comprehensive studies which include intuition in the studied field, despite existing much research with specific focus on intuition and management.

   This is an important finding since research also suggests that the importance of intuition may differ depending on the organizational context. Due to the empirical findings, it is therefore suggested that intuition in sales organizations may be more prominent when managing ethical behavior than it is in other organizations (section 5.6).

Concluding, by using GT as an approach, this study contributes a unique and integrated picture of the studied field that has to my knowledge not yet been presented. In the final chapter, a summary, contributions and suggestions for future research are presented.

6. Conclusion

The objective for the concluding chapter is to provide (1) a summary regarding the research process, (2) personal reflections, (3) theoretical- and (4) managerial contributions, (5) limitations and (6) suggestions for future research.

6.1 Summary

It was unveiled in chapter 1 that few, if any attempts seemed to have been made to conceptualize the social process of managing co-workers' ethical behavior in sales organizations, presenting it in an integrated comprehensive framework. The objective for this dissertation was to attempt to fill this gap in current research.

In chapter 2, orthodox GT was chosen as a methodology due to its appropriateness of being able to create a substantive theory that is a conceptually derived generalization based on the actors' subjective experiences. In chapter 3, the emergence process of the substantive theory is explained. In chapter 4, the substantive theory (Business Basics) for this dissertation is presented. It is characterized by the BSP of managing co-workers' ethical behavior in sales organization and is explained by its core category. The core category explains how the actors (managers) resolve their main concern – to continuously conduct business where managing co-workers' ethical behavior is a fundamental basis to achieve this.

The Business Basics theory consists of a conceptually integrated framework which describes the occurring dynamic social processes through five distinctive categories (conceptualizations), all relating to its core category (named Business Basics). It is important for the core category to have the characteristic of grabbing implications. The core category for this study is about where managing ethical behavior is a fundamental basis to achieve this. The social process of managers being able to continuously conduct business may very well be a condition that might be applied to other organizations as well.

As for the five categories, Bureaucratization, Relationship Investing, Educating, Monetary Managing and Intuiting, they represent different activities, tools and influences a manager can use to manage their co-workers' ethical behavior during their pursuit of resolving their main concern. The categories were conceptualized through interviews with the actors in the studied field. That is, Business Basics simplifies the complex social processes of managing co-workers' ethical behavior in sales organizations by making its inherent social process easier to understand and comprehend through its integrated framework and conceptualizations.

After generating the core category and five distinct categories of the substantive theory and saturation was reached, a theoretical validation process was conducted in chapter 5. Several notable existing and prominent theories and literature validated the different categories and sub-categories of the substantive theory. For example, the Bureaucratization category was validated in Max Weber's theory of bureaucracy, the Relationship Investing category was validated in Mayo's theory of human relations, the Educating category was validated in the social learning theory and the Monetary Managing category was validated in Herzberg's motivational theory. Consequently, the aim of this study to fill the gap in current literature has been fulfilled.

The validation chapter also constitutes new information where interesting discoveries, contributions, gaps and limitations are presented. For example, many prominent researchers related to the studied field (e.g. Bellizzi & Bristol, 2005; Schwepker & Good 2007; Stead et al. 1990; Wotruba, 1990) present sequential or linear frameworks (or models) based on quantitative data. In contrast to these, Business Basics describes a dynamic and social processes based on qualitative data.

Additionally, several of the different sub-categories in Business Basics can also be found in the existing models and frameworks but are often described somewhat differently in this dissertation. Unlike the five categories in Business Basics, existing literature of the studied field like Stead et al. (1990) often divides their material into three different theoretical themes (factors) influencing ethical behavior, i.e., organizational, individual and external influencing factors. What is also noteworthy is that the Intuiting category in Business Basics is not included or discussed in the existing models and frameworks that attempt to cover the studied field. Yet there is much literature on intuition in management and ethics.

6.1.1 Personal Reflections

Before undertaking this research, my initial thought was that while ethics as a topic might be somewhat important to some managers in sales organizations, I believed that ethics just was one of many things that were of importance. It was therefore surprising to me to find out about its importance, how seemingly all respondents in depth discussed their different strategies for managing ethical behavior. As a result, it became apparent to me from the conducted interviews that the engagement of the manager to appropriately manage their co-workers' ethical behavior is of great importance to them.

The overall sense is that the managers are genuinely engaged in ethical issues relating to their industry. They all seem to have a plan for how to foster desired ethical behavior in their co-workers. They simply articulated it differently. If the manager is less engaged in ethical issues it can, as I firmly believe, be potentially disastrous for that sales organization. This is also something that was stated by both the respondents and in current literature (e.g. Treviño & Brown, 2004; Huberts et al., 2007) that managers who care little for ethics can be directly harmful for their business.

However, I am not naive to think that all managers at all times when working focus on ethical practices or focus on managing ethical behavior. I realize that we are humans, we all make mistakes and we all have the potential to act deceptively if an opportunity presents itself. But I also contend that people in general are rational thinkers where the great majority of managers realize the importance of ethical behavior and therefore choose to act accordingly.

Another reflection I need to address is the respective experiences of the respondents. Appendix 2 shows that the respondents' average years of experience within the field is 19 years. While the average number of years as a manager in the field is likely to be lower, the overall experience within the industry is still high. As a result, due to the respondents' overall many years of experience in the field combined with that they all provide the overall same picture of how to manage co-workers' ethical behavior (albeit described differently), one can make the assumption that Business Basics reflects their reality quite well.

The final reflection I feel needed to be discussed concerns the early stages of the empirical collection. After having conducted three interviews the category of Brand protection was conceptualized (see section 3.1.1). However, after these three interviews, no other respondents brought the topic up for discussion. As a result, this conceptualization was removed since it did not seem to be in the respondents' interest to discuss the importance of protecting their brand.

It is noteworthy to address this reflection since I initially thought this conceptualization would be a prominent category for the substantive theory. Perhaps it could have been a preconception from my side for believing it was of importance. Another possible explanation as to why this category was not brought up in the remaining interviews can be that the importance of this topic was so central to all the respondents that they took it for granted when discussing. However, since I need to be aware of any potential preconceptions affecting me, I chose not to bring this topic up for discussion unless the respondents themselves first brought it up since I did not want to affect their answers with my own preconceptions. As a result, its importance when managing co-workers' ethical behavior in sales organizations can be further explored in future studies (see section 6.3.2).

6.2 Contributions

This dissertation provides three theoretical contributions along with two managerial contributions.

6.2.1 Theoretical Contributions

The following three theoretical contributions for this dissertation can be summed up as:

- *An integrated framework which describes social processes:*
  It is revealed that there do not appear to be any comprehensive and integrated frameworks based on the actors' subjective experiences that describe the social processes of managing co-workers' ethical behavior in sales organizations. The main objective for this study was to fill this gap by deriving empirical concepts based on the actors' subjective experiences and presenting them in an integrated framework.

  The integrated framework presented in Business Basics represents the managers' main concern and their recurrent resolution of it. It encompasses the social processes of continuously conducting business in sales organizations, where managing co-workers' ethical behavior is a fundamental basis to achieve this.

  As a result, Business Basics and its integrated framework can hopefully provide researchers with an increased understanding for how managers can manage co-workers' ethical behavior in sales organizations.
- *Illustrating the dynamism between categories:*
  The second theoretical contribution concerns the dynamism between the five different categories when managing co-workers' ethical behavior in sales organizations. It is revealed that:
  - The empirical findings suggest that there are dynamic processes between categories when managing co-workers' ethical behavior in sales organizations (e.g. sections 4.2.5, 4.3.4, 4.4.6 & 4.6.2).

    - In existing literature which aims to comprehensively describe the management process through an integrated framework or model, none seems to capture and describe these dynamic processes (see section 5.1).
    - Literature with a focus that is more closely related to one of the categories (instead of focusing on the whole process as in section 5.1) validates the dynamic processes in the empirical findings (see sections 5.2–5.6).
- *The importance of Intuition:*
  The third and final theoretical contribution concerning the importance of intuition when managing co-workers' ethical behavior in sales organizations. It is revealed that:
    - Intuition is a prominent category when managing co-workers' ethical behavior in sales organizations (section 4.6).
    - There is an abundance of research which validates the empirical data of the importance of intuition when managing ethical behavior (section 5.6).
    - However, there is a lack of comprehensive frameworks and models of the studied field that includes and discusses the importance of intuition in management (section 5.1.2).
    - There are indications in existing studies that the importance of intuition when managing is contextually dependent on the organization (section 5.6).

Hopefully, this finding may provide researchers with an increased understanding of the importance of intuition when managing co-workers' ethical behavior in sales organizations.

6.2.2 Managerial Contributions

As for the two managerial contributions for this dissertation, they can be summed up as:

- *A Practical Map when Managing:*
  Even though Business Basics is presented as a formal theory for academics, what is notable with the Business Basics theory is that it has previously not been known within research how these five distinct categories can help managers reach their main concern. Business Basics includes an integrated framework that allows managers to work systematically (both actively and proactively) when attempting to recognize

and seize opportunities that are beneficial to their main concern and the resolution of it.

This dissertation can therefore be useful as a practical "map" for managers to use both actively and proactively when managing ethical behavior. It can make it easier for them to orientate between the categories in the management process. This framework can help managers in sales organizations to improve co-workers' ethical behavior since they can see what important processes are needed to achieve this.

- *Finding the Source of Ethical Breaches:*
  This framework not only helps managers to proactively and actively work with managing co-workers' ethical behavior. If there is an ethical breach in a co-worker's behavior, the manager can with the help of this framework more easily pinpoint which process or processes (categories) that have contributed to the ethical breach. From there, the manager can gain a deeper understanding in how (s)he can proactively work to prevent similar potential breaches from recurring.

  In other words, managers can use this framework as an aerial photograph to understand where in the social process that might have contributed to unethical behavior.

6.3 Limitations and Future Research

This section aims to present encountered limitations for this dissertation ands well as suggestions for future research.

6.3.1 Limitations for the study

As in any research, flaws can be found and this dissertation is no exception. Four notable limitations were encountered during the process of writing which need to be addressed:

- The first *limitation* concerns the possibility of respondents being apprehensive to discuss ethical issues with an individual they had never met before, something that was earlier discussed. There might have been times that I asked questions which may have been perceived as a sensitive topic for the respondent. This can potentially have led to respondents adapting their answer or even avoiding answering certain questions. In order to solve this issue to the best of my abilities, several precautions were taken before and during the interview session:

1. All respondents were informed prior to their respective interviews that they were going to be anonymous and that all information would be cared for with full confidentiality, all in accordance with current research practices.
2. If a potential respondent was initially reluctant to participate in an interview, more information was offered via email, including a further explanation of my role and the topic (see Appendix 4 for an example). If the respondent to any extent felt uncomfortable with the topic, they had the option to cancel the interview. This precaution can potentially have affected the respondents during the interviews since they were better prepared and had more time to think of what to answer. However, I chose to see this as giving them time to be reflective on how they actually manage their co-workers' ethical behavior.
3. There were times questions were asked in a normative way (how things in general are supposed to be managed), since I believe it might be easier to discuss a potential sensitive topic like ethics in such a way.
4. Sometimes I found it easier to discuss the shortcomings of their competitors. Therefore, respondents were at times asked if they had heard about unethical practices competitors might have been involved in. If the respondent discussed this, I then proceeded to ask them how they would have solved such a situation. It was noted that the respondents tended to open up more at times when asking questions in such manner.

- The second limitation concerns the gender of the respondents and how it might have affected the conceptualizations process. The interviewed respondents consisted of twenty men and only five women (see Appendix 2). There is a chance that the outcome of this study would have turned out slightly different if the respondents' gender was more evenly represented.
- The third limitation concerns the concept of tabula rasa. It was established in chapter 2 that no person is completely tabula rasa. Working from an orthodox GT approach, the researcher should not have any preconceptions, not have any other knowledge about the subject so that (s)he can better conceptualize what the respondents are saying. The author of this dissertation tried to be as close to tabula rasa as possible in the research process where the measures to minimize potential preconceptions were presented in section 2.8.1. However, undertaking

these measures does not suggest that subconscious preconceptions and biases automatically are eliminated.
- The fourth and final limitation concerns the differences in salary systems across different industries and how as a result this may have affected the conceptualization process. Some industries have commission-based salary systems as praxis (e.g. real estate and car sales) while others have fixed salary systems as praxis (e.g. private investing). It was revealed in the empirical findings (later also confirmed in the validation chapter) that commission-based salaries are more likely to cause stress for the employees than fixed salaries. Stress can contribute to unethical decisions being taken. This can potentially lead to differences in how the managers manage their respective co-workers' ethical behavior. As a result, it is possible that the outcome of the conceptualization process would differ if this study would solely have focused on industries with either fixed or commission-based salary systems, not both.

Perhaps the definition of what a sales organization is should have been funneled further down in order to prevent the conceptualization process from being potentially affected.

6.3.2 Future Studies

This section presents six potential suggestions for future studies:

- While the field for this research focus on sales organizations, the same type of research approach (orthodox GT) with the same aim can be applied in another field and industry in order to find potential likenesses or differences. For example, a researcher can conduct research aimed at how businesses in general or how political leaders manage their co-workers' ethical behavior. One reason for conducting such a study can be to see the emergent fit of this dissertation's five categories in that area. One or perhaps several of the five categories in Business Basics may very well fit or be modified to fit into those areas as well.
- It is mentioned in the introduction (see chapter 1) that salespeople tend to be more exposed to unethical behavior than individuals in other organizations. Sometimes the managers in the sales organization also interact with customers. Customers can be dissatisfied with a particular salesperson or unhappy with a business transaction. In such scenarios, the manager can step in hoping to solve the issues. Additionally, franchisee managers in real estate organizations also often tend to work as

brokers themselves. As a result, they often interact with customers on a daily basis. Not all these customers might have the best of intentions.

Since the main concern of the managers in sales organizations is to continuously conduct business, unethical customers can become a potential problem. This suggests that it is likely that the manager can be forced to manage the customer's ethical behavior as well in order to prevent risking ethical scandals.

As a result, future studies can encompass conducting the same research approach as for this study. However, instead of focusing on managing their co-workers' ethical behavior, focus can instead be on managing their customers' ethical behavior. This may reveal whether this framework fits that social area as well. If that is the case, the Business Basics framework can be applied in an even broader context.

- It was revealed in chapters 4 and 5 that intuition is a prominent category managers can use when managing their co-workers' ethical behavior in sales organizations. Additionally, it is suggested in section 5.6 that the importance of intuition in management depends on the organizational context. Therefore, it is suggested for researchers to further investigate the importance of intuition in sales organizations compared to other organizations.
- Protecting their own brand was initially conceptualized as a category during the early stages of this research process. This was a topic the researcher believed would become central in the research process and the substantive theory. Since not many respondents discussed this, it was removed from the theory altogether. Therefore, a fifth suggestion for future studies can be to further investigate the importance of protecting the brand of their sales organizations as it is defined in this dissertation.
- The final suggestion for future research concerns differences in gender. It was earlier revealed that there was an unequal number between the genders of the participating respondents. It was also noted how some managers tended to favor certain aspects of the management process when discussing. It is possible this can be linked to gender. Consequently, this can potentially have affected the conceptualization process.

  Thus, a suggestion to future research is to conduct a deductive hypothesis test. The null hypothesis can be that there is no difference between genders, while another hypothesis can be that there are differences between men and women when managing co-workers' ethical behavior in sales organizations. Such a study can potentially provide important information regarding if the importance of the categories differs due to gender differences. Thereby, this can provide important insights into the field of management and gender studies.

6.4 The Researcher's Final Words

It has been over six years since I started my doctoral studies, before 2014, I had never heard of orthodox Grounded Theory. The learning of this methodology has been a transformative journey, making me more reflective today than I was back then. Learning to use a methodology that differs so greatly compared to other methodologies has been enriching, especially since earlier when I was more familiar with quantitative research procedures. I tried to the best of my abilities to adopt the traits and procedures of orthodox GT.

However, learning orthodox GT was a difficult process since I had to give up the theoretical and disciplinary autonomy that comes with quantitative research in favor of attempting to reach a new methodological autonomy. This resulted in long periods of confusion since I could not control the data. Instead, I needed to follow it where it led me, not the other way around. Gradually the processes of orthodox GT was learnt with expertise and coaching by scholars, including by Dr. Barney Glaser. It is my firm belief that it is a prerequisite to have a well-versed coach for any aspiring researcher not familiar with this methodology, due to the fundamental differences in orthodox GT compared to others. I was fortunate to have that coach as my main supervisor where he played a crucial part to my learning process.

If I was to conduct this research all over again, but with the knowledge I possess today, I would have done several things differently. For starters, I would have been even more careful to not ask such questions that could be perceived as preconceived notions. I would also have attempted to include a more diversified share of respondents. The lion's share of respondents in this dissertation consists mostly of middle-aged Swedish men. Finally, I would have been more reluctant with adding secondary data as early as I did with the ones I included in table 1.1 in chapter 1.

As I conclude this dissertation, I reflect over the great many things I have learned throughout this journey. To start, I have now become a firm believer of the old cliché that a satisfied customer is the best business strategy of all, and to achieve that, ethical conduct is quintessential. But the one thing that sticks out most of all in my mind is a question I got asked on several occasions.

Why do ethical breaches still occur when we have had for a long time ethical theories like deontology, teleology and virtue ethics that are supposed to help us understand why people act the way they act. Shouldn't people know better now?

From all that I have learned throughout this research process, I still go back to what I was taught by my very first teacher in Business Ethics. Mr. Gerard Betros once said:

> The reality is that people do not make decisions using rational methods of applying theory, they do things because they like to do things and justify their behavior after the event. (G. Betros, personal communication, November 30, 2017)

This means that ethical breaches are bound to happen again and again. However, the understanding of the management process of ethical behavior is important since it can help managers be more aware of why people do the things they do. Thereby these people can attempt to limit and better prevent these breaches from re-occurring.

While this journey now ends, it is with great anticipation I look at the future with a great desire to continue my contributions to research.

List of References

Adeyemi, A. (2013). Nigerian media and corrupt practices: The need for paradigm shift. *European Scientific Journal, ESJ, 9*(1).

Adom, A. (2018). The role of commission-based pay on employee retention in the Ghanaian banking industry: The case of GCB Bank Limited. *Africa's Public Service Delivery and Performance Review, 6*(1), 1–5.

Agor, W. (1986). The logic of intuition: How top executives make important decisions. Organizational Dynamics, 14(3): 5–18.

Ahearne, M., Haumann, T., Kraus, F., & Wieseke, J. (2013). It's a matter of congruence: How interpersonal identification between sales managers and salespersons shapes sales success. *Journal of the Academy of Marketing Science, 41*(6), 625–648.

Allén, S. (1986). *Svensk Ordbok*, 2nd ed. Solna: Esselte Studium.

Ambrose, M., & Kulik, C. 1999. Old friends, new faces: Motivation research in the 1990s. *Journal of Management*, 25: 231–292.

Anderson, E., & Oliver, R. L. (1987). Perspectives on behavior-based versus outcome-based salesforce control systems. *Journal of Marketing, 51*(4), 76–88.

André, R. (1995). Diversity stress as morality stress. *Journal of Business Ethics, 14*(6), 489–496.

André, R. (2008). *Organizational behavior – An introduction to your life in organizations.* London: Pearson Education.

Andreoli, N., & Lefkowitz, J. (2009). Individual and organizational antecedents of misconduct in organizations. *Journal of Business Ethics, 85*(3), 309.

Asgary, N., & Mitschow, M. C. (2002). Toward a model for international business ethics. *Journal of Business Ethics, 36*(3), 239–246.

Ashkanasy, N., Zerbe, W., & Härtel, C. (2016). *Managing emotions in the workplace.* Routledge.

Axberg, C. (1993). Franchising – en handbok. Malmö: Liber.

Axley, S. (1984). Managerial and organizational communication in terms of the conduit metaphor. *Academy of Management Review, 9*(3), 428–437.

Avital, M., & Te'Eni, D. (2009). From generative fit to generative capacity: exploring an emerging dimension of information systems design and task performance. *Information Systems Journal, 19*(4), 345–367.

Bass, B., & Steidlmeier, P. (1999). Ethics, character, and authentic transformational leadership behavior. *The Leadership Quarterly, 10*(2), 181–217.

Belak, J., & Milfelner, B. (2011). Informal and formal institutional measures of business ethics implementation at different stages of enterprise life cycle. *Acta Polytechnica Hungarica, 8*(1), 105–122.

Bellizzi, J., & Bristol, T. (2005). Supervising the unethical selling behavior of top sales performers: Assessing the impact of social desirability bias. *Journal of Business Ethics, 57*(4), 377–388.

Bellizzi, J., & Hite, R. (1989). Supervising unethical salesforce behavior. *Journal of Marketing, 53*(2), 36–47.

Bellizzi, J., & Hasty, R. (2003). Supervising unethical sales force behavior: how strong is the tendency to treat top sales performers leniently? *Journal of Business Ethics, 43*(4), 337–351.

Bennis W., & Manus, B. (1997). *Leaders: Strategies for Taking Charge.* New York: HarperCollins.

Bischoff, N., & Eppler, M. (2011). Caring for Clarity in Knowledge Communication. *J. UCS, 17*(10), 1455–1473.

Blatter, J. & M. Haverland (2012). *Designing Case Studies: Explanatory Approaches in Small N Research.* Basingstoke: Palgrave Macmillan.

Boedecker, K., Morgan, F., & Stoltman, J. (1991). Legal dimensions of salespersons' statements: A review and managerial suggestions. *Journal of Marketing, 55*(1), 70–80.

Bolander, W., Zahn, W. J., Loe, T. W., & Clark, M. (2017). Managing new salespeople's ethical behaviors during repetitive failures: when trying to help actually hurts. *Journal of Business Ethics, 144*(3), 519–532.

Bommer, M., Gratto, C., Gravander, J., & Tuttle, M. (1987). A behavioral model of ethical and unethical decision making. *Journal of Business Ethics, 6*(4), 265–280.

Bontis, N., Crossan, M. M., & Hulland, J. (2002). Managing an organizational learning system by aligning stocks and flows. *Journal of Management Studies, 39*(4), 437–469.

Brandl, P., & Maguire, M. (2002). Codes of ethics: A primer on their purpose, development, and use. *The Journal for Quality and Participation, 25*(4), 8.

Brief, A., Dietz, J., Cohen, R., Pugh, S., & Vaslow, J. (2000). Just doing business: Modern racism and obedience to authority as explanations for employment discrimination. *Organizational Behavior and Human Decision Processes, 81*(1), 72–97.

Brodhead, M., & Higbee, T. (2012). Teaching and maintaining ethical behavior in a professional organization. *Behavior Analysis in Practice, 5*(2), 82–88.

Brown, M. (2007). Misconceptions of ethical leadership: How to avoid potential pitfalls. *Organizational Dynamics.*

Brown, M., Treviño, L., & Harrison, D. (2005). Ethical leadership: A social learning perspective for construct development and testing. *Organizational Behavior and Human Decision Processes, 97*(2), 117–134.

Brown, M., & Treviño, L. (2006). Ethical leadership: A review and future directions. *The Leadership Quarterly, 17*(6), 595–616.

Brytting, T. (1991). *Organizing in the small growing firm a grounded theory approach.* Economic Research Institute, Stockholm School of Economics. Ekonomiska forskningsinstitutet vid Handelshögskolan.

Buckley, M. R., Beu, D. S., Frink, D. D., Howard, J. L., Berkson, H., Mobbs, T. A., & Ferris, G. R. (2001). Ethical issues in human resources systems. *Human resource management review, 11*(1–2), 11–29.

Cambridge Advanced Learners Dictionary (2008a). Franchising. 3rd ed. Cambridge University Press.

Cambridge Advanced Learners Dictionary (2008b). Business. 3rd ed. Cambridge University Press.

Cambridge Advanced Learners Dictionary (2008c). Basics. 3rd ed. Cambridge University Press.

Cambridge Advanced Learners Dictionary (2008d). Bureaucratic. 3rd ed. Cambridge University Press.

Carey, M. R. (1992). Transformational leadership and the fundamental option for self-transcendence. *The Leadership Quarterly, 3*(3), 217–236.

Carroll, A. B. (1991). The pyramid of corporate social responsibility: Toward the moral management of organizational stakeholders. *Business Horizons, 34*(4), 39–48.

Chakravarti, D., Mitchell, A., & Staelin, R. (1981). Judgment based marketing decision models: Problems and possible solutions. *Journal of Marketing, 45*(4), 13–23.

Challagalla, G., Shervani, T., & Huber, G. (2000). Supervisory orientations and salesperson work outcomes: The moderating effect of salesperson location. *Journal of Personal Selling & Sales Management, 20*(3), 161–171.

Charmaz, K. (2006). *Constructing grounded theory: A practical guide through qualitative analysis*. London: Sage Publications.

Chen, H. M., & Hsieh, Y. H. (2006). Key trends of the total reward system in the 21st century. *Compensation & Benefits Review*, 38(6), 64–70.

Christiansen, Ó. (2006). Opportunizing: A classic grounded theory study on business and management. *The Grounded Theory Review: An International Journal*, 109.

Christiansen, Ó. (2008). The rationale for the use of classic GT. *The Grounded Theory Review, 7*(2), 19–38.

Crane, A. & Matten, D. (2010). Business Ethics – Managing corporate citizenship and sustainability in the age of globalization, 3rd ed. Oxford: Oxford University Press.

Dainty, A., Moore, D., & Murray, M. (2007). *Communication in construction: Theory and practice*. Routledge.

Dane, E., & Pratt, M. (2007). Exploring intuition and its role in managerial decision making. *Academy of Management Review, 32*(1), 33–54.

Davenport, T., De Long, D., & Beers, M. (1998). Successful knowledge management projects. *Sloan Management Review, 39*(2), 43–57.

DeConinck, J. (1992). How sales managers control unethical sales force behavior. *Journal of Business Ethics, 11*(10), 789–798.

De George, R. (1987). The status of business ethics: past and future. *Journal of Business Ethics, 6*(3), 201–211.

De George, R. (2005, February). A history of business ethics. In *Papers delivered at the third biennial global business ethics conference. Santa Clara, CA: Markkula Center for Applied Ethics.*

Decoster, S., Camps, J., Stouten, J., Vandevyvere, L., & Tripp, T. M. (2013). Standing by your organization: The impact of organizational identification and abusive supervision on followers' perceived cohesion and tendency to gossip. *Journal of Business Ethics, 118*(3), 623–634.

DePree, M. (1997). *Leading Without Power: Finding Hope in Serving Community*. New York: JosseyBass.

Dickson, J. W. (1978). Perception of risk as related to choice in a two-dimensional risk situation. *Psychological Reports, 43*(3_suppl), 1059–1062.

Dubinsky, A. J., Yammarino, F. J., & Jolson, M. A. (1994). Closeness of supervision and salesperson work outcomes: An alternate perspective. *Journal of Business Research, 29*(3), 225–237.

Dwyer, F. R., Schurr, P. H., & Oh, S. (1987). Developing buyer-seller relationships. *Journal of Marketing, 51*(2), 11–27.

Eisenberger, R., & Cameron, J. (1996). Detrimental effects of reward: Reality or myth?. *American Psychologist, 51*(11), 1153.

Elarabi, H. M., & Johari, F. (2014). The impact of human resources management on healthcare quality. *Asian Journal of Management Sciences & Education, 3*(1), 13–22.

Epstein, M., McEwen, R., & Spindle, R. (1994). Shareholder preferences concerning corporate ethical performance. *Journal of Business Ethics, 13*(6), 447–453.

England, G. W. (1967). Personal value systems of American managers. *Academy of Management Journal, 10*(1), 53–68.

Fernlund, A. & Ideström, J. (2009). Franchise praktikant. Halmstad: Bulls Graphics.

Ferrell, O., & Skinner, S. (1988). Ethical behavior and bureaucratic structure in marketing research organizations. *Journal of Marketing Research, 25*(1), 103–109.

Ferrell, O., Fraedrich, J. & Ferrell, L. (2015). *Business Ethics: Ethical Decision Making and Cases*, 4th ed. Boston: Houghton Mifflin.

Ferrell, O., Ingram, T., & LaForge, R. (2000). Initiating structure for legal and ethical decisions in a global sales organization. *Industrial Marketing Management, 29*(6), 555–564.

Ferrell, O., Johnston, M. & Ferrell, L. (2007). A framework for personal selling and sales management ethical decision-making. *Journal of Personal Selling & Sales Management,* 27(4), 291–299.

Ferrell, O., Weaver, K., Taylor, J., & Jones, R. (1978). Ethical beliefs of marketing managers. *The Journal of Marketing*, 69–73.

Ferris, G. R., Arthur, M. M., Berkson, H. M., Kaplan, D. M., Harrell-Cook, G., & Frink, D. D. (1998). Toward a social context theory of the human resource management-organization effectiveness relationship. *Human Resource Management Review, 8*(3), 235–264.

Flaherty, K., & Pappas, J. (2000). The role of trust in salesperson – sales manager relationships. *Journal of Personal Selling & Sales Management, 20*(4), 271–278.

Foucault, M. (1977). *Discipline and punish: The birth of the prison*. Translated by A. Sheridan. New York: Pantheon.

Franchise Arkitekt (2011). Varför Franchising? Viewed November 14, 2015, Derived from: https://franchisearkitekt.se/vad-ar-franchise/

Gasson, S. (1998). Framing Design: A Social Process View of Information System Development. In Proceedings of the Nineteenth International Conference on Information Systems, Atlanta, GA: *Association for Information Systems* (AIS), 224–236.

Gellerman, S. W. (1989). Managing ethics from the top down. *MIT Sloan Management Review, 30*(2), 73.

Glaser, B. (1978), *Theoretical Sensitivity*. Mill Valley, CA: The Sociology Press.

Glaser, B. (1992). *Emergence vs Forcing: Basics of Grounded Theory Analysis*. Mill Valley, CA: Sociology Press.

Glaser, B. (1998). Att göra Grundad Teori: problem, frågor och diskussion, Translated by H. Thulesius and T. Åström. M., Sociology Press, Mill Valley, CA: Sociology Press.

Glaser, B. (2001). *The Grounded Theory Perspective: Conceptualization Contrasted with Description*. Mill Valley, CA: Sociology Press

Glaser, B. (2003). *The Grounded Theory Perspective II: Description's Remodeling of Grounded Theory Methodology*. Mill Valley, CA: Sociology Press.

Glaser, B. (2004). *Staying open,* Paper not published.

Glaser, B. & Strauss, A. (1967). *The Discovery of Grounded Theory: Strategies for Qualitative Research*. New York: Aldine.

Green, C. (2006). Trust Based Selling – Using Customer Focus and Collaborations to Build Long-Term Relationships. New York: McGraw Hill.

Grover, S. L. (1993). Lying, deceit, and subterfuge: A model of dishonesty in the workplace. *Organization Science, 4*(3), 478–495.

Grojean, M., Resick, C., Dickson, M. & Smith, D. (2004). Leaders, values, and organizational climate: Examining leadership strategies for establishing an organizational climate regarding ethics. *Journal of Business Ethics*, 55(3), 233–241.

Guiso, L., Sapienza, P., & Zingales, L. (2015). The value of corporate culture. *Journal of Financial Economics, 117*(1), 60–76.

Gustavsson, B. (1998). Metod: Grundad Teori för ekonomer – Att navigera i empirins farvatten. Lund: Academia Adacta.

Gustavsson, B. & Åge, L.-J. (2014). How and why managers use conceptual devices in B2B research, *Journal of Business and Industrial Marketing*, Vol. 29 No. 7/8.

Gustavsson, B. Åge, L.-J &, Cederlund, C. (2014). Conceptualizing for managerial relevance in B2B research: a grounded theory approach. *Journal of Business & Industrial Marketing.*

Haidt, J. 2001. The emotional dog and its rational tail: A social intuitionist approach to moral judgment. *Psychological Review, 108(4):* 814–834.

Harttman, J. (2001) *Grundad teori, teorigenerering på empirisk grund.* Lund: Studentlitteratur.

Hawes, J. M., & Rich, G. A. (1998). Selling and sales management in action: The constructs of sales coaching: Supervisory feedback, role modeling and trust. *Journal of Personal Selling & Sales Management, 18*(1), 53–63.

Heermance, E. (1924). *Codes of Ethics: A Handbook*. Burlington, VT: Free Press Printing.

Hegarty, W. & Sims, H. Jr. (1978). Some determinants of unethical decision behavior: An experiment. *Journal of Applied Psychology. 63,* 451-457.

Heres, L., & Lasthuizen, K. (2012). What's the difference? Ethical leadership in public, hybrid and private sector organizations. *Journal of Change Management, 12*(4), 441-466.

Herzberg, F. (1987). One more time: how do you motivate employees? *Harvard Business Review, 65*(5).

Heyler, S. G., Armenakis, A. A., Walker, A. G., & Collier, D. Y. (2016). A qualitative study investigating the ethical decision making process: A proposed model. *The Leadership Quarterly, 27*(5), 788–801.

Hit, M., Black, S. & Porter, L., (2005). *Management* – international edition. Pearson Education.

Hochwarter, W. A., Perrewe, P. L., Ferris, G. R., & Brymer, R. A. (1999). Job satisfaction and performance: The moderating effects of value attainment and affective disposition. *Journal of Vocational Behavior, 54*(2), 296–313.

Honeycutt, E. D., Glassman, M., Zugelder, M. T. and Karande, K. (2001). Determinants of ethical behavior: a study of auto salespeople. *Journal of Business Ethics*, Vol. 32, 69–79.

Huberts, L., Kaptein, M., & Lasthuizen, K. (2007). A study of the impact of three leadership styles on integrity violations committed by police officers. *Policing: An International Journal of Police Strategies & Management, 30*(4), 587–607.

Hummels, H. (1994). Management and the use of business ethics: Towards an investigative ethics. *International Journal of Value-Based Management, 7*(3), 239–253.

Ilgen, D., Hollenbeck, J., Johnson, M., & Jundt, J. (2005). Teams in organizations: From I–P–O models to IMOI models. *Annual Review of Psychology.*

Ingram, T., LaForge, R., & Schwepker, C. (2007). Salesperson ethical decision-making: The impact of sales leadership and sales management control strategy. *Journal of Personal Selling & Sales Management, 27*(4), 301–315.

Jaworski, B. (2011). On managerial relevance. *Journal of Marketing*, Vol. 75 No. 4, 211-224.

Jones, T. (1991). Ethical decision-making by individuals in organizations: An issue-contingent model. *Academy of Management Review*, *16*(2), 366–395.

José, A., & Thibodeaux, M. (1999). Institutionalization of ethics: The perspective of managers. *Journal of Business Ethics*, *22*(2), 133–143.

Joyner, B. E., & Payne, D. (2002). Evolution and implementation: A study of values, business ethics and corporate social responsibility. *Journal of Business Ethics*, *41*(4), 297–311.

Kaiser, R., Lindberg, J., & Craig, S. (2007). Assessing the Flexibility of Managers: A comparison of methods 1. *International Journal of Selection and Assessment*, *15*(1), 40–55.

Kalra, A., Shi, M. and Srinivasan, K. (2003). Salesforce compensation scheme and consumer inferences. *Management Science*, Vol. 49 No. 5, 655–72.

Kane-Urrbazo, C. (2006). Management's role in shaping organizational culture. *Journal of Nursing Management*, *14*(3), 188–194.

Khandelwal, P., & Taneja, A. (2010). Intuitive decision making in management. *Indian Journal of Industrial Relations*, 150–156.

Kotler, P., Armstrong G., Parment, A. (2011). *Principles of Marketing* Swedish Edition 1st ed. Prentice Hall, Pearson Education.

Kurbel, K. (2013). ERP: Enterprise Resource Planning. In *Enterprise Resource Planning and Supply Chain Management*. Berlin, Heidelberg: Springer, 95–126.

Kwok, A. (2014). The evolution of management theories: A literature review. *Nang Yan Business Journal*, *3*(1), 28–40.

Lawton, A. (2004). Developing and implementing codes of ethics. *Viesoji politika ir administravimas*, (7).

Laczniak, G. R., & Inderrieden, E. J. (1987). The influence of stated organizational concern upon ethical decision making. *Journal of Business Ethics*, *6*(4), 297–307.

Lee, S., & Cheng, I. (2012). Ethics management in public relations: Practitioner conceptualizations of ethical leadership, knowledge, training and compliance. *Journal of Mass Media Ethics*, *27*(2), 80–96.

Lee, J., Keil, M., & Wong, K. (2015). The effect of goal difficulty on escalation of commitment. *Journal of Behavioral Decision Making*, *28*(2), 114–129.

Levers, M. (2013). Philosophical paradigms, grounded theory, and perspectives on emergence. *Sage Open*, *3*(4), 2158244013517243.

Lewicki, R., & Bunker, B. (1996). Developing and maintaining trust in work relationships. *Trust in Organizations: Frontiers of Theory and Research*, *114*, 139.

Lewis, P. V. (1985). Defining 'business ethics': Like nailing Jello to a wall. *Journal of Business Ethics*, *4*(5), 377–383.

Longenecker, C. O., & Yonker, R. D. (2013). Leadership deficiencies in rapidly changing organizations: Multisource feedback as a needs assessment tool–Part I. *Industrial and Commercial Training*, *45*(3), 159–165.

MacInnis, D. (2011). A framework for conceptual contributions in marketing, *Journal of Marketing*, Vol. 75 No. 4, 136–154.

Macuh, B. (2015). Using quality educational approaches to implement new skills. *Sociološki diskurs*, *5*(10), 5–22.

Madhani, P. (2015). Ethical behavior in sales organizations: Key dimensions. World at Work Journal, Vol. 24, No. 1, pp. 55–69, January–March, 2015, Derived from: https://ssrn.com/abstract=2695725

Malloy, D., & Fennell, D. A. (1998). Codes of ethics and tourism: An exploratory content analysis. *Tourism Management, 19*(5), 453–461.

Mantel, S. (2005). Choice or perception: How affect influences ethical choices among salespeople. *Journal of Personal Selling & Sales Management, 25*(1), 43–55.

Manz, C. C, & Sims, H. R (1981). Vicarious learning: The influence of modeling on organizational behavior, *Academy of Management Review. 6,* 105–113.

Martin, M. (1999). Trust leadership. *Journal of Leadership Studies, 5*(3), 41–49.

Mayer, R., Davis, J., & Schoorman, F. (1995). An integrative model of organizational trust. *Academy of management review, 20*(3), 709–734.

Mayer, D., Kuenzi, M., Greenbaum, R., Bardes, M., & Salvador, R. (2009). How low does ethical leadership flow? Test of a trickle-down model. *Organizational Behavior and Human Decision Processes, 108*(1), 1–13.

Mayo, E. (2004). *The human problems of an industrial civilization*. Routledge.

Mayhew, R. (2019). What is a Salary System? Seen, 2020-02-02, derived from: https://smallbusiness.chron.com/salary-system-10652.html

McClelland, D. C. (1961). *The Achieving Society*. Simon and Schuster.

McDonald, G., & Nijhof, A. (1999). Beyond codes of ethics: an integrated framework for stimulating morally responsible behaviour in organisations. *Leadership & Organization Development Journal, 20*(3), 133–147.

McClaren, N. (2015). The methodology in empirical sales ethics research: 1980–2010. *Journal of Business Ethics, 127*(1), 121–147.

McPhail, K. (2009). Where is the ethical knowledge in the knowledge economy?: Power and potential in the emergence of ethical knowledge as a component of intellectual capital. *Critical Perspectives on Accounting, 20*(7), 804–822.

Meyer, I., & Nujjoo, A. (2012). The relative importance of different types of rewards for employee motivation and commitment in South Africa. *SA Journal of Human Resource Management, 10*(2), 1–10.

Micewski, E., & Troy, C. (2007). Business ethics–deontologically revisited. *Journal of Business Ethics, 72*(1), 17–25.

Miles, A., & Sadler-Smith, E. (2014). "With recruitment I always feel I need to listen to my gut": The role of intuition in employee selection. *Personnel Review.*

Mintzberg, H. (1973). *The Nature of Managerial Work.* New York: Harper & Row.

Moore, C., Wakeman, S., & Gino, F. (2014). Dangerous expectations: breaking rules to resolve cognitive dissonance. *Harvard Business School NOM Unit Working Paper*, (15-012).

Murphy, P. (1988). Implementing business ethics. *Journal of Business Ethics*, 907–915.

Neubert, M., Carlson, D., Kacmar, K., Roberts, J., & Chonko, L. (2009). The virtuous influence of ethical leadership behavior: Evidence from the field. *Journal of Business Ethics, 90*(2), 157–170.

Oneborg, T. (2019). Rekordmånga anmäler mäklare – svårt att få rätt. Retrieved from: https://www.svt.se/nyheter/lokalt/vasterbotten/rekordmanga-anmalningar-mot-maklare-2

Ordóñez, L., & Welsh, D. (2015). Immoral goals: How goal setting may lead to unethical behavior. *Current Opinion in Psychology, 6*, 93–96.

Paparoidamis, N., & Guenzi, P. (2009). An empirical investigation into the impact of relationship selling and LMX on salespeople's behaviours and sales effectiveness. *European Journal of Marketing, 43*(7/8), 1053–1075.

Parry, K. (1998). Grounded theory and social process: A new direction for leadership research. *The Leadership Quarterly, 9*(1), 85–105.

Pettijohn, C., Pettijohn, L., & Taylor, A. J. (2008). Salesperson perceptions of ethical behaviors: Their influence on job satisfaction and turnover intentions. *Journal of Business Ethics*, 78, 547–557.

Pielstick, C. D. (2000). Formal vs. informal leading: A comparative analysis. *Journal of Leadership Studies, 7*(3), 99–114.

Popper, K. (1972). *Objective knowledge* (Vol. 360). Oxford: Oxford University Press.

Porter, L., & Lawler, E. (1968). Managerial Attitudes and Performance. Homewood, IL: Dorsey Press.

Provis, C. (2010). Virtuous decision making for business ethics. *Journal of Business Ethics, 91*(1), 3–16.

Rich, G. (1997). The sales manager as a role model: Effects on trust, job satisfaction, and performance of salespeople. *Journal of the Academy of Marketing Science, 25*(4), 319–328.

Rich, G. (1998). The constructs of sales coaching: Supervisory feedback, role modeling and trust. *Journal of Personal Selling and Sales Management*, 18(01), 53–63.

Robertson, D., & Anderson, E. (1993). Control system and task environment effects on ethical judgment: An exploratory study of industrial salespeople. *Organization Science, 4*(4), 617–644.

Robertson, C., Gilley, K., & Street, M. (2003). The relationship between ethics and firm practices in Russia and the United States. *Journal of World Business, 38*(4), 375–384.

Román, S. (2011). Ethics in personal selling and sales management. *Sales Management–A Multinational Perspective,* Basingstoke, 147–170.

Román, S., & Munuera, J. (2005). Determinants and consequences of ethical behaviour: an empirical study of salespeople. *European Journal of Marketing, 39*(5/6), 473–495.

Rouziès, D., Anderson, E., Kohli, A., Michaels, R., Weitz, B., & Zoltners, A. (2005). Sales and marketing integration: a proposed framework. *Journal of Personal Selling & Sales Management, 25*(2), 113–122.

Ruppel, C., & Harrington, S. (2000). The relationship of communication, ethical work climate, and trust to commitment and innovation. *Journal of Business Ethics, 25*(4), 313–328.

Sadler-Smith, E., & Shefy, E. (2004). The intuitive executive: Understanding and applying 'gut feel' in decision-making. *Academy of Management Perspectives, 18*(4), 76–91.

Sargent, P. (2001). *Real men or real teachers?: Contradictions in the lives of men elementary school teachers*. Men's Studies Press.

Schnebel, E., & Bienert, M. (2004). Implementing ethics in business organizations. *Journal of Business Ethics, 53*(1–2), 203–211.

Schrodt, P., Witt, P., Turman, P., Myers, S., Barton, M., & Jernberg, K. (2009). Instructor credibility as a mediator of instructors' prosocial communication behaviors and students' learning outcomes. *Communication Education, 58*(3), 350–371.

Schweitzer, M., Ordóñez, L., & Douma, B. (2004). Goal setting as a motivator of unethical behavior. *Academy of Management Journal, 47*(3), 422–432.

Schwepker Jr, C., & Good, D. (2007). Sales management's influence on employment and training in developing an ethical sales force. *Journal of Personal Selling & Sales Management, 27*(4), 325–339.

Schwepker Jr, C., & Good, M. (2017). Reducing salesperson job stress and unethical intent: The influence of leader-member exchange relationship, socialization and ethical ambiguity. *Industrial Marketing Management, 66*, 205–218.

Shapiro, S., & Spence, M. (1997). Managerial intuition: A conceptual and operational framework. *Business Horizons, 40*(1), 63–69.

Shaw, W. & Barry, V. (2001). *Moral Issues in Business*, 8th ed. Belmont, CA: Wadsworth.

Shin, Y., Sung, S. Y., Choi, J. N., & Kim, M. S. (2015). Top management ethical leadership and firm performance: Mediating role of ethical and procedural justice climate. *Journal of Business Ethics, 129*(1), 43–57.

Shum, P., & Yam, S. (2011). Ethics and law: Guiding the invisible hand to correct corporate social responsibility externalities. *Journal of business ethics, 98*(4), 549–571.

Simon, H. (1959). Theories of decision-making in economics and behavioral science. *The American Economic Review, 49*(3), 253–283.

Simon, H. (1987). Making management decisions: The role of intuition and emotion. *Academy of Management Perspectives, 1*(1), 57–64.

Singh, V. (2013). Assignment on Sales Organization. Published Nov 30, 2013. Viewed January 4, 2016. Derived from: https://www.slideshare.net/vikram055/sales-organisation

Smith, J., Flowers, P. & Larkin, M. (2009). *Interpretative phenomenological analysis: Theory, method and research*. London: Sage.

Sonenshein, S. (2007). The role of construction, intuition, and justification in responding to ethical issues at work: The sensemaking-intuition model. *Academy of Management Review, 32*(4), 1022–1040.

Stathakopoulos, V. (1996). Sales force control: A synthesis of three theories. *Journal of Personal Selling & Sales Management, 16*(2), 1–12.

Stead, W., Worrell, D., & Stead, J. (1990). An integrative model for understanding and managing ethical behavior in business organizations. *Journal of Business Ethics, 9*(3), 233–242.

Stebbins, R. A. (2001). *Exploratory research in the social sciences* (Vol. 48). Sage.

Steidmeier, P. (1999). Gift giving, bribery and corruption: Ethical management of business relationships in China. *Journal of Business Ethics*, 121–132.

Stevens, B. (1999). Communicating ethical values: A study of employee perceptions. *Journal of Business Ethics, 20*(2), 113–120.

Stevens, B. (2008). Corporate Ethical Codes: effective instruments for influencing behavior. *Journal of Business Ethics*, 78, 601–609.

Strauss, A., & Corbin, J. (1990a). Grounded Theory Research: Procedures, canons, and evaluative criteria. *Qualitative Sociology, 13*(1), 3–21.

Strauss, A., & Corbin, J. (1990b). *Basics of Qualitative Research*. Sage Publications.

Strout, E. (2002). To tell the truth. *Sales and Marketing Management, 154*(7), 40–47.

Strömberg, A. (1998a). Utbilda. Stora synonymordboken. 1st ed. Stockholm: Strömbergs

Strömberg, A. (1998b). Påläst. Stora synonymordboken. 1st ed. Stockholm: Strömbergs

Strömberg, A. (1998c). Intuition. Stora synonymordboken. 1st ed. Stockholm: Strömbergs

Suchan, J., & Dulek, R. (1990). A reassessment of clarity in written managerial communications. *Management Communication Quarterly, 4*(1), 87–99.

Sundsten, P. (2006). Här avslöjas mäklarfusket. Published March, 23, 2006. Viewed January 13, 2016. Derived from: https://www.expressen.se/dinapengar/har-avslojas-maklarfusket/

Thompson, J., & McEwen, W. (1958). Organizational goals and environment: Goal-setting as an interaction process. *American Sociological Review*, *23*(1), 23–31.

Treviño, L. (1986). Ethical decision-making in organizations: A person-situation interactionist model. *Academy of Management Review*, *11*(3), 601–617.

Treviño, L., & Ball, G. (1992). The social implications of punishing unethical behavior: Observers' cognitive and affective reactions. *Journal of Management*, *18*(4), 751–768.

Trevino, L. & Brown, M. (2004). Managing to be ethical: Debunking five business ethics myths. *Academy of Management Perspectives*, *18*(2), 69–81.

Treviño, L., & Brown, M. (2005). The role of leaders in influencing unethical behavior in the workplace. *Managing Organizational Deviance*, 69–87.

Treviño, L., & Nelson, K. (2016). *Managing business ethics: Straight talk about how to do it right*. John Wiley & Sons.

Treviño, L., Brown, M., & Hartman, L. (2003). A qualitative investigation of perceived executive ethical leadership: Perceptions from inside and outside the executive suite. *Human Relations*, *56*(1), 5–37.

Trevino, L., Hartman, L., & Brown, M. (2000). Moral person and moral manager: How executives develop a reputation for ethical leadership. *California Management Review*, *42*(4), 128–142.

Treviño, L., Weaver, G., & Reynolds, S. (2006). Behavioral ethics in organizations: A review. *Journal of Management*, *32*(6), 951–990.

Treviño, L., Weaver, G., Gibson, D., & Toffler, B. (1999). Managing ethics and legal compliance: What works and what hurts. *California Management Review*, *41*(2), 131–151.

Uduji, J., & Onwumere, J. (2013). Supervisory behaviour and salesforce performance: an empirical investigation. *Developing Country Studies*, *3*(6), 141–148.

Ugurlu, C. (2013). School management related knowledge levels of primary school teachers. *Educational Sciences: Theory and Practice*, *13*(2), 907–912.

Vardi, Y., & Wiener, Y. (1996). Misbehavior in organizations: A motivational framework. *Organization Science*, *7*(2), 151–165.

Victor, B. & Cullen, J. (1988), The Organizational Bases of Ethical Work Climates. *Administrative Science Quarterly* 33, 101–125.

Viswesvaran, C., Deshpande, S., & Joseph, J. (1998). Job satisfaction as a function of top management support for ethical behavior: A study of Indian managers. *Journal of Business Ethics*, *17*(4), 365–371.

Weaver, G., Treviño, L., & Cochran, P. (1999). Corporate ethics practices in the mid-1990's: An empirical study of the Fortune 1000. *Journal of Business Ethics*, *18*(3), 283–294.

Weber, J. (1990). Measuring the impact of teaching ethics to future managers: A review, assessment, and recommendations. *Journal of Business Ethics*, *9*(3), 183–190.

Weeks, W., & Nantel, J. (1992). Corporate codes of ethics and sales force behavior: A case study. *Journal of Business Ethics*, *11*(10), 753–760.

Wiley, C. (1997). What motivates employees according to over 40 years of motivation surveys. *International Journal of Manpower*, *18*(3), 263–280.

Williams, J. (1995). *Style: toward clarity and grace* (Chicago guides to writing, editing, and publishing). Chicago University Press.

Williams, S., & Dewett, T. (2005). Yes, you can teach business ethics: A review and research agenda. *Journal of Leadership & Organizational Studies, 12*(2), 109–120.

Winstanley, D., & Woodall, J. (2000). The ethical dimension of human resource management. *Human Resource Management Journal, 10*(2), 5–20.

Wood, J., Boles, J., Johnston, W., & Bellenger, D. (2008). Buyers' trust of the salesperson: an item-level meta-analysis. *Journal of Personal Selling & Sales Management, 28*(3), 263–283.

Wotruba, T. (1990). A comprehensive framework for the analysis of ethical behavior, with a focus on sales organizations. *Journal of Personal Selling & Sales Management, 10*(2), 29–42.

Wotruba, T., Chonko, L., & Loe, T. (2001). The impact of ethics code familiarity on manager behavior. *Journal of Business Ethics, 33*(1), 59–69.

Xu, A., Loi, R., & Ngo, H. (2016). The mediating role of trust in organization. *Journal of Business Ethics, 134*(3), 493–504.

Yasir, M., & Azmi, M. (2016). Ethics and morality: Comparing ethical leadership with servant, authentic and transformational leadership styles. *International Review of Management and Marketing, 6*(4S), 310–316.

Yukl, G. (2012). Effective leadership behavior: What we know and what questions need more attention. *Academy of Management Perspectives, 26*(4), 66–85.

Yukl, G., & Mahsud, R. (2010). Why flexible and adaptive leadership is essential. *Consulting Psychology Journal: Practice and Research, 62*(2), 81.

Åge, L-J. (2009). Business Maneuvering – A Grounded Theory of Complex Selling Processes. Dissertation for the Degree of Doctor of Philosophy, PhD Stockholm, School of Economics.

Åge, L-J. (2011). Grounded theory methodology: Positivism, hermeneutics, and pragmatism. *Qualitative Report, 16*(6), 1599–1615.

Appendices

This is the appendix section. Here the reader will find additional texts, tables and readings that was previously referenced that relates to this dissertation.

Appendix 1
Key words used for identifying the gap in chapter 1

In order to find the gap in the study as presented in chapter 1, the following keywords were used in different combinations with each other to find relevant literature:

- Business ethics
- Controlling ethics
- Corporate Governance
- Controlling
- Ethical behavior
- Ethical compliance
- Ethics
- Foster/Fostering
- Governance and managing business ethics
- Governing
- Improving moral reasoning
- Management
- Managing
- Managing selling behavior/practices
- Moral/s
- Organizations
- Promoting ethical behavior
- Sales ethics
- Sales organizations
- Selling Organizations
- Stimulating morally responsible behavior
- Unethical behavior/practices

Below are examples of word combinations used:

- Managing unethical selling behavior
- Managing business ethics
- Managing ethical behavior
- Managing ethical compliance in sales organizations

The searches provided between 15 to 47.500 hits in electronic databases like Google Scholar, Emerald, and Discovery. In order to narrow down the searches, more specific search techniques were used. For example, using symbols like “ ” and [ ] before and after certain keywords allowed me to narrow down the searches considerably. In total, 21 articles and other relevant literature related to the studied field were used to find the gap (see Table 1.1).

An additional 45 references were used when investigating and explaining the current body of research in chapter 1. These references were collected through the same procedures as the literature in Table 1.1, also using the same words in different combinations. The references consist mainly of articles and research, but other relevant academic literature is also included. This includes borrowing academic books and dictionaries from the libraries of the University of Gävle and the University of Södertörn.

Appendix 2
Summary of the respondents

Date	Respondent Identifier	Title	Interview time	Gender	Age	No. of employees	Experience (in years)	Area
*20-Feb-16	A:1	CEO & HR Manager	Ca 6 hours	M/F	N/A	*Ca 1800*	N/A	Real Estate franchisor
**N/A	A:2	Former franchisee	N/A	M	53	9	32	Real Estate
16-Jun-16	A:3	Vice President	60:21	F	46	*Ca 1800*	20	Real Estate franchisor
18-Jun-16	A:4	Franchisee	40:41	M	33	7	7	Real Estate
14-Okt-16	A:5	Franchisee	46:41	M	47	14	19	Real Estate
25-Okt-16	A:6	Franchisee	47:54	M	43	14	17	Real Estate
07-Feb-17	A:7	Office Manager	46:07	M	40	7	14	Real Estate
21-Feb-17	A:8	HR Manager	47:45	F	34	*Ca 1500*	5	Real Estate franchisor
01-Mar-17	A:9	Franchisee	48:26	F	50	4	5	Real Estate
*20-Apr-17	A:10	CEO & HR Manager	Ca 6 hours	M/F	N/A	*Ca 1800*	N/A	Real Estate
20-Okt-17	A:11	Former franchisee	40:40	M	43	5	13	Real Estate
06-Feb-18	A:12	Office Manager/Franc hisee	62:49	M	42	9	12	Real Estate
**28-Jan-19	A:13	Former franchisee	85:58	M	53	9	32	Real Estate
05-Apr-17	B:1	Sales Manager	42:35	M	45	24	10	Car Sales
06-Apr-17	B:2	Sales Manager	45:43	M	45	25	25	Car Sales
10-Oct-17	B:3	Sales Manager	42:40	M	57	21	32	Car Sales
15-Nov-17	B:4	CEO	52:23	M	65	30	*42*	Car Sales
24-Nov-17	B:5	Sales Manager	24:05	M	40	14	3	Car Sales
04-Dec-17	B:6	Sales Manager	50:30	M	29	5	8	Car Sales
19-Dec-17	B:7	*CEO*	40:44	M	63	16	33	Car Sales
22-May-17	C:1	*CEO*	Ca 60:00	M	54	24	31	Window Sales
22-Jan-18	C:2	Account Manager	43:24	M	38	2	10	Business Advising

02-Feb-18	C:3	Assistant Bank Office Manager	42:47	F	52	75	33	Financial investing & private banking
07-Feb-18	C:4	Team Leader in Financial Advising	54:16	M	58	7	32	Financial Advising
17-May-18	C:5	District sales manager of Southern Norrland	46:00	M	50	21	20	Finance and Insurance
31-May-18	C:6	CEO	62:35	M	49	55	8	Pension Insurance Advisor
26-Jun-18	C:7	Bank Manager	51:57	M	51	185	24	Financial advising, Finance, Insurance and banking
20-Sep-18	C:8	Head of Local Bank	56:01	F	47	95	29	Banking and Finance
04-Okt-18	C:9	Branch manager with focus on private investing	69:49	M	40	14	18	Banking and Finance (Private Investing)

Note * Respondents, A:1, A:10 and C:1, are not interviews. A1 and A:10 are both one day seminars mentioned in the foreword and in chapter 2. The name of these annual seminars are "Ethics in practice". They focus on discussing the importance of ethics, ethical conduct and how to solve and manage complex ethical interactions brokers and managers alike may encounter when working.

Note ** Respondent A:2 is a colleague of the researcher for this dissertation to whom shorter conversations were conducted with throughout this research process. It was important that I did not get preconceived due to this individuals knowledge in parts of the authors area of research. It was therefore decided to conduct a deep interview at a later stage in the research process with this individual. For the actual interview with this respondent, he was re-listed as Respondent A:13.

Appendix 3
Examples of questions asked during the interviews

Since the interviews were open-ended, the nature of questions could differ depending on the answer from the respondent. In no particular order, below is a list with typical questions asked in the beginning of the research process. While the questions were asked in Swedish, these examples have been translated.

- *Tell me about how a normal working day progresses for you in your role as a manager*
- *In regards to your role as a manager, what is most important to you and why?*
- *Tell me about challenges and potential challenges you may face in your role as a manager*
- *Can you tell me about one or more complex situations you were involved in and how you solved it/them.*
- *By reading newspapers, I got the feeling that your industry has a negative stigma attached to it due to unethical practices occurring. Is this something you can relate to and elaborate on?*
- *If so, how would you in your role as a manager work to move away from this and prevent it from happening in the future?*
- *How do you get your employees to behave?*
- *Have you ever been exposed to unethical behavior from employees, customers or other stakeholders? If so, how did you manage that situation? Would you have done it differently today?*
- *Have you ever encountered an employee acting inappropriately at work? What did you do?*
- *Tell me about ethics in regards to this industry*
- *Has it ever come to your attention that a customer has felt that they were treated wrongfully by a co-worker? If so, how did you solve this situation?*
- *How do you ensure that your salespeople do not conduct business in ways that are only beneficial to them and not the customers?*
- *Can you tell me about an instance of an ethical breach you have heard done by a competitor?*
    - How did the management in that organization act?
    - How would you have acted if you were to be put in such a scenario?

As the interview session progressed, the respondent could raise certain areas for discussion. Depending on the direction of the given answer, typical follow-up questions were:

Example 1:
Author: *Earlier you spoke about trust and that mutual trust was important as a manager*
Respondent X: *Yes I did.*
Author: *In what ways are you working on trying to create and maintain trust?*

Example 2:
Author: *What type of help are you talking about?*
Respondent Y: *We have an* ***HR*** *department. There is a person who will come and help you (to manage) since they know the law and rulebook like the palm of their hand.*

The study became delimited once the core category was discovered. As a result, all further discovered categories related to the core category are either delimited or disposed. In later interviews as more data was collected, along with the constant comparing of the data, different categories, sub-categories and properties emerged.

It is during this stage of the research process that the interviews and collection of data became not only more selective, but the interview questions themselves became more grounded (precise). It was possible that I wanted respondent X to further elaborate on a particular subject to which respondents Y and Z had previously discussed. Below are examples of different questions that could have been asked during these later stages:

- Earlier respondents have been discussing that (e.g. staff welfare, written guidelines, gut feeling) is important when managing the ethical behavior of the co-workers. Can you also please elaborate on this?
- Please explain the bureaucracy in your work, how it affects you and your co-workers and how it is expressed in work routines.
- Can you tell me if you have an external entity monitoring the conduct of the organization, and if so, how does it affect you in your work?
- How do you communicate these changes in the law and routines to the co-workers, what was that procedure?

- How do salaries affect the ethical behavior of the employees? Is there something you as a manager can do to prevent co-workers from acting unethically?
- Several respondents have earlier discussed the importance of written guidelines and their effect on their co-workers' ethical behavior. Can you tell me your point of view on these, including both pros and cons?
- Tell me about trust in this business, its importance, why it is important/unimportant and how you as a manager can create it.

Appendix 4
E-mail sent to respondents

The initial contacts with the respective respondents were usually conducted either via phone conversations or via email. While the original emails were written in Swedish, these examples have been translated to provide the reader of how a first approach might appear.

> *Hello*
> *I am a PhD candidate admitted at the University of Södertörn, but am working from the University of Gävle.*
> *My research targets sales organizations from a managerial perspective. I want to know more about how you manage complex and challenging situations, along with what your drive and passion are as a manager.*
> *The questions are open-ended. Some questions may be asked hypothetically about how you would act in complex scenarios.*
> *All interviews are conducted with full confidentially. This means that no names of individuals or organizations can be identified by others than me and my supervisor.*
> *I also wonder if it is possible to record the interview since it will be easier for me to analyze the answers.*
> *If you have any questions, do not hesitate to contact me.*
> *Sincere regards//Benny*

Of the respondents that agreed to be interviewed, two respondents were initially slightly apprehensive about participating. In an attempt to gain their trust to have them agree to being interviewed, I emailed them examples of typical questions that could be asked. On three other occasions, the respondents had already agreed to do an interview, but still wanted examples of questions to be emailed beforehand. Examples of the questions I sent to the these respondents are seen below:

- *Tell me about how a normal working day progresses for you in your role as a manager*
- *In regards to your role as a manager, what is most important to you and why?*
- *Tell me about challenges and potential challenges you may face in your role as a manager*

- *Can you tell me about one or more complex situations you have been involved in and how you solved it/them.*
- *Have you ever been exposed to unethical behavior from employees, customers or other stakeholders. If so, how did you manage that situation. Would you have done it differently today?*
- *Has it ever come to your attention that a customer has felt that they were treated wrongfully by a co-worker? If so, how did you solve this situation?*

Appendix 5a–e
Different codes

In the following appendices (5a-e) examples of sub-categories, keywords in incidences and descriptive incidences are provided to each category of the Business Basics theory to exemplify the conceptualization processes and the conceptual levels.

5a Codes related to Bureaucratization

Category: Bureaucratization		
Sub-categories	**Empirical Examples**	**Descriptive Incidences in the data**
Laws	GDPR	"Take the GDPR for example. There we have a new bureaucratic law... that we need to implement… then you will find new ways of creating relations in order to sell"
	Regulations	"It comes constantly, new regulations from everywhere – from the car producers themselves, or from the banks due to money laundry."
Written Guidelines	Ethical Guidelines	"We have our guidelines on how we should work… they (the co-workers) got themselves a copy of the guidelines to bring with them. And they are revived every now and then."
	Codes of Conduct	"We have clear guidelines for both, us as a franchisee and for those who are co-workers. There we have a model, and it can be developed of course with your own ideas and so on."
Documentation	Documentation procedures	"The bureaucracy has become almost… well the banks have more bureaucracy, but we are not far behind. So after a sale, you have a huge pile of papers that are required to be there, it is extremely controlled. But it is also a business where it is extremely important that everything is ethical."
	Keeping protocols	"When we implement (new protocols)... We are good at involving the co-workers and ask them how they want to do it. It is seldom we managers come with a complete "map". We have a kit of pictures we leave to the co-workers… When we have found the

		best way to do it, we try to spread (information) that so every does the same."
External Control	FMI	"We have a governmental organ… who do check-ups to ensure we are doing our job properly. If you don't do it properly, you lose your registration."
	Octroi	"We are a licensed business. An octroi is required to run a bank. Which means that were are under constant supervision, where the Finance inspection has that task (to ensure ethical proceedings)"

5b Codes related to Relationship Investing

Category: Relationship Investing		
Sub-categories	**Empirical Examples**	**Descriptive Incidences in the data**
Trust	Trust	"Trust is incredibly important... It is important to us that it (business transactions) is done correctly, you need people whom do a good job and you trust."
	Adapting trust	"If I have ten co-workers, I have ten different *needs*, *thoughts* and *ideas* of what is right and not. I need to adapt. In order to gain *Trust* to one and another, a lot is about creating an understanding. Since all people are different, I need to adapt. I cannot break my own moral values, but I can adapt my way of communicating myself, expressing myself, and asking questions in order to reach results."
Enterprise Culture	Having Core Values	"We have our core values and key values what we have to live by (at work)... We work with these core values, have workshops."
	Fellowship Building	"We work a lot with Team Building, where you decide how personal you want to be. But a little bit private you need to be, or else you won't build any relationship."
Staff Welfare	Focusing on welfare for co-workers	"This is staff Welfare... We can attend Hockey with some, attend football, do some activities."
	Nursing for co-workers	"It's funny because people say that I've changed profession from working as a nurse. And I reply saying no, this business is still about taking care of people

5c Codes related to Educationing

Category: Educationing		
Sub-categories	**Empirical Examples**	**Descriptive Incidences in the data**
Well-Read	Process on reading up on a topic before teaching it	"First and foremost I try to understand it myself… I read-up on it quite simply."
	Reading instructions on regular basis	"In our case as a real estate agent, there is something called FMI which sends out monthly or quarterly letters which I read-up on… (Sometimes) it could be that things that are legally correct are not ethically correct. But by reading these instructions, court rulings and praxis from FI in order to get guidelines for that is at least is legally correct and not."
Communication	Regular meetings	"An ordinary day I have my meetings so that they start directly in the morning… Once a week we have an informational meeting, which is for the whole office - The classic meeting hour so to say… On page two in the material (for up-coming meetings), there it is written exactly how the work group has been involved and how our values translates into our everyday workdays. Every time I have a meeting and come to page two, I stop there and go thru some of these definitions and work with it in the group."
	E-mail	"Send it out (via email to the co-workers) and tell them that this is our plan (For how to work)"
Clarity	Provide extra information	"When we take in new co-workers… we have these introduction days, information about the company and what we stand for, and how it works. We have a program where we have theoretical education combined

		with practice – in these education about codes of conduct is included… how we should behave towards each other and towards customers… ethics is also included here."
	Making things clear	"We should be high on morals and in everything we do, ethics should permeate it all. But it is very floating, and now I try to get everything down so it becomes more clearly (to the co-workers)."
Role Modeling	Being a role model	"A manager should always act as he or she was constantly filmed by a hidden camera."
Termination	Letting a co-worker go	"One can have to relieve an employee from his or her duties"
	Fire an employee	"If I would find out that an employee for a fact had acted badly ethically speaking… I would fire that person."

5d Codes related to Monetary Managing

Category: Monetary Managing		
Sub-categories	**Empirical Examples**	**Descriptive Incidences in the data**
Salary Systems	Performance-based salary	"… it is *performance-based pay* most often… we also sell to *fixed* price as well, but most often because it is the seller (of the house) who wants that (performance based pay), because he wants the real estate agent to sell to as high price as possible and that the real estate agent should really do anything to sell."
	Implementing fixed monthly salary	"We are not allowed to have this (performance-based salary) anymore…
Rewards	Win a hotel weekend due to good sales	"**A** bonus I recall is that we tried to increase our housing sales. The winner would get a hotel weekend… It was new and we did it locally at our office."
	Monetary Rewarding systems	"One can control co-workers (ethical) behavior via monetary rewarding systems. Especially if you use in the everyday work some sort of bonus system and such things"
Goals	Adapting Financial goals	"…the co-worker could feel very stressed by them (High financial goals)… so they are driven towards higher sales where the consequence can be that they are selling the wrong products to the customer… So yes, we could say that we adapt our sales goals"
	Budget goals	"Her little daughter of 1,5 years of age died, got an apple stuck in her throat… then you have to look between the fingers since you cannot demand that they should meet the budget for some time."

5e Codes related to Intuiting

Category: Intuiting		
Category & Sub-category	**Empirical Examples**	**Descriptive Incidences in the data**
Intuiting (Category)	Gut Feeling	"If you look beyond the merits where two candidates are exactly the same on paper, the bottom line is that I would go on chemistry… (I) use my Gut-feeling."
	Fingertip Feeling	"There is a lot of using the finger-tip feeling (When recruiting ethically desired people)"
	Get a feeling	"We must get a feeling for how we connect (So the manager will know how to manage that individual)"
	Compass	"everyone has an inner compass to use when separating right from wrong"
Ethical Flexibility (Sub-category)	Dilemmas	"You have the right to have whatever opinion you want as long as it is legal… and there I can encounter dilemmas… especially when managing."
	Conflicts of interest	"I've ended up in some conflicts of interest… there I ended up in a situation where everyone around you (thought), what's happening, how come that the one who was always celebrated gets let go. It is a very fine line for me to walk. I would want nothing than to explain that everything is not about hunting for revenue. It also has to be done the right way."
	Different points of view, but manger let employee continue with behavior	"If a co-worker votes for a certain political party does not mean they are automatically a racist…if one is that on their spare time, and are nice to all customers help all customers… then it is… (ok)."

Appendix 6
Theoretical codes of Glaser for Orthodox GT Methodology

In this part of the appendix, the originator of orthodox GT methodology - Barney Glaser's own perception on the theoretical codes are given. The distinction between theoretical codes and substantive codes according to Glaser (1998) is as follows:

> Substantive codes are the categories and properties of the theory, which images the substantive area researched. They are used to build the conceptual theory but are not theoretical codes. This is a little bit confusing for people, especially those with little or no theoretical training. Theoretical codes implicitly conceptualize how the substantive codes will relate to each other as interrelated, multivariate hypotheses in accounting for resolving the main concern. They are emergent and weave the fractured story, turned into concepts, back to an organized whole theory. They provide the models for theory generation and emerge during coding, memoing and especially in sorting. Theoretical codes, too, must pattern out to be verified to provide grounded integration. (Glaser, 1998, p.163)

The substantive codes as concepts are placed on a lower level of abstraction than the theoretical codes since the substantive codes are less abstract of place, time people etc. By this argument, a listing of them is justified. Therefore, for researchers using an orthodox GT approach, who are interested in a sample of possible theoretical codes, the reader is advised to read Glaser (1978, pp.73-82; 1998, pp. 170-175; 2005, pp.7-30) in order to be further enlightened about discovered theoretical coding families. Regarding these coding families, Glaser (1978) express that they are:

> not mutually exclusive, they overlap considerably. Also, one family can spawn another. Their conceptual level in relation to each other is also arbitrary by their use. Some are different ways of saying the same thing. The reader may think of other words for each family as well as discover new families. But in the final effort, they make the analyst very sensitive what to write at which point, when in fact, he must take a stand to try to theoretically render an empirical pattern. (Glaser, 1978, pp.73-74)

Appendix 7
Notes about methodology literature

Much literature for the methodology chapter (chapter 2) was included where the main focus was on orthodox GT methodology. Glaser (1978; 1992; 1998) and Gustavsson (1998) are for this dissertation considered as being the most essential sources for information about the orthodox GT methodology – both for my learning process of the methodology but also when writing chapter 5.

Other important sources to orthodox GT methodology are of course Glaser and Strauss (1967) as well as Glaser (2001; 2003). Additionally, I have also used both Harttman (2001) as an important subsidiary source, as well as been inspired by Christiansen (2006; 2008).

If the reader want to know more about orthodox GT, and/or conduct a study using this approach, the reader are recommended to read the mentioned literature above.

Moreover, I have also had other important sources for my learning about orthodox GT through inspirational and informative discussions with several well-versed academic GT users. For example, I have had two Skype-sessions with Dr. Barney Glaser as well as discussions with Professor Andy Lowe at the University of Århus back in May 2016 during a course focusing on orthodox GT. I have also had several ongoing discussions throughout the whole research process with my supervisor Professor Lars-Johan Åge who is also well-versed in orthodox GT.

Appendix 8
Key words used for the validation chapter

In order to find the appropriate articles and related literature to validate the empirical findings presented in chapter 5, several additional keywords relating to the emerged categories and sub-categories were used. These key-words were often used in different combinations, often in conjunction with the previous used keywords in appendix 1 to refine the search for relevant literature. The following new key-words which were used are:

- Bureaucracy
- Bureaucratic leadership
- Clarity
- Clarity, importance of displaying
- Codes of ethics
- Codes of conduct
- Communication
- Communication channels
- Communicating ethics
- Communication tools
- Corporate ethical codes
- Education ethics
- Educating ethical behaviour
- Effective communication skills
- Ethical climate
- Ethical guidelines
- Ethical leadership
- Ethical norms
- Fingertip-feeling
- Flexible leadership
- Goals, organizational
- Goals, monetary
- Gut-feeling
- Human resource management
- Human Resource practices
- HRM
- Intuition, Management via
- Intuition management, effects of
- Learning processes
- Management theory
- Organizational culture
- Panopticon
- Preparing, importance of
- Preparation
- Profit maximization, effects of
- Relationship
- Role model organization
- Role model manager
- Salary, Commission-based
- Salary, fixed
- Salary, performance-based
- Social learning theory
- Termination/terminating
- Trust
- Rewards, remuneration, discipline systems
- Written guidelines

The searches provided between 11 to 158 365 hits on Google-scholar, Emerald, and Discovery depending on the used key-words. In order to narrow down the searches as in chapter 1, the same specific search techniques were used. In total, 110 scientific articles and relevant literature were included. This also includes borrowing academic books and dictionaries from the libraries of the university of Gävle, the university of Södertörn and Uppsala University.

Fin.

Södertörn Doctoral Dissertations

1. Jolanta Aidukaite, *The Emergence of the Post-Socialist Welfare State: The case of the Baltic States: Estonia, Latvia and Lithuania*, 2004
2. Xavier Fraudet, *Politique étrangère française en mer Baltique (1871–1914): de l'exclusion à l'affirmation*, 2005
3. Piotr Wawrzeniuk, *Confessional Civilising in Ukraine: The Bishop Iosyf Shumliansky and the Introduction of Reforms in the Diocese of Lviv 1668–1708*, 2005
4. Andrej Kotljarchuk, *In the Shadows of Poland and Russia: The Grand Duchy of Lithuania and Sweden in the European Crisis of the mid-17th Century*, 2006
5. Håkan Blomqvist, *Nation, ras och civilisation i svensk arbetarrörelse före nazismen*, 2006
6. Karin S Lindelöf, *Om vi nu ska bli som Europa: Könsskapande och normalitet bland unga kvinnor i transitionens Polen*, 2006
7. Andrew Stickley. *On Interpersonal Violence in Russia in the Present and the Past: A Sociological Study*, 2006
8. Arne Ek, *Att konstruera en uppslutning kring den enda vägen: Om folkrörelsers modernisering i skuggan av det Östeuropeiska systemskiftet*, 2006
9. Agnes Ers, *I mänsklighetens namn: En etnologisk studie av ett svenskt biståndsprojekt i Rumänien*, 2006
10. Johnny Rodin, *Rethinking Russian Federalism: The Politics of Intergovernmental Relations and Federal Reforms at the Turn of the Millennium*, 2006
11. Kristian Petrov, *Tillbaka till framtiden: Modernitet, postmodernitet och generationsidentitet i Gorbačevs glasnost' och perestrojka*, 2006
12. Sophie Söderholm Werkö, *Patient patients? Achieving Patient Empowerment through Active Participation, Increased Knowledge and Organisation*, 2008
13. Peter Bötker, *Leviatan i arkipelagen: Staten, förvaltningen och samhället. Fallet Estland*, 2007
14. Matilda Dahl, *States under scrutiny: International organizations, transformation and the construction of progress*, 2007
15. Margrethe B. Søvik, *Support, resistance and pragmatism: An examination of motivation in language policy in Kharkiv*, Ukraine, 2007
16. Yulia Gradskova, *Soviet People with female Bodies: Performing beauty and maternity in Soviet Russia in the mid 1930–1960s*, 2007
17. Renata Ingbrant, *From Her Point of View: Woman's Anti-World in the Poetry of Anna Świrszczyńska*, 2007
18. Johan Eellend, *Cultivating the Rural Citizen: Modernity, Agrarianism and Citizenship in Late Tsarist Estonia*, 2007
19. Petra Garberding, *Musik och politik i skuggan av nazismen: Kurt Atterberg och de svensk-tyska musikrelationerna*, 2007

20. Aleksei Semenenko, *Hamlet the Sign: Russian Translations of Hamlet and Literary Canon Formation*, 2007
21. Vytautas Petronis, *Constructing Lithuania: Ethnic Mapping in the Tsarist Russia, ca. 1800–1914*, 2007
22. Akvile Motiejunaite, *Female employment, gender roles, and attitudes: the Baltic countries in a broader context*, 2008
23. Tove Lindén, *Explaining Civil Society Core Activism in Post-Soviet Latvia*, 2008
24. Pelle Åberg, *Translating Popular Education: Civil Society Cooperation between Sweden and Estonia*, 2008
25. Anders Nordström, *The Interactive Dynamics of Regulation: Exploring the Council of Europe's monitoring of Ukraine*, 2008
26. Fredrik Doeser, *In Search of Security After the Collapse of the Soviet Union: Foreign Policy Change in Denmark, Finland and Sweden, 1988–1993*, 2008
27. Zhanna Kravchenko. *Family (versus) Policy: Combining Work and Care in Russia and Sweden*, 2008
28. Rein Jüriado, *Learning within and between public-private partnerships*, 2008
29. Elin Boalt, *Ecology and evolution of tolerance in two cruciferous species*, 2008
30. Lars Forsberg, *Genetic Aspects of Sexual Selection and Mate Choice in Salmonids*, 2008
31. Eglė Rindzevičiūtė, *Constructing Soviet Cultural Policy: Cybernetics and Governance in Lithuania after World War II*, 2008
32. Joakim Philipson, *The Purpose of Evolution: 'struggle for existence' in the Russian-Jewish press 1860–1900*, 2008
33. Sofie Bedford, *Islamic activism in Azerbaijan: Repression and mobilization in a post-Soviet context*, 2009
34. Tommy Larsson Segerlind, *Team Entrepreneurship: A process analysis of the venture team and the venture team roles in relation to the innovation process*, 2009
35. Jenny Svensson, *The Regulation of Rule-Following: Imitation and Soft Regulation in the European Union*, 2009
36. Stefan Hallgren, *Brain Aromatase in the guppy, Poecilia reticulate: Distribution, control and role in behavior*, 2009
37. Karin Ellencrona, *Functional characterization of interactions between the flavivirus NS5 protein and PDZ proteins of the mammalian host*, 2009
38. Makiko Kanematsu, *Saga och verklighet: Barnboksproduktion i det postsovjetiska Lettland*, 2009
39. Daniel Lindvall, *The Limits of the European Vision in Bosnia and Herzegovina: An Analysis of the Police Reform Negotiations*, 2009
40. Charlotta Hillerdal, *People in Between – Ethnicity and Material Identity: A New Approach to Deconstructed Concepts*, 2009
41. Jonna Bornemark, *Kunskapens gräns – gränsens vetande*, 2009
42. Adolphine G. Kateka, *Co-Management Challenges in the Lake Victoria Fisheries: A Context Approach*, 2010

43. René León Rosales, *Vid framtidens hitersta gräns: Om pojkar och elevpositioner i en multietnisk skola*, 2010
44. Simon Larsson, *Intelligensaristokrater och arkivmartyrer: Normerna för vetenskaplig skicklighet i svensk historieforskning 1900–1945*, 2010
45. Håkan Lättman, *Studies on spatial and temporal distributions of epiphytic lichens*, 2010
46. Alia Jaensson, *Pheromonal mediated behaviour and endocrine response in salmonids: The impact of cypermethrin, copper, and glyphosate*, 2010
47. Michael Wigerius, *Roles of mammalian Scribble in polarity signaling, virus offense and cell-fate determination*, 2010
48. Anna Hedtjärn Wester, *Män i kostym: Prinsar, konstnärer och tegelbärare vid sekelskiftet 1900*, 2010
49. Magnus Linnarsson, *Postgång på växlande villkor: Det svenska postväsendets organisation under stormaktstiden*, 2010
50. Barbara Kunz, *Kind words, cruise missiles and everything in between: A neoclassical realist study of the use of power resources in U.S. policies towards Poland, Ukraine and Belarus 1989–2008*, 2010
51. Anders Bartonek, *Philosophie im Konjunktiv: Nichtidentität als Ort der Möglichkeit des Utopischen in der negativen Dialektik Theodor W. Adornos*, 2010
52. Carl Cederberg, *Resaying the Human: Levinas Beyond Humanism and Antihumanism*, 2010
53. Johanna Ringarp, *Professionens problematik: Lärarkårens kommunalisering och välfärdsstatens förvandling*, 2011
54. Sofi Gerber, *Öst är Väst men Väst är bäst: Östtysk identitetsformering i det förenade Tyskland*, 2011
55. Susanna Sjödin Lindenskoug, *Manlighetens bortre gräns: Tidelagsrättegångar i Livland åren 1685–1709*, 2011
56. Dominika Polanska, *The emergence of enclaves of wealth and poverty: A sociological study of residential differentiation in post-communist Poland*, 2011
57. Christina Douglas, *Kärlek per korrespondens: Två förlovade par under andra hälften av 1800-talet*, 2011
58. Fred Saunders, *The Politics of People – Not just Mangroves and Monkeys: A study of the theory and practice of community-based management of natural resources in Zanzibar*, 2011
59. Anna Rosengren, *Åldrandet och språket: En språkhistorisk analys av hög ålder och åldrande i Sverige cirka 1875–1975*, 2011
60. Emelie Lilliefeldt, *European Party Politics and Gender: Configuring Gender-Balanced Parliamentary Presence*, 2011
61. Ola Svenonius, *Sensitising Urban Transport Security: Surveillance and Policing in Berlin, Stockholm, and Warsaw*, 2011
62. Andreas Johansson, *Dissenting Democrats: Nation and Democracy in the Republic of Moldova*, 2011

63. Wessam Melik, *Molecular characterization of the Tick-borne encephalitis virus: Environments and replication*, 2012
64. Steffen Werther, *SS-Vision und Grenzland-Realität: Vom Umgang dänischer und „volksdeutscher" Nationalsozialisten in Sønderjylland mit der „großgermanischen" Ideologie der SS*, 2012
65. Peter Jakobsson, *Öppenhetsindustrin*, 2012
66. Kristin Ilves, *Seaward Landward: Investigations on the archaeological source value of the landing site category in the Baltic Sea region*, 2012
67. Anne Kaun, *Civic Experiences and Public Connection: Media and Young People in Estonia*, 2012
68. Anna Tessmann, *On the Good Faith: A Fourfold Discursive Construction of Zoroastripanism in Contemporary Russia*, 2012
69. Jonas Lindström, *Drömmen om den nya staden: stadsförnyelse i det postsovjetisk Riga*, 2012
70. Maria Wolrath Söderberg, *Topos som meningsskapare: retorikens topiska perspektiv på tänkande och lärande genom argumentation*, 2012
71. Linus Andersson, *Alternativ television: former av kritik i konstnärlig TV-produktion*, 2012
72. Håkan Lättman, *Studies on spatial and temporal distributions of epiphytic lichens*, 2012
73. Fredrik Stiernstedt, Mediearbete i mediehuset: produktion i förändring på MTG-radio, 2013
74. Jessica Moberg, *Piety, Intimacy and Mobility: A Case Study of Charismatic Christianity in Present-day Stockholm*, 2013
75. Elisabeth Hemby, *Historiemåleri och bilder av vardag: Tatjana Nazarenkos konstnärskap i 1970-talets Sovjet*, 2013
76. Tanya Jukkala, *Suicide in Russia: A macro-sociological study*, 2013
77. Maria Nyman, *Resandets gränser: svenska resenärers skildringar av Ryssland under 1700-talet*, 2013
78. Beate Feldmann Eellend, *Visionära planer och vardagliga praktiker: postmilitära landskap i Östersjöområdet*, 2013
79. Emma Lind, *Genetic response to pollution in sticklebacks: natural selection in the wild*, 2013
80. Anne Ross Solberg, *The Mahdi wears Armani: An analysis of the Harun Yahya enterprise*, 2013
81. Nikolay Zakharov, *Attaining Whiteness: A Sociological Study of Race and Racialization in Russia*, 2013
82. Anna Kharkina, *From Kinship to Global Brand: the Discourse on Culture in Nordic Cooperation after World War II*, 2013
83. Florence Fröhlig, *A painful legacy of World War II: Nazi forced enlistment: Alsatian/Mosellan Prisoners of war and the Soviet Prison Camp of Tambov*, 2013
84. Oskar Henriksson, *Genetic connectivity of fish in the Western Indian Ocean*, 2013

85. Hans Geir Aasmundsen, *Pentecostalism, Globalisation and Society in Contemporary Argentina*, 2013
86. Anna McWilliams, *An Archaeology of the Iron Curtain: Material and Metaphor*, 2013
87. Anna Danielsson, *On the power of informal economies and the informal economies of power: rethinking informality, resilience and violence in Kosovo*, 2014
88. Carina Guyard, *Kommunikationsarbete på distans*, 2014
89. Sofia Norling, *Mot "väst": om vetenskap, politik och transformation i Polen 1989–2011*, 2014
90. Markus Huss, *Motståndets akustik: språk och (o)ljud hos Peter Weiss 1946–1960*, 2014
91. Ann-Christin Randahl, *Strategiska skribenter: skrivprocesser i fysik och svenska*, 2014
92. Péter Balogh, *Perpetual borders: German-Polish cross-border contacts in the Szczecin area*, 2014
93. Erika Lundell, *Förkroppsligad fiktion och fiktionaliserade kroppar: levande rollspel i Östersjöregionen*, 2014
94. Henriette Cederlöf, *Alien Places in Late Soviet Science Fiction: The "Unexpected Encounters" of Arkady and Boris Strugatsky as Novels and Films*, 2014
95. Niklas Eriksson, *Urbanism Under Sail: An archaeology of fluit ships in early modern everyday life*, 2014
96. Signe Opermann, *Generational Use of News Media in Estonia: Media Access, Spatial Orientations and Discursive Characteristics of the News Media*, 2014
97. Liudmila Voronova, *Gendering in political journalism: A comparative study of Russia and Sweden*, 2014
98. Ekaterina Kalinina, *Mediated Post-Soviet Nostalgia*, 2014
99. Anders E. B. Blomqvist, *Economic Natonalizing in the Ethnic Borderlands of Hungary and Romania: Inclusion, Exclusion and Annihilation in Szatmár/Satu-Mare, 1867–1944*, 2014
100. Ann-Judith Rabenschlag, *Völkerfreundschaft nach Bedarf: Ausländische Arbeitskräfte in der Wahrnehmung von Staat und Bevölkerung der DDR*, 2014
101. Yuliya Yurchuck, *Ukrainian Nationalists and the Ukrainian Insurgent Army in Post-Soviet Ukraine*, 2014
102. Hanna Sofia Rehnberg, *Organisationer berättar: narrativitet som resurs i strategisk kommunikation*, 2014
103. Jaakko Turunen, *Semiotics of Politics: Dialogicality of Parliamentary Talk*, 2015
104. Iveta Jurkane-Hobein, *I Imagine You Here Now: Relationship Maintenance Strategies in Long-Distance Intimate Relationships*, 2015
105. Katharina Wesolowski, *Maybe baby? Reproductive behaviour, fertility intentions, and family policies in post-communist countries, with a special focus on Ukraine*, 2015
106. Ann af Burén, *Living Simultaneity: On religion among semi-secular Swedes*, 2015
107. Larissa Mickwitz, *En reformerad lärare: konstruktionen av en professionell och betygssättande lärare i skolpolitik och skolpraktik*, 2015
108. Daniel Wojahn, *Språkaktivism: diskussioner om feministiska språkförändringar i Sverige från 1960-talet till 2015*, 2015

109. Hélène Edberg, *Kreativt skrivande för kritiskt tänkande: en fallstudie av studenters arbete med kritisk metareflektion*, 2015
110. Kristina Volkova, *Fishy Behavior: Persistent effects of early-life exposure to 17α-ethinylestradiol*, 2015
111. Björn Sjöstrand, *Att tänka det tekniska: en studie i Derridas teknikfilosofi*, 2015
112. Håkan Forsberg, *Kampen om eleverna: gymnasiefältet och skolmarknadens framväxt i Stockholm, 1987–2011*, 2015
113. Johan Stake, *Essays on quality evaluation and bidding behavior in public procurement auctions*, 2015
114. Martin Gunnarson, *Please Be Patient: A Cultural Phenomenological Study of Haemodialysis and Kidney Transplantation Care*, 2016
115. Nasim Reyhanian Caspillo, *Studies of alterations in behavior and fertility in ethinyl estradiol-exposed zebrafish and search for related biomarkers*, 2016
116. Pernilla Andersson, *The Responsible Business Person: Studies of Business Education for Sustainability*, 2016
117. Kim Silow Kallenberg, *Gränsland: svensk ungdomsvård mellan vård och straff*, 2016
118. Sari Vuorenpää, *Literacitet genom interaction*, 2016
119. Francesco Zavatti, *Writing History in a Propaganda Institute: Political Power and Network Dynamics in Communist Romania*, 2016
120. Cecilia Annell, *Begärets politiska potential: Feministiska motståndsstrategier i Elin Wägners 'Pennskaftet', Gabriele Reuters 'Aus guter Familie', Hilma Angered-Strandbergs 'Lydia Vik' och Grete Meisel-Hess 'Die Intellektuellen'*, 2016
121. Marco Nase, *Academics and Politics: Northern European Area Studies at Greifswald University, 1917–1992*, 2016
122. Jenni Rinne, *Searching for Authentic Living Through Native Faith – The Maausk movement in Estonia*, 2016
123. Petra Werner, *Ett medialt museum: lärandets estetik i svensk television 1956–1969*, 2016
124. Ramona Rat, *Un-common Sociality: Thinking sociality with Levinas*, 2016
125. Petter Thureborn, *Microbial ecosystem functions along the steep oxygen gradient of the Landsort Deep, Baltic Sea*, 2016
126. Kajsa-Stina Benulic, *A Beef with Meat Media and audience framings of environmentally unsustainable production and consumption*, 2016
127. Naveed Asghar, *Ticks and Tick-borne Encephalitis Virus – From nature to infection*, 2016
128. Linn Rabe, *Participation and legitimacy: Actor involvement for nature conservation*, 2017
129. Maryam Adjam, *Minnesspår: hågkomstens rum och rörelse i skuggan av en flykt*, 2017
130. Kim West, *The Exhibitionary Complex: Exhibition, Apparatus and Media from Kulturhuset to the Centre Pompidou, 1963–1977*, 2017
131. Ekaterina Tarasova, *Anti-nuclear Movements in Discursive and Political Contexts: Between expert voices and local protests, 2017*

132. Sanja Obrenović Johansson, *Från kombifeminism till rörelse: Kvinnlig serbisk organisering i förändring, 2017*

133. Michał Salamonik, *In Their Majesties' Service: The Career of Francesco De Gratta (1613–1676) as a Royal Servant and Trader in Gdańsk*, 2017

134. Jenny Ingridsdotter, *The Promises of the Free World: Postsocialist Experience in Argentina and the Making of Migrants, Race, and Coloniality*, 2017

135. Julia Malitska, *Negotiating Imperial Rule: Colonists and Marriage in the Nineteenth century Black Sea Steppe*, 2017

136. Natalya Yakusheva, *Parks, Policies and People: Nature Conservation Governance in Post-Socialist EU Countries*, 2017

137. Martin Kellner, *Selective Serotonin Re-uptake Inhibitors in the Environment: Effects of Citalopram on Fish Behaviour*, 2017

138. Krystof Kasprzak, *Vara – Framträdande – Värld: Fenomenets negativitet hos Martin Heidegger, Jan Patočka och Eugen Fink*, 2017

139. Alberto Frigo, *Life-stowing from a Digital Media Perspective: Past, Present and Future*, 2017

140. Maarja Saar, *The Answers You Seek Will Never Be Found At Home: Reflexivity, biographical narratives and lifestyle migration among highly-skilled Estonians*, 2017

141. Anh Mai, *Organizing for Efficiency: Essay on merger policies, independence of authorities, and technology diffusion*, 2017

142. Gustav Strandberg, *Politikens omskakning: Negativitet, samexistens och frihet i Jan Patočkas tänkande*, 2017

143. Lovisa Andén, *Litteratur och erfarenhet i Merleau-Pontys läsning av Proust, Valéry och Stendhal*, 2017

144. Fredrik Bertilsson, *Frihetstida policyskapande: uppfostringskommissionen och de akademiska konstitutionerna 1738–1766*, 2017

145. Börjeson, Natasja, *Toxic Textiles – towards responsibility in complex supply chains*, 2017

146. Julia Velkova, *Media Technologies in the Making – User-Driven Software and Infrastructures for computer Graphics Production*, 2017

147. Karin Jonsson, *Fångna i begreppen? Revolution, tid och politik i svensk socialistisk press 1917–1924*, 2017

148. Josefine Larsson, *Genetic Aspects of Environmental Disturbances in Marine Ecosystems – Studies of the Blue Mussel in the Baltic Sea*, 2017

149. Roman Horbyk, *Mediated Europes – Discourse and Power in Ukraine, Russia and Poland during Euromaidan*, 2017

150. Nadezda Petrusenko, *Creating the Revolutionary Heroines: The Case of Female Terrorists of the PSR (Russia, Beginning of the 20th Century)*, 2017

151. Rahel Kuflu, *Bröder emellan: Identitetsformering i det koloniserade Eritrea*, 2018

152. Karin Edberg, *Energilandskap i förändring: Inramningar av kontroversiella lokaliseringar på norra Gotland*, 2018

153. Rebecka Thor, *Beyond the Witness: Holocaust Representation and the Testimony of Images - Three films by Yael Hersonski, Harun Farocki, and Eyal Sivan*, 2018
154. Maria Lönn, *Bruten vithet: Om den ryska femininitetens sinnliga och temporala villkor*, 2018
155. Tove Porseryd, *Endocrine Disruption in Fish: Effects of 17α-ethinylestradiol exposure on non-reproductive behavior, fertility and brain and testis transcriptome*, 2018
156. Marcel Mangold, *Securing the working democracy: Inventive arrangements to guarantee circulation and the emergence of democracy policy*, 2018
157. Matilda Tudor, *Desire Lines: Towards a Queer Digital Media Phenomenology*, 2018
158. Martin Andersson, *Migration i 1600-talets Sverige: Älvsborgs lösen 1613–1618*, 2018
159. Johanna Pettersson, *What's in a Line? Making Sovereignty through Border Policy*, 2018
160. Irina Seits, *Architectures of Life-Building in the Twentieth Century: Russia, Germany, Sweden*, 2018
161. Alexander Stagnell, *The Ambassador's Letter: On the Less Than Nothing of Diplomacy*, 2019
162. Mari Zetterqvist Blokhuis, *Interaction Between Rider, Horse and Equestrian Trainer – A Challenging Puzzle*, 2019
163. Robin Samuelsson, *Play, Culture and Learning: Studies of Second-Language and Conceptual Development in Swedish Preschools*, 2019
164. Ralph Tafon, *Analyzing the "Dark Side" of Marine Spatial Planning – A study of domination, empowerment and freedom (or power* in, of *and* on *planning) through theories of discourse and power*, 2019
165. Ingela Visuri, *Varieties of Supernatural Experience: The case of high-functioning autism*, 2019
166. Mathilde Rehnlund, *Getting the transport right – for what? What transport policy can tell us about the construction of sustainability*, 2019
167. Oscar Törnqvist, *Röster från ingenmansland: En identitetsarkeologi i ett maritimt mellanrum*, 2019
168. Elise Remling, *Adaptation, now? Exploring the Politics of Climate Adaptation through Post-structuralist Discourse Theory*, 2019
169. Eva Karlberg, *Organizing the Voice of Women: A study of the Polish and Swedish women's movements' adaptation to international structures*, 2019
170. Maria Pröckl, *Tyngd, sväng och empatisk timing - förskollärares kroppsliga kunskaper*, 2020
171. Adrià Alcoverro, *The University and the Demand for Knowledge-based Growth The hegemonic struggle for the future of Higher Education Institutions in Finland and Estonia*, 2020
172. Ingrid Forsler, *Enabling Media: Infrastructures, imaginaries and cultural techniques in Swedish and Estonian visual arts education*, 2020
173. Johan Sehlberg, *Of Affliction: The Experience of Thought in Gilles Deleuze by way of Marcel Proust*, 2020

174. Renat Bekkin, *People of reliable loyalty…: Muftiates and the State in Modern Russia*, 2020
175. Olena Podolian, *The Challenge of 'Stateness' in Estonia and Ukraine: The international dimension a quarter of a century into independence*, 2020
176. Patrick Seniuk, *Encountering Depression In-Depth: An existential-phenomenological approach to selfhood, depression, and psychiatric practice*, 2020
177. Vasileios Petrogiannis, *European Mobility and Spatial Belongings: Greek and Latvian migrants in Sweden*, 2020
178. Lena Norbäck Ivarsson, *Tracing environmental change and human impact as recorded in sediments from coastal areas of the northwestern Baltic Proper*, 2020
179. Sara Persson, *Corporate Hegemony through Sustainability – A study of sustainability standards and CSR practices as tools to demobilise community resistance in the Albanian oil industry*, 2020
180. Juliana Porsani, *Livelihood Implications of Large-Scale Land Concessions in Mozambique: A case of family farmers' endurance*, 2020
181. Anders Backlund, *Isolating the Radical Right – Coalition Formation and Policy Adaptation in Sweden*, 2020
182. Nina Carlsson, *One Nation, One Language? National minority and Indigenous recognition in the politics of immigrant integration*, 2021
183. Erik Gråd, Nudges, *Prosocial Preferences & Behavior: Essays in Behavioral Economics*, 2021
184. Anna Enström, *Sinnesstämning, skratt och hypokondri: Om estetisk erfarenhet i Kants tredje Kritik*, 2021
185. Michelle Rydback, *Healthcare Service Marketing in Medical Tourism – An Emerging Market Study*, 2021
186. Fredrik Jahnke, *Toleransens altare och undvikandets hänsynsfullhet – Religion och meningsskapande bland svenska grundskoleelever*, 2021
187. Benny Berggren Newton, *Business Basics – A Grounded Theory for Managing Ethical Behavior in Sales Organizations*, 2021
188. Gabriel Itkes-Sznap, *Nollpunkten. Precisionens betydelse hos Witold Gombrowicz, Inger Christensen och Herta Müller*, 2021

www.ingramcontent.com/pod-product-compliance
Ingram Content Group UK Ltd.
Pitfield, Milton Keynes, MK11 3LW, UK
UKHW021838270726
14058UKWH00002B/217

9 789189 109575